The Cult of Individualism
A History of an Enduring American Myth

AARON BARLOW

 PRAEGER

AN IMPRINT OF ABC-CLIO, LLC
Santa Barbara, California • Denver, Colorado • Oxford, England

Library of Congress Cataloging-in-Publication Data

Barlow, Aaron, 1951–
   The cult of individualism : a history of an enduring American myth / Aaron Barlow.
     page cm
   Includes bibliographical references and index.
   ISBN 978–1–4408–2829–4 (cloth : alk. paper) — ISBN 978–1–4408–2830–0
(ebook) 1. Individualism—United States. 2. Culture—United States. I. Title.
HM1276.B373   2013
306—dc23   2013014048

ISBN: 978–1–4408–2829–4
EISBN: 978–1–4408–2830–0

17 16 15 14 13   1 2 3 4 5

This book is also available on the World Wide Web as an eBook.
Visit www.abc-clio.com for details.

Praeger
An Imprint of ABC-CLIO, LLC

ABC-CLIO, LLC
130 Cremona Drive, P.O. Box 1911
Santa Barbara, California 93116-1911

This book is printed on acid-free paper ∞

Manufactured in the United States of America

For Jan . . .
Always

Contents

Acknowledgments

First and foremost, I would like to thank New York City College of Technology's President Russell Hotzler and Provost Bonne August for the support they gave this project through the sabbatical I was granted for the fall semester of 2012. Without it, I would not have been able to finish for another year or more. Also deserving thanks is my editor at Praeger, Michael Millman. Rodger Cunningham of Alice Lloyd College in Pippa Passes, Kentucky, provided me with a copy of a recent presentation of his, a paper that proved quite valuable to me, especially in writing Chapter 7. Thanks, Rodger. I should not forget Wayne Franklin, whose tutelage at the University of Iowa many decades ago got me started thinking about American culture. An article I wrote for the *ePluribus Media Journal* that was published online on April 18, 2008 under the title "How the West Was Changed: Degradation of the Townspeople after World War II in the American Western" became, after *much* change, a part of Chapter 6. Though the journal is no longer available, I want to thank its former staff, especially Roxy Caraway, for their efforts in that endeavor. My uncle, Joel Dimmette of Wilksboro, North Carolina, helped in my exploration of Borderer culture by telling me tales of my grandfather's youth in Wilkes County. That connection proved valuable as I tried to gain a better understanding of the culture of my ancestors. Finally, I must once more thank my wife, Jan Stern. Though she sometimes gets frustrated by my focus on my work, she remains ever supportive, making actual completion of it possible.

Introduction: Starting from the Individual

The cult of individualism is something every American sees but few even try to understand. We pass it off as simply as an aspect of greed or blame it on a misunderstanding of religion—or dismiss it with any of a dozen other simplistic excuses. Yet we all partake in it, and most of us even come to believe that individualism is a natural human state—sometimes even arguing that it is the job of society to counter the worst excesses of individualism or even that this is what government is *for*.

What we rarely consider is that individualism, as practiced in America (as practiced anywhere), is as much a cultural phenomenon as a human one. Everything we do is predicated on interaction with others, from language to land use and even to the barriers we create around us, including walls of shelter and weapons. It may all start with the individual, but all of it ends up enmeshed in culture. In fact, the very *idea* of the individual has its roots in culture and the myths it engenders.

My own quest to understand these myths began at the end of 2006, when I read an article by novelist Jane Smiley on the *Huffington Post* website, one that wakened me to things about myself, to those myths of mine, of my culture, and of my country that had long slumbered within me. It also introduced me to David Hackett Fischer's *Albion's Seed: Four British Folkways in America* and, by a circuitous route, to Rodger Cunningham's *Apples on the Flood: Minority Discourse and Appalachia*, great influences on me since, negatively and positively.

Smiley and Fischer angered me, making me feel that I, my family, and our past were somehow being insulted, though I did not quite know how.

Cunningham explained why I felt that way. Together, the three piqued my interest in the myths and cultures of my ancestors—not simply as Americans but as "Borderers," one of the four folkways of Fischer's book. They have also led me to examine quite a number of cultural assumptions I had bought into, including those behind Richard Hofstadter's brilliant *Anti-Intellectualism in American Life*. What had been one of my favorite books was now appearing problematic, especially in its depiction of the various types of Americans. I could not leave that alone.

*****

Philosopher Richard Rorty once lashed out against one of the myths engendered by the Enlightenment: "The idea that liberal societies are bound together by philosophical beliefs seems to me ludicrous. What binds societies together are common vocabularies and common hopes."[1] He is right, of course. It is not ideas—or even a lack of them—that gird cultures but common aspirations and the ability to share them. But language, which allows those common vocabularies, can also mask deep cultural divides, the scars of generations of conflict. That has happened in America. The particular injuries I am considering here first occurred there in the 18th century—though the new lacerations often proved to be nothing more than means of reopening of much older wounds. These injuries have set up one of the great oppositions—and conundrums—of the American experience.

In *The Machine in the Garden*, one of the seminal works of the field of American Studies, Leo Marx writes that "a most striking fact about the New World was its baffling hospitality to radically opposed interpretations. If America seemed to promise everything that men always had wanted, it also threatened to obliterate much of what they already had achieved."[2] Even today, not only do we never know for sure how to "read" America as promise or as threat, but America itself often seems to promote both contradictory outcomes, further complicating any attempt at generating understanding. America, as we have discovered, can *stop* achievement at the same time as it promotes it. Its dominant cultures, as the New World grew older, nearly obliterated (or tried to) the cultures on the continent with not quite so much power—from Native American to African and even to the less powerful cultures from the British Isles themselves. The hazards of America, just as Marx says, are as myriad as its possibilities, the hazards of attempting to make sense of it all equally so.

*****

There were two major groups of immigrants into the North American British colonies of the 18th century. Neither of these came with the same bright promise of Renaissance and then Enlightenment ideals that had preceded them. One of these we all know about: Their descendants can't be missed, even today. These, of course, were the slaves purchased or stolen from Africa, people not even considered people, branded in their supposed "inferiority" by the color of their skin. Forever marked in a white-dominated society, they have had to struggle against odds that few others, even slaves elsewhere, have faced. That struggle still marks the culture of their descendants.

The other group looked no different than the earlier immigrants from the British Isles. They could be "cleaned up," if need be, to pass into "society." Indentured servants, people fleeing the Ulster Plantation that had proved unwelcoming to their parents and grandparents, and others escaping the poverty of the borderland between Scotland and England, these people found little welcome among the established colonies and soon fled to a new border, this one between those colonies and the Native Americans whom the Europeans were muscling toward the interior of the continent.

Today, we recognize that the umbrella American culture includes the African American. Distinct from white American culture, it is still related, still combines with it to create one whole American culture. Many people—too many—still don't like this, but they cannot deny it: The evidence is ever before our eyes. On the other hand, over the centuries, there has certainly been some success in the struggle for recognition of the place and importance of the African American in and for American society. However, we have all but forgotten that other culture stemming from 18th-century immigrants, the culture of those Scots-Irish Borderers.

Today, the WASP, the White Anglo-Saxon Protestant, has come to be seen as a monolith. Many still believe that all of the immigrants from Europe from the period before the great Irish influx of the potato famine starting in the decades before the Civil War have melded into one great American white culture. But that never happened. The "melting pot" was more of a myth than we recognize even today, and for reasons we don't want to consider. Just look at Electoral College results from 1824 on: What's remarkable is the continual reemergence of one pattern, New England plus the expanding northern tier of states and, later, the West Coast against most of the rest of the country, elections often decided by states in the West or directly south of that northern tier. Why does this happen? It's not simply politics but is culture. And it denies that there ever was a melting pot.

In his cultural history of African Americans through their music, *Blues People*, Amiri Baraka (LeRoi Jones) writes, "Each man, in whatever 'type' of culture he inhabits, must have a way of looking at the world—whatever that means to him—which is peculiar to his particular culture."[3] This is clearly true in America and, as we shall see, it is the base behind our "red state" and "blue state" split. The ways of each culture seem "peculiar" to the others. Baraka goes on to comment that "Africans were forced into an alien world where none of the references or cultural shapes of any familiar human attitudes were available ... [and this determined] the *kind* of existence they had to eke out here: not only slavery itself but the particular circumstances in which it existed."[4] Though the Scots-Irish faced no break of that magnitude, they did find themselves in a new land where they were unwelcome, either by the earlier colonists or by the indigenous population they soon found themselves pitted against. And, a little like the Africans, they had no real understanding of the mores and ways of the dominant culture. Like most observers of American culture, however, Baraka lumps the white population into one:

> One of the most persistent traits of the Western white man has always been his fanatical and almost instinctive assumption that his systems and ideas about the world are the most desirable, and further, that people who do not aspire to them, or at least think them admirable, are *savages* or *enemies*. ... [T]hey ... were certainly in a position to declare that all thought outside their known systems was at least "backward."[5]

And they did, but not all of them—and not just to the thought of black folk.

*****

The culture of what is roughly half of white America was also long ago deemed "backward" by the people who write the histories and who control the discussions and media of American society. As dialects merged and mass production made physical appearance less and less distinctive, that culture, spawned by the Scots-Irish push to the west, became less and less apparent in the record. After all, in the eyes of those who wrote, it was nothing more than a "backward" culture, not worth commenting on, certainly not in any positive light. It was ignored.

Ignore someone right next to you for long enough and they will start to resent you.

This book is, in part, an attempt to explore that resentment, a resentment that manifests itself today in a "cult of individualism" that shrugs off the federal government as a creature of the "East Coast liberals" and as the bearer of restrictive and degrading "entitlements" that are used only to solidify its own power. The emotions behind such feelings have a long history beginning even before the American Revolution. It is a history that started in 18th-century struggles like those of the Regulators in North and South Carolina.

Today's passionate defense of gun rights by the cult of individualism is just one of the outcomes of the imbalance that the spiritual inheritors of the Scots-Irish Borderers see in an America they believe should be theirs alone but that is, in their eyes, dominated by people—including African Americans—foreign to their own American culture. Feeling alienated, strangers in their own land, their guns, they believe, may be the only things standing between them and further encroachment by those who have taken over their country. Guns and individualism, in their eyes, are almost one and the same—the former making the latter possible.

*****

Paradoxically, the best way to look into the cult of individualism in America is to study it as an ethnic and cultural phenomenon, not simply as an aspect of the individual—as many studies of individualism have done. Though American individualism arises to a great extent through the Scots-Irish Borderer, it is not even theirs exclusively—certainly not anymore. Vast numbers of others from divergent ethnicities have been enfolded into the Borderer culture to the extent that only a minority retains a genetic connection to what are the spiritual ancestors of almost half of America. Not only that, but a second great strain of American individualism, one that is perhaps even better known, arose through the secular-liberal culture, as is evidenced in the writings of Benjamin Franklin, Ralph Waldo Emerson, and more. The two strains are related, compounding the difficulty in exploring this complex American trait, for they are also distinct.

Questions of individualism and selfishness so pervade the study of American history and culture that no single work can cover them adequately. Almost by definition, none could. This book is a limited work by necessity, and any point I make could be made just as well through documents and writers other than those I use. Still, I don't think I am far off in the pattern I present of the development of individualism in America.

*****

In his preface to *Internal Colonialism: The Celtic Fringe in British National Development, 1536–1966*, Michael Hechter tells what *didn't* bring him to *his* topic: "Autobiography had nothing to do with it: none of my ancestors were English, Welsh, Scottish, or Irish—of either hue. Neither am I of Roman Catholic, Presbyterian, Calvinist, Methodist, or Anglican descent."[6] In my case, autobiography has *everything* to do with it. My ancestors were English, Welsh, Scottish, and Irish—of both hues (and German and French—but who's counting?). And I am of Roman Catholic, Presbyterian, Calvinist, Methodist, and Anglican (and Quaker) descent. My myths descend from the myths of all of these. And this book is about them, their myths of individualism and mine. I am no outside observer but rather a participant, for better and for worse.

Taking a cue from "participatory journalism," as Jason Mosser calls it, I am working in a tradition of "participatory history" here—not in the sense of the making, as with the journalists, but in the studying. In other words, this is no objective work. Furthermore, what Mosser has to say about journalism and the New Journalism of the 1960s could just as easily be applied to conventional history, particularly conventional cultural history anyway, and to what I am attempting here:

> Readers of conventional journalism perceive events in the same context, that of the standard journalistic formula. The form of the conventional news story attempts to assure the reader that the writer has carefully weighed each discrete bit of information and determined its importance prior to composition. This style encourages a passive reading and does not invite the reader to actively engage with the text, to interrogate its meaning. The closed, formulaic style and structure of a routine news story imply a static, authoritarian view of history. Alternatively, because New Journalists view history dialectically, their texts therefore remain open.[7]

I want this openness and dialogue. I recognize that I am neither alone nor unique but experience a set of cultural influences that also have an impact on millions of my own generation, not to mention generations before and after. My myths are not simply my own.

★★★★★

After a brief initial overview chapter, I focus Chapter 2 on that single trait at the heart of my study and the one most associated with the Borderer culture: individualism itself. Chapter 3 is an attempt to show the basis of the strength of Borderer culture and why, even early on in American history, it was clearly destined to have an influence far beyond the numbers of actual Borderer immigrants. As Fischer writes,

The people of these four cultures shared many traits in common. Nearly all spoke the English language, lived by British laws, and cherished their ancestral liberties. Most dwelled in nuclear households and had broadly similar patterns of marital fertility. Their prevailing religion was Christian and Protestant. Their lands were privately owned according to peculiar British ideas of property which were adopted throughout much of the United States. But in other ways these four British cultures were very different from one another.[8]

Yes. And not all (not even a majority) of "white" people from the British Isles would be assimilated into any uniform American culture (itself a mythical idea). But Fischer's explanations for this in his book seem simplistic and, frankly, biased. Still, Chapter 2 does owe a great deal to Fischer. After all, he did provide one of the sparks for my exploration.

Certainly, being white in America never did make one part of a single great WASP culture—a fact that, by itself, accounts for a portion of the resentment that Borderer descendants feel today toward what they call the "East Coast elite" (much as their great-great-grandparents probably did). White "privilege" has given them . . . what? Though I have not the room in this study to try to answer that, the very fact of the question points to a great deal of the resentments exhibited in American politics in the early 21st century. It also points to the retreat into individualism.

Most histories of the "English" in America start with Jamestown and Plymouth Rock. Mine starts with Ulster Plantation. Again, I make no pretense that I am telling the entire story, simply that I am trying to work from a different vantage point. When I was preparing the proposal for this book, one person suggested that I be more inclusive, adding in more women, for example, and minorities. But I am simply trying to reenvision a *part* of history, not to tell the whole of it—or even to be fair or inclusive. After all, I am dealing with individualism, not inclusivity. Borderers often see the demand for inclusivity as an incursion on individual rights and attempts at fairness simple as cover for redistribution—of credit as well as of wealth.

Especially as I am dealing with myth, I need to be honest about lacks and limitations, not trying to sugarcoat imagined history by trying to be fair by focusing on *all* the groups that have been ignored, mistreated, or worse. I am interested, for this project, in only two broad cultures, one much more dominant than the other, and their myths of individualism as well as the impact of those. I do not have room to consider their parts or the other American cultures, however worthy of study they most certainly are. Besides, trying to sanitize older myths to fit contemporary visions of how the past *should* be seen would be counterproductive. Yes, we create the past—but we should not deliberately misshape it to make it fit contemporary sensibilities.

In Chapter 4, I use Daniel Boone as my touchstone. After all, the great individualist moved down the Great Wagon Road with a large Borderer migration, ending up (for a time, at least) settling with them in western North Carolina. Boone became more than a man, of course, becoming a myth even in his own lifetime. He becomes the spark for Natty Bumppo in James Fenimore Cooper's Leatherstocking Tales, helping create another myth, one of particular self-sufficiency and individualism in westward expansion (and in America in general) that also continues, though in new forms, into the present. The chapter continues with a look at the impact of Andrew Jackson, who became the first Borderer president, and ends with a brief introduction to John Brown as another Borderer icon—though his antislavery stance may seem at odds with prevalent Borderer racism.

Next, in Chapter 5, I give a quick look at the writings on individualism coming out of New England but in the context of the growing myth of the West. Most histories of this time, naturally enough, focus on the North/South divide and the issues surrounding slavery. For my purpose, I am more concerned with the West as seen from the East.

As the greater topic of individualism in America was becoming just too big for me to conceivably handle in a single book (it would take much more than a lifetime), I move quickly on in this chapter, skipping much, to the myths centering on the writings of Horatio Alger and the idea of pulling oneself up by one's bootstraps. These myths concern an urban environment quite far removed from Borderer rural and small-town experiences. This contrasting and complementary vision of individualism led to other boys' books, particularly the Tom Swift series and, here, on to Charles Lindbergh, one of the 20th century's great icons of American individualism.

Lindbergh was mythical, representing the heights that Americans could achieve and in so many ways. Though he called his bestseller about his trip across the Atlantic *We*, he was writing not of a group but simply of himself and his airplane, the now-iconic *Spirit of Saint Louis*. Lindbergh was no saint, however, no matter how much he was mythologized. His involvement in the isolationist America First movement on the eve of World War II had teetered on the edge of anti-Semitism. In one speech, he said, "Their [the Jews] greatest danger to this country lies in their large ownership and influence in our motion pictures, our press, our radio, and our government."[9] Both his positive and his negative reputations often represent Borderer sensibilities and are still important to us today—witness his use in Philip Roth's 2005 novel *The Plot against America*.

Lindbergh's mythological opposite number is, perhaps, that fictional Jewish screenwriter and Hollywood producer Sammy Glick of Budd Schulberg's 1941 novel *What Makes Sammy Run?* Yet Sammy's answer to the narrator's question toward the end of the book, except for the facial expressions, certainly could also have come from Lindbergh:

> "Sammy," I said quietly, "how does it feel? How does it feel to have everything?"
>
> He began to smile. It became a smirk, a leer.
>
> "It makes me feel kinda ..." And then it came blurting out of nowhere—"patriotic."[10]

Both manage to make the leap from personal success to, essentially, politics. The Borderers, through the cult of individualism, make that leap, too.

Chapter 6 arises from the movies, particularly cowboy movies, now grandly called "westerns." Before World War II, most westerns were made for small-town and rural audiences by the third-tier studios of Poverty Row. Just before the war, westerns began to be co-opted by the majors. The changing presentations of populations in the West in these movies, especially as they began to be made for other audiences, illustrate the disdain for the Borderer culture by the Americans of the coasts and also illustrate competing myths of individualism.

Chapter 7 brings us back to the discussions of Chapter 2 but, this time, with an even stronger focus on contemporary debates on culture and ethnicity in relation to individualism. I hope that, given the chapters preceding it, Chapter 7 makes a convincing case that our understandings today of cultural divides are weak and poorly conceived. As a culture, we almost completely ignore the importance of the Borderer in defining a major part of white America and what was once a near majority of Americans as a whole.

*   *   *   *   *

The questions raised in this book are particularly important to me for two reasons. First, as a child of Appalachia who grew up, for the most part, outside of the areas of greatest Borderer influence (primarily what are now seen as the "red states"), I am interested in the odd disconnect I feel in much of "blue state" culture—and in exploring the reasons for it. Second, I see the influence of the Borderers in almost all of the political divisions of the early 21st century and have long wondered about it and about why the cultural descendants of the other English "folkways" (as Fischer calls them) continue to view the Borderer descendants with such dislike and condescension, exacerbating what would be a difficult political opposition anyway. Just as coastal Americans of English descent long looked down on the backcountry people, "blue state" Americans still view the people of the "red states" as more backward than they.

Few on either side of the divide are willing to give an inch, as Henry Stamper of Ken Kesey's *Sometimes a Great Notion* would have said it. The Stampers of Oregon are a classic Borderer clan, though far from Appalachia, as classic as William Faulkner's Snopes family of Mississippi and John Steinbeck's Joads of Oklahoma and California. American literature is filled with others, most of them presented as nasty and perverse, though occasionally a Borderer can be presented as ultimately standing honorably—as is Mark Twain's Huck Finn of Missouri. Though they are often a focus of literature, the Borderers, as a distinct culture, are rarely examined by scholars working beyond the restrictive field of Appalachian Studies.

Though there is necessary reference to the scholarship of the field of Appalachian Studies throughout this book, this is not a book specifically about the people of that region or those beyond it who (like me) trace their cultural roots in America to those mountains. Instead, it is about the myths of these people and of the other great American culture—and about how images of the Borderer have been manipulated, furthering a cultural divide that has served all of us poorly.

An image of American individualism that had once "belonged" to small-town audiences is theirs no longer. America is no longer theirs either, if it ever was. It does not belong exclusively to their opposite numbers, the secular liberals, nor did it ever.

Michael Ignatieff writes, "All forms of nationalism vest political sovereignty in 'the people'—indeed, the word 'nation' is often a synonym for 'the people'—but not all nationalist movements create democratic regimes, because not all nationalisms include all of the people in their definition of who constitutes the nation."[11] And therein lies the problem and the genesis of the cult of individualism.

CHAPTER 1

Myths, Cults ... and Cultures

"Myth is a four-letter word to most social critics," writes Appalachian Studies specialist Rodger Cunningham. True, but we should never forget that, as he goes on to say, "myth-patterns can be forced into the mold of power structures, to which these myth-patterns give strength."[1] Ignoring myth means ignoring the roots of power, and that would be irresponsible. The result of this forcing of patterns, often, is not simply the rise of a "cult" but also the development of a unifying belief, a myth, often one becoming distinct from those of the broader society from whence it comes. And *that* can change the course of history.

"Myth" and "cult" are intertwined, the former a necessary creation for the development of the latter. Referring to the word "myth" in Henry Nash Smith's *Virgin Land*, Leo Marx writes, "As he uses the term, myth is a mode of belief."[2] If this is so, discussion of myth cannot be avoided in examination of society, for society is based on belief. This study centers on backgrounds to the pattern and process through which myth is forced into politics, among other things, and has, in one particular American case (that of individualism), resulted in what can best be described as a "cult" (though one lacking a single charismatic leader), but a cult that is manifest today in the so-called Tea Party and the right wing of the Republican Party. It is also necessarily about the myth of individualism itself, not just about how it becomes a foundation for power and power's cult. This process of incorporation has been going on, in one form or another, throughout the history of the United States and even before, culminating in a situation, in this particular case, where the myth, driven by the power of the cult, has trumped truth as the deciding factor in almost every political debate. It has had the effect of changing the terms of American political discussion from what they were just 40 years ago when a "conservative" Richard Nixon could put forward policies that, today, would be seen as decidedly "liberal."

The cultural imperatives behind myths, cults, and their power—even when these are apparently emasculated within the public sphere—drive a great deal more of our public discussions than most of us ever imagine. Myth *can* drive debate, and its power controls whether we can learn from each other— making a real and whole American culture finally possible. But, so far in American history, myth has generally done the opposite, competing myths keeping us apart.

The country needs to change that, to stop relying so much on myth and the power of the cult, to develop means of understanding, one group to another, back and forth. As Peter Marin claims, "Reciprocity is identical to culture: a collective creation and habitation of value sustained by what we carelessly call the 'individual' self."[3] We can certainly believe in the individual, even in distinct ways, but if we cannot compromise our myths or step outside of them to the point where they are discernible to the "other," we will never achieve a whole American culture that includes a debate that is based on fundamental understanding, one individual to another, one group to another.

Myths and cults, as I said, have a great deal to do with each other. It is internal cultural myths, myths that individuals have made their own, that are played on for the creation of cults, even cults like the cult of individualism without charismatic leaders and purposeful genesis. Even the most private myth arises from factors external to the individual; nothing is truly personal. On the other hand, as Michael Rogin tells us, "Disembodied cultural myths do not act; individual men living out myths do."[4] So, any focus on the myths of a culture must also include the individual. Products of their social upbringing, no matter what sort that might have been, individuals are the ones who make myths real. They are the ones, also and dangerously, who combine to create cults.

History—and especially cultural history—always is personal to some degree. After all, we use our personal judgment when we write. As liberal political commentator E. J. Dionne tells us, reflecting the understanding of historians for generations now, "In their interpretations, in the stories they tell, and in the evidence they select, America's historians are powerfully influenced by the political culture in which they work."[5] Just so. And the influence, again, is personal, individual. Perhaps it does not reach the level of a cult, but it is crucial to keep this in mind nonetheless.

Dionne subtitles the chapter containing the above quote "Why the Past Can Never Escape the Present." It cannot, as we are always remaking it in the image of our myths and even for the use of our cults (all of us partake in cults of some sort). The contemporary and the personal, then, are the best starting points for exploration and rethinking of the past and of some of the myths and cults that shaped it and that shape the present.

*****

In a review of Charles Murray's *Coming Apart: The State of White America, 1960–2010*, Nicholas Confessore writes that "a popular conservative narrative of modern America has gone something like this: Our center-right nation, devout and industrious, is ruled by a politically liberal elite that disdains family, despises religion and celebrates indolence with government handouts."[6] This, both sides of this, are myths, too—but, like all myths, both sides also contain a certain amount of truth. That truth, or an attempt to find it, is the heart of any exploration of the cultural or ethnic identities accompanying and opposing such myths and their cults. There is even truth in Murray's conservative vision, though perhaps not quite what he imagines it to be.

There are two major cultures in white America, both with cultlike aspects, and two visions or myths of individualism. One of the cultures is that "liberal elite" with its ideal of an individual as a creature of the web of community given equal chance with all and fair, universal treatment. I call this the "secular-liberal" culture. The other is that of the supporters of the "Reagan Revolution," the people who believe that one should rely only on oneself, one's family, and one's friends. This, basing the name on the Scots-Irish ethnic roots of that culture, I call the "Borderer" culture. Though these two cultures may sound like they *could* be compatible, they often are not—as we see through the rancorous political squabbling of the major American political parties, each associated with one of these cultures—the Republicans with the Borderers and the Democrats with the secular-liberals. Instead, the cultures are each growing more and more unable to reach out and connect to the other, not understanding what the other means even when using the same words (including that apparently simple word "individualism").

How did this happen? And why is it that America, which has always been assumed to have one dominant white culture, actually has two? What makes these two so different? And, again, why?

*****

To find the answers, one must go back to the 18th century. In an online essay published during the Bush administration, novelist Jane Smiley provided a hint to where this comes from. Taking her cue from David Hackett

Fischer's *Albion's Seed: Four British Folkways in America* with its four
Colonial-American folkways (Puritan, Cavalier, Quaker, and Borderer),
she wrote that, over the past 20 years or so, we had experienced the ascendancy of

> the Borderers/Appalachian culture of hot-blooded and violent populism that is xenophobic, religiously aggressive, fundamentalist, and sectarian, that is suspicious of learning, antagonistic towards "elites," and antipathetic to women's autonomy. It defines itself by masculinity and arms-bearing, is belligerent by nature and quick to take offense. Its natural (and historic) enemy is the outgrowth of Quaker culture, liberalism.[7]

If such language were not incendiary enough on its own, Smiley continues on
in the same vein, drawing a line between her own secular-liberal culture and
that of the Borderers: "For Borderers and their descendants, patriotism is
about passionate loyalty to the group, alert self-defense, and domination in
every sphere."[8] This, to her, is despicable.

On some level, Smiley herself must have been a little uncomfortable with
what she was writing (which verges on indulging in attitudes not far different
from racism), for she does ultimately try to move from the stereotypes she has
thrown about to questions of allegiance and choice:

> If Al Gore had been elected, would we have gone to war in Iraq? Al Gore and George W. Bush, according to Fischer, present an interesting contrast. The Bush family is a Yankee family and the Gore family is Appalachian. But Gore grew up in Washington and went to Harvard, where he enthusiastically took up and was changed by a New England sort of education. Bush grew up in Texas, did not care for a New England sort of education, and had a typical Borderers alcohol addiction/religious conversion. He reacted to 9-11 belligerently. Gore did not, and, by his own testimony, would not have triggered the war machine as Bush has done. Who they seem to be as men reflects their affinities and allegiances rather than their inheritances.[9]

What of this was true? Part of the answer can be found in the work of
Appalachian Studies scholars, including Cunningham, who first might seem
to agree with Smiley, writing (referring to a much earlier situation but one
similar to our current political divide) that "the basic identities and conflicts
of the situation are not 'ethnic'—at least not in any vulgar generic sense—
but *regional*."[10] However, he carefully goes on to claim that

"identification" is not the same as identity ... ; the very nature of the Scotch-Irish identity had been formed by repeated forced abandonments of identification. Now, however, within this "nonexistent" zone of the mountains, a new identity was being fostered. ... Here, in this area ignored by the rhetoric and mentality of American expansion, having no "real" place in the American sense of identity, this new identity began to take shape. Though rooted largely in the collective experience of the Scotch-Irish, it was no more to remain confined to those of Scotch-Irish descent than the "general American" mentality has remained confined to Anglo-Americans.[11]

There was much more going on in this American past than most American history classes, Smiley, regionalism, or even simple ethnic identity would lead us to believe. Choice has something to do with it, but little. History and culture have much more.

The traditional and received historical progression of American culture shows, speaking loosely, a progression jumping from William Bradford and John Winthrop to Benjamin Franklin and Thomas Jefferson to Ralph Waldo Emerson and Henry David Thoreau and so forth. But this is not the whole of it. There was always much more going on in America than a focus on the touchstone luminaries and thinkers of its past can show. One of the questions that the traditional emphasis cannot answer is this: Why do these Borderers, these children of the backwoods (who are a far greater percentage of Americans than most of us have ever imagined), *seem* as they do? And why do others react so negatively to them?

This is a particularly important question even in the broader American culture, for, as Smiley points out, the Borderers appeared, before 2012, to have won out as the premier culture in the country, their myths dominating the greater political discourse even when elections are won by the other side. This is true, paradoxically, even as their power seems to wane with the rise in influence of other ethnic groups. It is true even as the domination by the "white males" associated with Borderer culture (though the "liberal elite" is dominated by white males, too) begins to collapse.

*****

Most postmortems of the Obama/Romney presidential race assumed that "white" voters belong together as a voting bloc. This is a mistake. Even beyond the Borderer/secular-liberal split, there are other splits, other groups within that bloc. More than a few of these, perhaps uncomfortable with being lumped together, have distanced themselves from Borderer culture. Though they often share political affinities, they have opted to stress, for example, European ethnic-ities that, though they may have been their parents', are theirs today only by ancestry and not by lifestyle. Still, in a sense, these people are merely reverting to—or simply exposing—their own separate ethnicities, ones that had been overcome by a "symbolic Americanism" adopted in order to blend in with the broader American culture and allowing for the mistaken assumption of white solidarity. Part of the electoral success of the Borderers over the past generations came from what looked like a coalition with these urban white ethnic groups—even though those groups appear culturally far removed from the rural-based Borderers. Part of their failure today may be a loosening of this coalition. Cultural and ethnic blendings, we see, are as complex as they are real.

The two largest nonwhite minorities in America are, of course, Latinos and African Americans. Unlike the white ethnics, some of whom identify with Borderer mind-sets and some of whom have become secular-liberals, these have not split their allegiances between the two European-descended American cultures. Also, each retains identity in ways far beyond the symbolic ethnicity of many white ethnics (though they both do indulge in that, too). For various reasons, a majority of Latino voters have now allied themselves with the secular-liberals, as have the African Americans (who fled the Republican Party in the Great Depression and who closed the door on it as it welcomed the Borderers who were themselves abandoning the Democrats in the wake of 1960s civil rights legislation). These have formed a new tripart political coalition centered on the Democratic Party that portends future demographic muscle that the Republicans will not be able to match—unless things change and Republicans find a way to reach out beyond their "base." Still, the power of the Borderer-dominated right has been unmatched for 40 years, and its influence is not going to ebb quickly.

How did these changes in alliance and dominance happen, and what, besides demographics, lies behind them? Certainly, it is not the Borderers alone who make up the "red state" political population. In fact, neither the "red states" nor the "blue states" are exclusively red or blue. The divide in each is fairly close: Rare are the states where the majority consistently com-mands anywhere near 60 percent of the vote.

* * * * *

In any discussion that touches on ethnic distinctions or, indeed, on ethnic uni-ties, it is worth remembering what Max Weber wrote just about a century ago:

> The belief in group affinity, regardless of whether it has any objective foundation, can have important consequences especially for the formation

of a political community. We shall call "ethnic groups" those human groups that entertain a subjective belief in their common descent because of similarities of physical type or of customs or both, or because of memories of colonization and migration; this belief must be important for the propagation of group formation; conversely, it does not matter whether or not an objective blood relationship exists.[12]

This is particularly significant to any discussion of the Borderers as a cultural or ethnic group in America, for, as Smiley intuits, they have never been defined accurately by blood—any more than they have been defined by what we normally think of as the extended trappings of ethnicity.

Generally, the Borderers have been defined by what they are not or, more accurately, by what others imagine they lack. At the same time, they are usually described in terms of class structures better suited to older, more stratified European societies than to America. Rather than being seen as a distinct culture, the Borderers become, in many minds, nothing more than American versions of European lower classes. Richard Hofstadter, a case in point, finds them to be the lack of all that a gentleman should be. He cannot even name them, not more than by calling them things like "unschooled" and "western squatters" whose leaders "were pushed up from the bottom [rather] than selected from the top."[13] In the 19th century, he writes, the better sort of people

> were born in the Northeast—mainly in Massachusetts, Connecticut, New York, and Pennsylvania—although a scattered few lived in those parts of the Middle West which had been colonized by Yankees and New Yorkers. Morally and intellectually these men were the heirs of New England, and for the most part its heirs by descent. They carried on the philosophical concerns of Unitarianism and transcendentalism, the moral animus of Puritanism, the crusading heritage of the free-soil movement, the New England reverence for education and intellectualism, the Yankee passion for public duty and civil reform.[14]

In his eyes, these were all things the Borderers, most clearly, were not. These were the hallmarks of an eastern elite, of the secular liberals, the people who were the only hope for civilizing the unwashed masses who had settled the rest of the country.

Though the accepted wisdom, ever since Nathan Glazer and Daniel Moynihan's *Beyond the Melting Pot* was published in the 1960s, has been that American "ethnics" are qualitatively different from the Borderers and the other descendants of Fischer's four British folkways, they are really less of a distinct grouping than ancestry may make it may appear. Politically, as I have said, most of the various ethnics have become allied either with the Borderers or with the secular-liberals, many of them coming to feel a real comfort with one or the other of the older American cultures. In fact, Herbert Gans goes so far as to name the remaining little ethnicity of many of them "symbolic ethnicity," arguing that assumed ethnicity, after a generation or two, rests simply on easy symbols, on things that make their adherents appear to be apart from the mainstream of white America, giving them a cachet in what many still see as an increasingly homogeneous "white" America. The actual difference, Gans might argue, may be only in assumable appearance.

Still, though Gans does make an important point about the way ethnicity is sometimes worn, I am not completely convinced that "symbolic ethnicity" cannot also be "real ethnicity." Richard Alba follows up on Gans more strongly, arguing that the loss of "real" rather than "symbolic" ethnicity heralds "the formation of a new ethnic group: one based on ancestry from anywhere on the European continent."[15] Though the various groups have indeed developed affinities, I think Alba is wrong, and for a simple reason: His argument ignores the fact that ethnicity covers not only those whites from more recent immigration waves (those beginning with the Irish Potato Famine of the decades before the Civil War) but also those whose families came before. It may be in fact that our older ethnic cultures and these newer ethnics are joining together, but not as if into a melting pot of the whole—for there was never a unified American culture or ethnic group in the first place, not even a "white" one.

This is not to say that various cultural groups within a larger framework do not influence one another, their cultural myths never spilling from one group into another. They certainly do. Contemporary African American culture does not owe its development solely to Africa and its children. It was shaped as much by Europe. The reverse is just as true: White Americans without a drop of African blood have been as surely influenced by Africa as by Europe. American cultures cannot be defined exclusively by so-called race any more than they can be defined by ethnic origin. All of them, also, are strongly tainted by myth—probably more than by reality—and, though they can be cultlike in their exclusionary attitudes, none is ruled by absolutes. The influential rhythm-and-blues musician Johnny Otis, for example, was born to Greek immigrants in California as Ioannis Alexandres Veliotes. Growing up in a black neighborhood, he adopted African American culture and lived his life within it. The very idea of race, we realize, is itself mythical—and sometimes even race itself becomes a cult.

The myth of an American cultural unity *did* grow into a dominating force, of course, but it was also a myth that was blown apart over the last half of the 20th century, to a degree by the work of Glazer and Moynihan and their followers but also by the civil rights movement itself and subsequent emphasis on a different set of ethnic myths, ones that also had a direct impact on American politics. Certainly, "the enactment of Civil Rights legislation by the Democratic Kennedy and Johnson administrations, opposed by Barry Goldwater, the 1964 Republican candidate for the presidency, generated a new race-based divide between the parties"[16] and within America as a whole. The divide was never based on reality, of course, but rather on perception. And the impact was much greater that simply politics: "Only with the Civil Rights successes of 1964 and 1965 did the dominant discourse of national civic life acknowledge the salience of group experience and standing."[17] Certainly, the focus of politics was once again on race and, subsequently, on ethnicity in ways that it had not been before. Nonracially or nonethnically (in terms of visible symbols) distinct groups began to be ignored or were lumped together—and many of them often began to feel that they were left out of the discourse completely.

Though, admittedly, there are not many actual Borderers in New York City, Glazer and Moynihan, for example, include them (by omitting any mention of them) where they don't belong, with the one group that they dismiss from their serious consideration, calling them "white Protestants," who

> are a distinct ethnic group in New York, one that has probably passed its low point and will now begin to grow in numbers and probably also in influence. It has its special occupations, with the customary freemasonry. This involves the banks, corporation front offices, educational and philanthropic institutions, and the law offices who serve them. It has its own social world (epitomized by, but no means confined to, the *Social Register*), its own churches, schools, voluntary organizations and all the varied institutions of a New York minority.[18]

Though obviously not a description of Borderers, this stereotype of the WASP (with its tacit Borderer inclusion) has been, since the 1960s, carried through as an assumption behind much of America's discussion of race, culture, and ethnicity. It has affirmed that the Borderers should remain invisible and ignored, allowing creation of a myth of universal "white privilege" while ignoring the reality of white poverty outside of specified ethnic bounds.

Though they were not a huge presence in New York City in the 1960s, the Borderers still did live in the city, and in numbers. The same is true today.

Taking them out of the picture has not only skewed any discussion of ethnicity but has also helped leave Borderers with an increasing feeling that their position in America has been eroding. Since the 1960s, the country they once viewed as theirs has begun to seem to slip away from their grasp. And, it is true, the nation today can appear to be dominated by a combination of the children and grandchildren of immigrants and racial minorities. This perception has slowly become closer to reality, and this reality is part of the reason for the political change going on in the second decade of the 21st century, the ebbing of recent Borderer political clout.

By not making distinctions between the Borderers and other early American folkways, students of ethnicity such as Alba are subsequently unable to see that the cultural intermarriage they view as critical to the diffusion of real ethnicity into symbolic ethnicity is also a continuation of an American process of enculturation. They are unable to make note of the process of enfolding a portion of the newer Americans into the Borderer mindset. Again, the new immigrants and their children as often develop allegiance to Borderer culture as they do to the secular-liberal culture, but they do divide—and not simply on class lines (in America, social classes are, themselves, something of a myth). And why not? If Johnny Otis could choose his culture, others certainly can. Smiley, then, is not completely off base in arguing that culture is assumable.

Contrary to the popular image of the Borderer, their culture has always welcomed newcomers—as long as they accept Borderer ways and do not try to change them. Through their experiences with the high percentage of single males following in their footsteps during the push west into the frontier, the Borderers learned early on how to assimilate others, even if they were from distant ethnicities, into their own culture. Once the limits of the frontier had been established, this ability to assimilate allowed Borderer culture to reach back to the East Coast to some degree, to ethnics of the newer immigration movements. Brooklyn, New York, neighborhoods like Marine Park, long an Irish and Italian Catholic bastion (though now becoming more and more Orthodox Jewish), share many of the attitudes of the Borderers, for example. People who see only racism, religious intolerance, and cultural exclusionism in the Borderers might find this surprising, imagining that the predominantly Catholic ethnicities would be unlikely candidates for inclusion in Borderer culture or among its friends. That would be a misreading of Borderer attitudes. However racist they might be (and xenophobic), the Borderers have assimilated many from outside or have developed bonds with them. Again, as long as the "others" are not perceived as a threat, Borderers will accept them. African Americans, as a group, have long been held to them as vying to share in or take away any prosperity they might have gathered. This makes the African Americans seem as though they connive to steal things away from the Borderers. So, as a group, African Americans are distrusted, and the old pattern of racism is furthered. Individual blacks, though, often find themselves welcomed (or, at least, tolerated) in Borderer communities—as long as they are perceived as sharing Borderer values and as wanting nothing from them beyond joining them.

The election of Barack Obama as president has accented this distinction. As a figure distant from daily lives, Obama becomes a symbol and not an individual. For many from the Borderer culture, he represents the contemporary iteration of a combination of forces that have long sought to take something away from the predominantly white Borderer communities. In the past, in Borderer minds, the goal was to give what was taken from them to the bankers and moguls of the East. Today, and since the rise of the "welfare state," another goal has been added: to give Borderer assets to those from cultures (and races) centered on "taking," not working. Mitt Romney reflected this attitude, of course, in his famous remarks about the supposed 47 percent of Americans "who are dependent upon government, who believe that they are victims, who believe the government has a responsibility to care for them, who believe that they are entitled to health care, to food, to housing, to you-name-it. That that's an entitlement. And the government should give it to them."[19] This, of course, is a myth based on a faceless (or, rather, blackfaced) "them" who threaten the largely white "us." It is in reaction to this perceived threat that many Borderers have retreated into a belligerent individualism, one that does, it is true, carry a certain type of racism with it—and a hatred of Obama.

*****

The reaction to the perceived selfishness on the part of others is often an increase in selfishness of one's own. This develops into an ever-growing cycle of selfishness and anger, one often also cloaked in a more idealistic individualism. It is true, as Eric Hoffer writes, that

> the inordinately selfish are particularly susceptible to frustration. The more selfish a person, the more poignant his disappointments. It is the inordinately selfish, therefore, who are likely to be the most persuasive champions of selfishness.
>
> The fiercest fanatics are often selfish people who were forced, by innate shortcomings or external circumstances, to lose faith in their own selves. They separate the excellent instrument of their selfishness from their ineffectual selves and attach it to the service of some holy

cause. And though it be a faith of love and humility they adopt, they can be neither loving nor humble.[20]

When this is extended to an entire culture, the results can be extreme. In the case of the Borderers, the cause chosen is often an aggressive and exclusionary individualism—even when cloaked in religion, as it sometimes is.

The movement toward individualism has been aided by religion, of course, for it can be used to create a barrier between the self and the rest of the world—especially when relations with the rest of the world have not been particularly good. Other things have served the same function, for Borderers and for others, including political movements, of course, and the various self-improvement and therapy cults that have sprung up in America over at least the last two centuries, with promises of better futures based on belief and self-confidence. However, as Peter Marin, resonating Hoffer, has pointed out, even "Our therapies become a way of hiding from the world, a way of easing our pangs of conscience. What lies behind the form they now take is neither simple greed nor moral blindness; it is, instead, the unrealized shame of having failed the world and not knowing what to do about it."[21] This often lies behind the cult of individualism as well: find someone else to blame for one's own failings in the broader world and hide your own culpability. Such blame, of course, often focuses on those who are clearly "other," people of different religions or origins—or race.

A study by Michael Tesler and David Sears attempts to show the impact of racism spilling over into political attitudes. They claim that "the spillover of racialization mechanism is premised in large part on the fact that most Americans do not have well-developed political belief systems, but instead formulate their opinions about public policy from cues provided by groups and politicians who share their political views."[22] Though this can lead to a classic "which came first" argument, Tesler and Sears certainly do have a point when they claim that Obama's election has amplified the impact of race on political affiliations, that "racial resentment is causing changes in partisan attachments rather than party identification changing respondents' underlying levels of racial resentment."[23] What they do not deal with is the reasons for the fixation on race, reasons coming from a long history of American cultural—and not just racial—divides and from the myths that have furthered those divides.

The easy and common reaction to this, of course, is to ignore all else and fall back onto the charge of racism—but it really is not so simple. Yes, race is a factor, but the cultural divide that race has come to exemplify is an even greater one. In many cases, racism is the result of a confluence of forces, both mythical and real, that have resulted in retreat from interaction with others into aggressive individualism. Many of these forces arise from real abuses, especially on Borderers. The reality of these does not excuse racist attitudes, of course, but recognition of them can allow those attitudes to be more effectively addressed.

Most Borderers, probably as far back as their arrival in America or before, mistrusted the idea of "equality," racial or otherwise, in the first place. Not only do they feel they have never experienced it, but it is something, in their eyes, that cannot be legislated or tied to group struggle. Not only that, but it is an impossibility, given the limitations of human life and interaction—and Borderers know this. It is no wonder, then, that Austrian-born economist Friedrich Hayek found an appreciative audience within the Borderer culture with works like *The Constitution of Liberty*, where he writes,

> Equality of the general rules of law and conduct . . . is the only kind of equality conducive to liberty and the only equality which we can secure without destroying liberty. Not only has liberty nothing to do with any other sort of equality, but it is even bound to produce inequality in many respects. This is the necessary result and part of the justification of individual liberty: if the result of individual liberty did not demonstrate that some manners of living are more successful than others, much of the case for it would vanish.[24]

This is the heart of Borderer hesitation to embrace the concept of equality as put forward in America from the successes of the civil rights movement of the 1960s on. It also points to the distinction between "dream" and "myth" in terms of "success," as a Borderer might see it. Each person has the right to dream and to have the possibility of seeing those dreams realized, but no person has the right to success. So, dreams can remain dreams without consequence.

The myth of success is something else, the idea of something actually achievable by anyone. This concept goes far back in American considerations of individualism and success—and in both major white American cultures. Writing about the writer of 19th-century motivational novels for juveniles Horatio Alger, Richard Weiss states that,

> the "dream" and the "myth" [of success] represent two separate and distinct threads in the fabric of American culture, and the use of them as synonyms assumes an identity where none exists. The "dream" grew out of the new possibilities for wealth and power that industrialization brought in its wake. It was fired by the advent of Napoleons of the market-pace, men who commanded industrial armies, controlled vast resources, and

lived in lordly opulence. The "myth," by contrast, reflected the values of a merchant-agrarian society, religious, moderate, and simple in tone.[25]

The goals of the dream, in most lives, superseded those of the myth.

*****

Fischer sees four British influences in America: the Pilgrim, the Cavalier, the Quaker, and the Borderer. Three of these he presents with tacit sympathy. After all, they came to the colonies as groups with idealistic visions, visions with a variety of roots and manifestations, but all imagining a new and better sort of life along lines that were often well defined. The Borderers, however, came to the colonies primarily as a result of economic exigency, escaping poverty rather than dreaming of a city on a hill. Unfortunately, the other groups were generally much more literate than the Borderers, and, as a result, it is only through the lens of their writings and their ideals that we see the 18th-century Borderers. As they did not much care for the Borderers, the image we have is a negative one.

This is one of the legacies of colonial America that keeps us, today, from recognizing the extent of Borderer success. The Borderers who arrived early in America were vilified, as contemporary descriptions show, and then were ignored before being vilified again. The impact of this on the later development of what amounts to a Borderer cult of individualism can hardly be overstated. If the other groups thought of the Borderers at all, it was generally as debased refugees from English culture in need of training in the niceties of society and a little formal education. However, as if that were not enough, by the 1960s they were seen as having no culture or ethnicity of their own *at all*—outside of Appalachia, at any rate (and most Borderer descendants were no longer Appalachian). This lack grew in importance as the idea of "ethnicity" itself rose to greater prominence during the 20th century, becoming one of the mainstays of the popular perception of the American character. Certainly, since the 1960s and Glazer and Moynihan, the quest for and study of "ethnicity" has been all the rage among those examining American identity. But the contemporary popular concept of "ethnicity," for some reason, generally assumes that all of the European Americans whose ancestors arrived before the Revolution were one and the same, subsuming the Borderers as a distinctive group. Fischer's great saving grace is that he, like scholars in the field of Appalachian Studies, recognizes that "ethnicity" extends well beyond the grandchildren of Ellis Island, his book remedying this omission at least a little.

Two of the most interesting books of the last few decades on white ethnicity in America are Alba's *Ethnic Identity: The Transformation of White
America* and Matthew Frye Jacobson's *Roots Too: White Ethnic Revival in
Post-Civil Rights America*. In both cases, "ethnicity" is limited to more
recent immigrants than the Borderers. In fact, there is only passing mention
of Scots in the former, none of Appalachia, and only a single reference to
"Scots-Irish" in a footnote, saying, "The Scots-Irish combination can be
more troublesome, in the sense that it can be difficult to decide in any individual case whether the ancestry represents a single group (the Scots-Irish,
persons of Scots background who were transplanted to Ireland after English
conquest of the island) or a mixture."[26] Troublesome it surely is, but not
quite in the way Alba meant. There is no mention at all of Appalachia, the
Scots, or the Scots-Irish in Jacobson's book. Though both books do deal
extensively with the Irish, it is the Irish of later waves of immigration.

Difficult to define precisely because they have welcomed so many outsiders
into the fold, the Borderers (as a culture) evidently also become more easily
ignored. It should not cause any wonder that they, more than other Americans,
now wrap themselves in a cult of individualism that allows them, in turn, to
ignore all of the others.

Conveniently ignoring them or conflating the Scots-Irish experience with
that of other European groups has a long and illustrious pedigree. Margaret
Mead, writing in the 1940s, claimed that "Americans establish . . . ties by
finding common points on the road that all are expected to have traveled,
after their forebears came from Europe one or two or three generations
ago, or from one place to another in America, resting for long enough to
establish for each generation a 'home town' in which they grew up and which
they leave."[27] The roads of internal migration are far different from those of
the millions who come from abroad. Pairing the two, as Mead does, can make
one feel that the former is little more than a pale shadow of the latter.

Mead goes on to say that Europeans do not understand that an American
hometown "is not where one lives but where one did live."[28] This assumes
that Americans move around while Europeans do not, that people came to
America from places their ancestors had been for many generations. In the
case of the Borderers, this was not true. Not only had many of them been
recently displaced from Scotland to Ireland before coming to America, but
their lives in the Scottish lowlands had never been as securely tied to place
as in other areas of Europe. Mead continues, "Life had ceased to be expressed
in static, spatial terms as it was in Europe, where generation after generation
tied their security to the same plot of ground, or if they moved to a city, acted

as if the house there, with its window plants, was still a plot of ground anchored, by fruit trees."[29] Borderers never had that security before coming to
America or, for many of them, even after. Their only trust lay in themselves
and their families. Everything outside could be lost—and often was.

*****

The "slighting" of the Borderer, in Borderer perception of the Borderer role
in American society, may have receded somewhat over the years since the
founding of the republic but it was renewed with a vengeance shortly after
the first moves toward affirmative action by President Kennedy in 1961,
moves amplified by the 1964 Civil Rights Act. As the Borderers (and the
descendants of the other "folkways," for that matter) began to be dismissed
as "white bread" by those clearly different (or who, like the "counterculture"
of the time, made themselves *appear* clearly different), they began to feel
newly marginalized within their own land as attention to minorities and "ethnics" grew. They were being told, or so they believed, that they had no real
culture, no real standing with those outside of their immediate social groups.
Even their self-perception as core Americans was being cast into doubt. Few
Borderers could embrace an Italian, Jewish, Irish, or Polish heritage (even
those with actual genetic ancestry in such "ethnics" often could not, now
being too far removed by generations and intermarriage)—but the media
could. Television and movies were suddenly filled with romanticized
"ethnics," and the assumption began to grow that *these* were the "real"
Americans. Ellis Island became the touchstone for American authenticity.
The older "real" Americans now found themselves on the outside looking
in. And they resented it.

Generally urban based, the "ethnics," in their first generation, had very little in common with the descendants of the Borderers. Many of them, particularly those who rose in the professions—in business, the arts, and education—
integrated (with a few bumps along the way) with the secular-liberal culture
that had grown from the other three folkways, further alienating the
Borderers from what seemed to be a possible new American majority. Even
though just as many of the "ethnics," as generations progressed, moved
closer to Borderer mind-sets and became their political allies, the general perception of the Borderers was that power in America was now in the hands of
minorities and "ethnics"—a perception that moved a step closer to reality
with the 2008 and 2012 elections.

While others are encouraged to be proud of their ethnicity, Borderer children have found that they can hardly ever claim their own Scots-Irish or

Appalachian heritage as their part of the mania for ethnic identification. I have rarely heard anyone disparage anyone—not over the last 25 or 30, at any rate—for being proud of their ethnicity—except in one case: In most of America, when anyone starts to talk about their Appalachian background, they get laughed at. Outside of the Appalachian Studies programs at colleges and universities in the mountains, the Borderer culture is not considered an "ethnicity" worth studying or even examining. In most minds, it is not a real ethnicity at all, simply a devolved culture—or an unevolved one of "contemporary ancestors" that the rest of us have moved beyond. It has become the butt of jokes and even self-parody, certainly on television, starting at least as early as the *Beverly Hillbillies* of the 1960s and *Hee Haw* of the 1970s and 1980s and continuing through such present-day Country Music Television programs as *My Big Redneck Vacation* and *Chainsaw Gang*.

Yet, for all their continuing setbacks, the individualism of the Borderers, perhaps their defining characteristic, is proving to be one of the driving forces of 21st-century American politics—even in its decline. Inability to understand that contemporary political contentiousness arises in part from a long-standing cultural divide, one that has been widening since the 1960s, only makes matters worse. The Borderers are not throwbacks thrown forward but rather a dynamic and integral part of the American public sphere—no matter how regressive some others may view their positions. Whoever wins elections, the Borderers—and their individualism—are perhaps the most potent and important single force in American politics today.

CHAPTER 2

The Individual in Two American Cultures

As philosophy professor Stephen Asma reminds us, "If you want to know what is *good* for human beings, Aristotle thought, you don't study *The Good* (as Plato tried). Instead, you study *human beings*."[1] Just so, if you want to know what makes a good *individual* human being, you do not study abstractions; rather, you study people and the societies they form. Yet "individualism," as understood in America, stems both from an unrealistic abstraction taken away from ideals of community and born of rejection and from "we, the people," a concept embracing the importance of the person to the group. The two primary white cultures of the country, roughly the "red state" and the "blue state" ones, can be differentiated by the relative origins and emphasis of their own conceptions of the word.

The irony of individualism arises from the fact that the concept exists only within cultural contexts. An absolutist individualist would have no need of language or of distinction—and could not exist, not as a human being, at least, for all of us humans are dependent on others. Individualism arises only as an aspect of community, as an aspect of a society's vision of its individual parts.

In political and cultural terms, both "individualism" and its sometimes synonym "selfishness" are filled with problems—and with nuance that is often missed. Though they are much the same, generally speaking, the most obvious difference between these two words is that the former frequently carries a sense of pride and accomplishment, while the latter makes us think first of the miser. "Individualism," in the minds of many of her citizens, is what made America great, while a certain sort of "selfishness" (often attributed to political enemies) is what tears it apart. The one is good, the other bad. Both of the major white American cultures accuse the other of a miserly sort of selfishness while lauding its own grand individualism.

It is not so simple, of course, for either Borderer or secular liberal.

To begin to see the complexity and to understand the difficulty of establishing a clear distinction between the competing senses of the words, we need do no more than look at the start of chapter 2 of volume 2, part 2, of *Democracy in America*, where Alexis de Tocqueville makes one of the earliest uses of the word "individualism" ("individualisme" in the original French):

> *Individualism* is a recent expression arising from a new idea. Our fathers knew only selfishness.
>
> Selfishness is a passionate and exaggerated love of self that brings man to relate everything to himself alone and to prefer himself to everything.
>
> Individualism is a reflective and peaceable sentiment that disposes each citizen to isolate himself from the mass of those like him and to withdraw to one side with his family and his friends, so that after having thus created a little society for his own use, he willingly abandons society at large to itself.
>
> Selfishness is born of a blind instinct; individualism proceeds from an erroneous judgment rather than a depraved sentiment. It has its source in the defects of the mind as much as in the vices of the heart.
>
> Selfishness withers the seed of all the virtues; individualism at first dries up only the source of public virtues; but in the long term it attacks and destroys all the others and will finally be absorbed in selfishness. Selfishness is a vice as old as the world. It scarcely belongs more to one form of society than to another.
>
> Individualism is of democratic origin, and it threatens to develop as conditions become equal.[2]

Though there is a conflict between the two terms, de Tocqueville says that "selfishness" ("egoïsme") is ultimately the victor, consuming the weaker "individualism." And, indeed, this does seem to be the case in the United States today, taken most cynically. Certainly it can seem to be so—in how we view ourselves and in how we imagine our own self-sufficiency, whichever side of the cultural divide we fall on.

*****

The impact of the myth of individual effort as the primary basis for individual success in America has grown only stronger over the years. So strong (and so evolved into selfishness) has this become that, over at least the past 30 years, many of us on one side of the divide, the "red state" side, the Borderer side, are no longer even willing to recognize the very real help that others (particularly government) give us. We each did it *all*—alone!

This is an impossibility, as I have said and as we all know when we stop and think about it. But, according to Suzanne Mettler, this startling unwillingness to recognize the support we have received over our lives has had the surprising result of actually driving a good deal of the communitarian efforts of the federal government of the United States—and more—underground: "In the lives of most Americans other than seniors, the impact of visible governance has diminished while that of the submerged state has grown."[3] Our sense of self-creation has grown so important to many of us that we deliberately fool ourselves as a group in order to maintain it.

So cultlike has the belief in individualism become that few people associated with the contemporary Borderer culture seem to be able to admit that, indeed, they have succeeded in their lives because of the support of others, particularly if these others include government. In fact, one can go further: On *either* side of the cultural divide, we want to believe that we did it all by ourselves. As de Tocqueville knew would happen, many of us go further still, using the cloak of "individualism" to cover a much more coarse vision of "selfishness." Here again, though, we do not want to admit to a desire to take whatever we can get, no matter the source—so much so that we have institutionalized the disguising and subverting of government's role in our lives. Indeed, as Mettler says, we go so far as

> making the real actors appear to be those in the market or private sector —whether individuals, households, organizations, or businesses. The mechanisms or tools through which such activities occur have proliferated to include a great variety, such as loans subsidized and guaranteed by government but offered through private banks and government-sponsored enterprises; social benefits in the form of tax incentives and tax breaks for those engaging in activities that government wishes to reward; and benefits and services provided by nonprofits and private third-party organizations that are subsidized or "contracted out" by government.[4]

Government has become, in many minds on the "red state" side of the cultural divide, the opposite of individualism, the representative of attempts to take away a person's freedom of action in favor of an amorphous "common good" promoted by "blue state" adherents. The government, in this view, suppresses family and favoritism, basic building blocks of society and culture, in favor of a mythological and impossible equality. Asma explains the conundrum as arising from the fact that, for generations now, Americans have been "taught, from an early age, that no one is intrinsically 'higher' or 'lower' than anyone else, that everyone is equally valuable. Philosopher Martha Nussbaum says, 'Our nation is built on the idea that all citizens as citizens are of equal worth and dignity.' So how do we reconcile our favoritism with our conflicting sense of equality for all?"[5] The "red state" people, spiritual descendants of the Scots-Irish Borderers, have been asking this question for centuries. In a sense, we all have. Not only are the conflicts between individualism and community within each of us, but we have never even acknowledged the existence of two major American white cultures, one with family and community at its center and the other based on values stemming from the Enlightenment, of dignity and equality for all—each with its own vision of the role and possibilities of the individual, each with its own competing myth of individualism.

The split between these cultures has led to differing interpretations of "individualism" and to constant misunderstanding between the two sides. Over the past several generations, views on the novelist and self-proclaimed "philosopher" Ayn Rand have come to be one of the tests of which side any person may fall—though, of course, the divide extends far beyond her, both in time and in ideas. Today, many of her followers take the split to extremes, taking it beyond culture and *embracing* "selfishness" in even its most negative connotations, pushing away any distinction with "individualism" or, rather, making the latter just one part of a whole. Rand proclaimed the "virtue of selfishness," after all, extolling it as the foundation of American—indeed, human—success.

Rand writes that "selfishness," in her vision, is often misunderstood:

> It is not a mere semantic issue nor a matter of arbitrary choice. The meaning ascribed in popular usage to the word "selfishness" is not merely wrong: it represents a devastating intellectual "package-deal," which is responsible, more than any other single factor, for the arrested moral development of mankind.
>
> In popular usage, the word "selfishness" is a synonym of evil; the image it conjures is of a murderous brute who tramples over piles of corpses to achieve his own ends, who cares for no living being and pursues nothing but the gratification of the mindless whims of any immediate moment.
>
> Yet the exact meaning and dictionary definition of the word "selfishness" is: *concern with one's own interests.*[6]

Rand was not simply being provocative by proclaiming "selfishness" a virtue. She believed it and wished to sweep away any timid reliance on a tepid or constrained "individualism." Rather than being a way to hide "selfishness" before being subsumed by it, "individualism" becomes, for her, simply an aspect of selfishness or a weak synonym.

"Individualism" is, in the words of Rand's erstwhile follower, colleague, and lover Nathaniel Branden,

> at once an ethical-political concept and an ethical-psychological one. As an ethical-political concept, individualism upholds the supremacy of individual rights, the principle that man is an end in himself, not a means to the ends of others. As an ethical-psychological concept, individualism holds that man should think and judge independently, valuing nothing higher than the sovereignty of his intellect.[7]

He continues, "An individualist is a man who lives for his own sake and by his own mind; he neither sacrifices himself to others nor sacrifices others to himself; he deals with men as a trader—not as a looter; as a Producer—not as an Attila."[8]

Writing a decade later than Branden, in the mid-1970s, social commentator and activist Peter Marin described what he saw as a new narcissism in America in which "the individual will is all powerful and totally determines one's fate."[9] Of course, this was not a new idea even with Rand; it was common in 19th-century America and even earlier. No matter how much many Americans want to believe it, however, this is simply so much window dressing in most of their lives—no matter which side of the cultural divide they fall on. Believers in it see themselves standing tall as traders while really they are also looters—of, among other things, the submerged government they strive to ignore.

*****

The impact of government programs is certainly often unseen, as Mettler argues, or at least unacknowledged, with the intended result that people can easily and without any feeling of discomfort ignore their own reliance on them. In many respects, Rand notwithstanding, the individualism we are seeing today has no high sensibility behind it but is simply the playing out of what de Tocqueville described nearly two centuries ago. If anything, for many of her contemporary American followers, Rand becomes an excuse after the fact rather than a light to a new path. There is more to the cult of individualism than that—as we shall see—but Rand is often the starting point and the excuse for a contemporary defense of what is, actually, a much older and deeper cultural attitude of individualism held by a large percentage of Americans.

As we certainly see in America and as Steven Lukes illustrates in his study of individualism, the meaning of the word differs in different cultures and settings. In "France, it usually carried, and indeed still carries, a pejorative connotation, a strong suggestion that to concentrate on the individual is to harm the superior interests of society."[10] This, of course, is quite different from many American conceptions of the word—and different from de Tocqueville's description. Lukes discusses a number of somewhat distinct European and American views and their changes over time before turning to a presentation of the "basic ideas" of individualism. He sees these as five:

1. The Dignity of Man: This, he takes back to the Bible, showing its decline in the Middle Ages and its subsequent resurgence, culminating in Immanuel Kant's *The Moral Law* and maintained today.

2. Autonomy: The idea that one's thoughts and actions are the responsibility of the self, it "is a value central to the morality of modern Western civilization, and it is absent or understressed in others (such as many tribal moralities or that of orthodox communism . . .)."[11]

3. Privacy: A modern aspect of individualism, it "refers to a sphere that is not of proper concern to others. It implies a negative relation between the individual and some wider 'public,' including the state—a relation of non-interference with, or non-intrusion into, some range of this thoughts and/or action."[12]

4. Self-Development: Lukes traces this to the Italian Renaissance, moving forward through the Romantics and even into Marxism. He concludes that the "notion of self-development thus specifies an ideal for the lives of individuals—an ideal whose content varies with different ideas of the *self* on a continuum from pure egoism to strong communitarianism."[13]

5. The Abstract Individual: "According to this conception, individuals are pictured abstractly as given, with given interests, wants, purposes, needs, etc.; while society and the state are pictured as sets of actual or possible social arrangements."[14]

He further divides individualism into the political, the economic, the religious, the ethical, the epistemological, and the methodological. Relating to American individualism in particular, he writes that it "had, by the end of the Civil War, acquired an important place in the vocabulary of American ideology. Indeed, even those who criticized American society, from New England Transcendentalists to the Single Taxers and the Populists, often did so in the name of individualism."[15] This, of course, remains true today.

However, a "perusal of the various American uses of the term reveals a quite distinctive range of connotations."[16]

Taking a slightly different tack from Lukes, Stephanie Walls divides individualism into "radical" or "popular" individualism and "authentic" individualism, the latter being community based and the former much more in keeping with Rand's idea of selfishness. She also sees a progression in how individualism has been defined:

> The three main phases in the evolution of individualism will be classified in terms of "ideals": individualism as a political ideal, an economic ideal and a social ideal. The literature documents the view of individualism as a political ideal and then as an economic ideal. The third category concerns individualism as a social ideal, and I believe that this is the phase Americans transitioned into during the last half of the twentieth century.[17]

Like de Tocqueville, she argues for a progression from the authentic to the radical but bases her argument on an Enlightenment ideology in early America that I am not sure could be applied to those Scots-Irish Borderers whose influence is at the center of much of this book and from whom comes one of our contemporary American sense of "individualism." They were not a particularly well-educated group. Their poverty and constant movement kept them away from many of the intellectual conversations elsewhere in the British Isles and the colonies. Enlightenment thinking pretty much passed them by.

Walls also presents the more convincing argument that this individualism is as much a product of space as it is distant ideology, something that *does* fit the Borderers and the early America that Walls describes:

> There was simply plenty of physical space for citizens to spread out and literally take care of themselves. I believe that individualism as a political ideal can be classified as an "authentic" form of individualism. While the emphasis was placed on the individual, no part of this ideal blatantly disregarded the interests of others. Political individualism did not necessarily force people to turn against the best interests of others to pursue their own best interests. The amount of land available at that time was vast, and those with sufficient "rugged" characteristics were free to depart from society and live as individuals. The concept of individualism as a political ideal was able to grow and thrive in this environment, because it was literally possible to leave civilized society, however one wished to define it.[18]

In addition, Walls sees there being political, economic, and social individualism, much as Lukes does, but she warns that

> the American notion of individualism is not one that is easy to quantify. It is an ideological concept that has evolved over our country's history from a purely political concept to a complex social ideal. It is a facet of classical liberalism that is at once latent in our political history and active in our cultural habits. Previous attempts at explaining declining participation have focused on logistical issues and external conflicts that make participation less feasible. The American tradition of individualism and the empirical evidence presented herein make obvious the need to include internal ideological attitudes in any discussion of non-participation.
>
> The success of our democracy requires an open dialogue on the topic of non-participation. It is worth investigating whether or not one of America's founding ideological concepts is undermining that success. In the political realm, individualism has a history of empowering citizens. In the social realm, however, individualism is partially responsible for the neglect of community and political matters. It is an ideological concept many Americans embrace but do not apply consistently. Individualism has evolved into an incongruous concept, given the interconnected world we live in. Our democracy requires participation, yet individualism encourages withdrawal. We must deal directly with this ideological phenomenon if we hope to explain non-participation in political and community matters. And we must create a full explanation of non-participation if we hope to correct it.[19]

Perhaps this is the crux of the problem in trying to define individualism in an American context: Its meaning changes even as one person uses it in different situations. And it has certainly changed over the centuries, even though aspects of it have remained strong and sometimes the same. Still, its meaning is clearly different in different cultural situations, especially in those as distinct as the two major American cultures are, at heart.

Oddly enough, neither Lukes nor Walls deals at all with John Dewey's 1930 book *Individualism Old and New*. Lukes ignores Dewey completely, while Walls discusses only *The Public and Its Problems*, a slightly earlier book. Perhaps the reason is simple: At first glance, Dewey does not seem to add much to our understanding of early American individualism, and his proposal for a new type of individualism in the face of the corporatization of society can seem hopelessly out of date. Dewey places individualism squarely within a system of cultural support, a vision opposite to the libertarian viewpoint that has dominated much of American discussion since. He writes that

"assured and integrated individuality is the product of definite social relationships and publicly acknowledged functions."[20] Unlike those within the contemporary American conservative movement, Dewey saw the corporation as
an enemy of individualism rather than one of its possible extensions, and he
wanted to find ways to develop new protections for individualism in a
changed environment: "Individualism has been identified with ideas of initiative and invention that are bound up with private and exclusive economic
gain. As long as this conception possesses our minds, the ideal of harmoniz-
ing our thought and desire with the realities of present social conditions will
be interpreted to mean accommodation and surrender."[21] He summed up
his view of the possibilities of individualism:

> Individuality is at first spontaneous and unshaped; it is a potentiality, a
> capacity of development. Even so, it is a unique manner of acting in
> and with a world of objects and persons. It is not something complete
> in itself, like a closet in a house or a secret drawer in a desk, filled with
> treasures that are waiting to be bestowed on the world. Since individu-
> ality is a distinctive way of feeling the impacts of the world and of show-
> ing a preferential bias in response to these impacts, it develops into
> shape and form only through interaction with actual conditions; it is
> no more complete in itself than is a painter's tube of paint without rela-
> tion to a canvas.[22]

There is no supreme or absolute individualism possible in Dewey's conception of the word, only something that grows from interaction and that is,
therefore, never alone or self-made.

What Branden misses in *his* definition of "individualism" but that is clear
from de Tocqueville and the evidence of American cultural history, not to
mention Lukes's and Walls's more considered studies or Dewey's somewhat
iconoclastic vision, is that "individualism" is not simply ethical-political or
ethical-psychological—and it is certainly not so easily encapsulated. It is definitely cultural and ethnic in how we view it and use it and so must be flexible
and encompassing of many uses. Let me give just one simple illustration, one
of how individualism can even stretch beyond the single person, one even
mentioned in the passage above from de Tocqueville's book: the family.

*****

The family, of course, has biological roots, but growing out of that—and in
any cultural or ethnic situation—the "family" takes on specific societal meanings, its definition changing culture by culture. In American society, the
individual is extended to include various American concepts of family (often,

as de Tocqueville says, it even includes friends), and, as a result, an individual is also often able to turn things around, to take credit for what the family has done and vice versa. Donald Trump may consider himself a self-made man, but he inherited control of a vast real estate empire. That does not count, though: It is family. The same is true, on much smaller scales, for most of us. It was even true for that mythical American loner Daniel Boone: "A hunter who loved the solitude of the forest, Boone was also a part of an extended, close-knit community of relatives and friends that stayed with him in different combinations throughout his many moves on the Yadkin [River], across the mountains into Kentucky, and eventually all the way to Missouri."[23]

* * * * *

When, during the 2012 presidential campaign, candidate Mitt Romney said, "I had inherited nothing. Everything that Ann and I have we earned the old-fashioned way, and that's by hard work,"[24] he was able to justify his statement by explaining that he and his wife gave away their monetary inheritances when their parents died. But Romney's inheritance was much greater than dollars. Not only did it include the secure upbringing and fine education he was provided, but it also encompassed an entire cultural background— including his Mormon religion—that was provided for him. Following from Mettler, this is a "submerged inheritance," but an inheritance it remains.

Also during the 2012 presidential campaign, Romney blasted Barack Obama for suggesting that it takes more than an individual to build a company:

> To say that Steve Jobs didn't build Apple, that Henry Ford didn't build Ford Motor, that Papa John didn't build Papa John pizza, that Ray Kroc didn't build McDonald's, that Bill Gates didn't build Microsoft ... to say something like that is not just foolishness, it's insulting to every entrepreneur, every innovator in America, and it's wrong.[25]

What Obama had said was,

> If you were successful, somebody along the line gave you some help. There was a great teacher somewhere in your life. Somebody helped to create this unbelievable American system that we have that allowed you to thrive. Somebody invested in roads and bridges. If you've got a business—you didn't build that. Somebody else made that happen. The Internet didn't get invented on its own. Government research

created the Internet so that all the companies could make money off the
Internet.[26]

This is a key difference in attitude between the two cultures toward
individualism.

A blogger on the progressive political site *Daily Kos* responded to
Romney:

> Did Steve Jobs stand on an assembly line and assemble the iPod? No.
> Did Henry Ford attach motors to the Model T? No. Thousands of ordi-
> nary folks who get up in the morning and with calloused hands and
> sweaty brows … they are the ones who built those companies. Sales-
> men and customer service reps and repairmen and ordinary consumers.
> That's who built those companies. Mitt Romney seems to think that it's
> the team owners who win championships and not the team.[27]

What we see in this exchange is the crux of the "red state"/"blue state"
divide as it plays out in competing visions of the place of the individual in
society.

My father liked to tell a story of when he was teaching at Denison
University in the 1950s. At that time, attendance at Sunday chapel was
required—and the deans and their staffs had to round up the numerous students shirking the service, which generally included an outside speaker. One
semester, they noticed that no one was avoiding chapel. Curious, the deans
decided to explore. What they discovered rather shocked them: It seems that
the university had agreed to host a series of speakers from an Ohio club of
self-defined, self-made millionaires. Quickly, the students discovered that
the men were not self-made at all—and developed a betting pool based on
what minute into the talk the speaker would let the cat out of the bag. One
might have worked his way up from the mailroom but let slip that it was
Dad who had promoted him to the executive suite. Or he had swept the
floors at Taylor Motors, working hard every day—dating Julie Taylor on
weekends until their wedding. Each one, at one point or another, inadver-
tently indicated that they had had a special advantage. The fun was in betting
on *when* they would admit it, not *if*. This is not surprising. For most of us, as
Asma claims, "families literally prepare the pumps of emotional chemistry and
smooth the pathway to later social connection."[28] Success, no matter how we
might try to submerge the connection, often depends on family or friends—
and it does so in ways far beyond even the sort of nepotism so easily identified
by those Denison students.

This example shows the power of what can seem to be an American schizo-phrenia—if the fact of dueling American cultures is ignored, that is (as it so often is). Even Asma frequently puts the situation into an exclusively family perspective (though he does later mention in passing that "rural" Americans see the situation differently from "urban" ones): "The idea that everyone deserves equal treatment, that everyone has equal claim upon resources, or that everyone has equal value as my kin are all foreign to the intrinsically hierarchical emotional brain."[29] He goes on to challenge traditional liberal thinking on human development:

> We don't come into the world as selfish Hobbesian mercenaries. Contrary to the usual pessimistic contract theory, we mammals don't start out as self-serving egotistical individuals who then need to be socialized (through custom, reason, and law) to endure the com-promises of tribal living. Rather, we start out in a sphere of emotional-chemical values—created by family care—in which feelings of altruistic bonding are preset before the individual ego even extricates itself. ... I think there is an ancient favoritism instinct, and it's not the usual indi-vidualistic selfish instinct that veneer theorists might call "human nature." It's a tribal instinct that has altruism already built in (caring and being cared for are intrinsically, even intoxicatingly rewarding).[30]

This faith in an intrinsic "goodness" of human beings raised within family environments has been disparaged as simple tribalism by the Enlightenment-based culture of half of America, the culture that, because of its stress on language and on education, once dominated the political and philosophical discussions within America (though the other side has always been present to some degree). Ideas such as Asma's had long been sublimated or ignored as a result.

*****

Submerged connection, especially family connection: This went under-ground because of competing idolatries of individualism. There are, as we have seen, two types in America—and not simply "individualism" and "self-ishness" but the individual as an Ayn Rand independent actor or the individ-ual as Benjamin Franklin might have drawn him or her, as someone operating within a social framework but through the power of individual initiative.

Horace Kallen wrote almost a century ago, "Respect for ancestors, pride of race! Time was when these would have been repudiated as the enemies of democracy, the antithesis of the fundamentals of the North American

Republic, with its consciously proclaimed belief that 'a man's a man for a' that.'"[31] Though Kallen was both wrong and naive, the fact remains that the two forces, family and democracy, remain incredibly strong—and have been for centuries—as is illustrated not only by de Tocqueville's melding of the individual and family but also by contemporary political debate where the libertarian individualist and the promoter of family values often turn out to be one and the same.

If our dependence on government is submerged, as Mettler claims, our dependence on family and all that it implies in terms of culture and ethnicity is also often ignored, as in Romney's case, or forgotten—or subsumed in the individual. In fact, history itself is almost completely forgotten in this context. Likewise, the sanctity of "family" (look, for example, at the debates over gay marriage), in terms of political debate, shows right where our examinations stop and where we are unwilling to look. Certainly, no politician would challenge the contemporary importance of today's American vision of family or of the "right" to contribute to one's family's future. But, for the most part, we do not examine its past, simply claiming (if thinking about it at all) that "family," as imagined now, was always the meaning of "family." We do a lot of this and in many realms, even extending the idea of the unity of the family *with* the individual to our concept of intellectual property, including the inheritor as the equivalent of the creator. We now take the U.S. Constitution's article I, section 8, governmental power "To promote the Progress of Science and useful Arts, by securing for limited Times to Authors and Inventors the exclusive Right to their respective Writings and Discoveries" far beyond the initial purpose of promoting progress to protecting inheritance (does lifetime plus 70 years promote progress more than the much older 14 years renewable once? I doubt it). Older meanings, including constitutional ones, have become irrelevant. The family, as representative of the individual, trumps all. Fairness, in terms of the public sphere, has disappeared. The liberal tradition, at least in this instance, has lost out.

Strangely, this attitude concerning the family's connection to the individual does not seem to extend to education, not among the "reformers" of the first decades of the 21st century, at least. Perhaps this is because education is one arena where secular liberalism has remained strong. Or perhaps this is because there is a mendacious aspect to our conceptions of "family" (see Donald Trump). It seems, at least, that we are willing to abandon the concept when it requires effort apart from gain or *for* the gain. Joel Klein and Michelle Rhee, former heads of the New York City and Washington, D.C., public schools, respectively (writing with a group of other education administrators) go so far as to claim that "the single most important factor determining whether students succeed in school is not the color of their skin or their ZIP code or even their parents' income—it is the quality of their teacher."[32] Not only does this deflect responsibility from the family, but it flies in the face of scholarship on learning and becomes a parody, not a reflection, of liberal sensibilities. Take, in contrast to Klein and Rhee, what Betty Hart and Todd Risley discovered well over a decade ago:

> We found we could easily increase the size of the children's vocabularies by teaching them new words. But we could not accelerate the rate of vocabulary growth so that it would continue beyond direct teaching; we could not change the developmental trajectory. However many new words we taught the children in the preschool, it was clear that a year later, when the children were in kindergarten, the effects of the boost in vocabulary resources would have washed out. The children's developmental trajectories of vocabulary growth would continue to point to vocabulary sizes in the future that were increasingly discrepant from those of the professors' children. We saw increasing disparity between the extremes—the fast vocabulary growth of the professors' children and the slow vocabulary growth of the … [poorer] children. The gap seemed to foreshadow the findings from other studies that in high school many children from families in poverty lack the vocabulary used in advanced textbooks.[33]

In other words, the family you come from *does* make a tremendous difference in how likely you are to succeed in school—or in life, as the successes of Romney and so many others show. It is not just a question of economic status: Families with a great interest in seeing their children succeed in education tend to expose them to a greater range of experiences and language than do others and teach them necessary skills at home. When I was growing up it was even a cliché: There was a mother or grandmother pushing every successful student, no matter the socioeconomic background. When expectations for education were high and parents provided the necessary early exposure to words and ideas, children did well. It is the family, in other words, that makes the scholar, not the teacher. It is the family that makes the individual, with the resulting strong connection between individual and family. This is a major problem for proponents of state-created equality in education just as it is elsewhere.

It is an odd thing about American individualism and its protectiveness of family and family rights that it does not extend to all of our discussions of society, education, culture, and ethnicity. Instead, we again submerge the connection as Klein and Rhee have done. Over the centuries, we have created a myth through our focus on individuality (but, again, not *really* individuality, for it includes family and friends), a myth of the individual who does it all himself or herself, the very myth that Romney, again, was promoting during the 2012 election and, paradoxically, that Klein and Rhee manipulate to create their own vision of education. This long, cultlike tradition in America dates back, of course, to the earliest movements to the new colonies, even though many of the first immigrants, like the Pilgrims, were strongly communitarian. By the time of the Revolution, the myth of the individual had become stronger, perhaps, than the competing ideal of community— or, rather, community now served the individual in the vision of many, not vice versa.

* * * * *

In Letter III of his *Letters from an American Farmer* of 1782, J. Hector St. John de Crèvecoeur wrote,

> *He* is an American, who leaving behind him all his ancient prejudices and manners, receives new ones from the new mode of life he has embraced, the new government he obeys, and the new rank he holds. He becomes an American by being received in the broad lap of our great *Alma Mater*. Here individuals of all nations are melted into a new race of men, whose labours and posterity will one day cause great changes in the world. Americans are the western pilgrims, who are carrying along with them that great mass of arts, sciences, vigour, and industry which began long since in the east; they will finish the great circle. The Americans were once scattered all over Europe; here they are incorporated into one of the finest systems of population which has ever appeared, and which will hereafter become distinct by the power of the different climates they inhabit. The American ought therefore to love this country much better than that wherein either he or his forefathers were born. Here the rewards of his industry follow with equal steps the progress of his labour; his labour is founded on the basis of nature, *self-interest*; can it want a stronger allurement? Wives and children, who before in vain demanded of him a morsel of bread, now, fat and frolicsome, gladly help their father to clear those fields whence exuberant crops are to arise to feed and to clothe them all; without any part being claimed, either by a despotic prince, a rich abbot, or a mighty lord. ... The American is a new man, who acts upon new principles; he must therefore entertain new ideas, and form new opinions.[34]

De Crèvecoeur's book, described by Leo Marx as "simple-minded,"[35] leaves out the fact that, even if he is right, every immigrant to the colonies and then the new nation also carried within him or her the culture of the homeland, even going back to the first settlers. As Randolph Bourne wrote a year before American involvement in World War I (and when there was still an ever so *slight* chance that the United States could go in on the side of the Germans, not the English),

> The truth is that no more tenacious cultural allegiance to the mother country has been shown by any alien nation than by the ruling class of Anglo-Saxon descendants in these American States. English snobberies, English religion, English literary styles, English literary reverences and canons, English ethics, English superiorities, have been the cultural food that we have drunk in from our mothers' breasts. The distinctive American spirit—pioneer, as distinguished from the reminiscently English—that appears in Whitman and Emerson and James, has had to exist on sufferance alongside of this other cult, unconsciously belittled by our cultural makers of opinion.[36]

The past is in all the presents and futures that Americans, old or new, have built, even when they have integrated into the new culture. In spite of all the new allegiances that were formed, ancestors were not left behind and forgotten but continue to hold sway in each individual and individual family. Yet it is also true that simple genealogy itself never covers enough ground, not really. There are just too many ancestors of too many types. Most of the time, even those who explore them limit themselves to certain strands, often just patronymics, and ignore the rest. But the rest is huge and by itself puts the lie to the concept of the self-made man.

No person is immune to the past; no one makes an independent fresh start. The American myth, though, allows us to imagine that we can leave our past and our ancestors behind by moving to a new continent or its expanding frontier. At the start of *The Fountainhead*, Rand presents a conversation between her hero Howard Roark and a dean at the school that has just expelled him. The dean argues for a continuity of human experience and creativity:

> "We must learn to adapt the beauty of the past to the needs of the present. The voice of the past is the voice of the people . . ."
> "But you see," said Roark quietly, "I have, let's say, sixty years to live. Most of that time will be spent working. I've chosen the work I want to do. If I find no joy in it, then I'm only condemning myself

to sixty years of torture. And I can find the joy only if I do my work in the best way possible to me. But the best is a matter of standards— and I set my own standards. I inherit nothing. I stand at the end of no tradition. I may, perhaps, stand at the beginning of one."[37]

The individualism shown in this passage, American in spirit but tempered by Rand's own experiences as a youth in revolutionary Russia, imagines that the real self-made person can be exactly that. The weaknesses of such an attitude, of course, are myriad. First, and most obviously, all humans share in languages whose creation they have had no part in, whose development they affect only incidentally, at most. Just by talking to the dean, Roark is standing on tradition. In addition, a real individualist of the sort Rand thinks she is showing would never even consider tradition, either start or finish. It would be irrelevant: The real self-made person would care no more to influence than to have been influenced.

The irony of the imagined self-contained and complete individual is unintentionally accented by the last line of the book: "Then there was only the ocean and the sky and the figure of Howard Roark."[38] Yet Roark is standing atop a building, one that, even though it is "his" creation, is the work of many and is "his" only through cultural convention.

*****

A generation before Rand immigrated to America came another Russian of Jewish background, Mary Antin, whose autobiography about growing up an immigrant in America and the process of assimilation, *The Promised Land*, made her famous. She wrote in what seems to be a similar vein to Rand's at the start of her book, "*I* emerged a new being, something that had not been before. And when I discovered my own friends, and ran home with them to convert my parents to a belief in their excellence, did I not begin to make my father and mother, as truly as they had ever made me? Did I not become the parent and they the children, in those relations of teacher and learner?"[39] The idea of the opportunity to become the creator both of one's past and one's future had, we see, already become an established part of American mythology by the time of Rand. In a subsequent book, Antin wrote,

> There is a phrase in the American vocabulary of approval that sums up our national ideal of manhood. That phrase is "a self-made man." To such we pay the tribute of our highest admiration, justly regarding our self-made men as the noblest product of our democratic institutions.

Now let any one compile a biographical dictionary of our self-made men, from the romantic age of our history down to the prosaic year 1914, and see how the smell of the steerage pervades the volume! *There* is a sign that the practical man finds it easy to interpret. Like fruit grows from like seeds. Those who can produce under American conditions the indigenous type of manhood must be working with the same elements as the native American who starts out a yokel and ends up a senator.[40]

The self-made person (as it has become today). The rugged individualist. It would take some time to unpack this quote with its claim that the very land of America is what makes American individualism—and that allows the individual to overcome ethnic, class, and cultural barriers. But the intent is clear: The opportunity of America is that of the individual, and the institutions of America allow opportunity to be seized. This is related, as we will see, to the secular-liberal tradition of older New England.

Although 19th-century immigrants from countries outside of English/ American cultural traditions gravitated equally toward either American tradition, their base experience was with the confluent rags-to-riches traditions of the time, traditions that can lead to affinity with either the secular-liberal or the Borderer culture and traditions that grew out of parts of both.

At first, in America, the ideal individual *was* presented, by the likes of Benjamin Franklin and Thomas Jefferson, as a character within a social context and compact. As Bourne writes,

If freedom means the right to do pretty much as one pleases, so long as one does not interfere with others, the immigrant has found freedom, and the ruling element has been singularly liberal in its treatment of the invading hordes. But if freedom means a democratic cooperation in determining the ideals and purposes and Industrial and social institutions of a country, then the immigrant has not been free, and the Anglo-Saxon element is guilty of just what every dominant race is guilty of in every European country: the imposition of its own culture upon the minority people.[41]

Freedom, reflecting this more cynical depiction, generally meant the latter in early America. People like the Scots-Irish Borderers, who were not willing to conform, were relegated to the frontier. Certainly, the demanded conformity, even to many others beside the Borderers, seemed to be rather confining, especially when couched in terms of domination. It carries the reminder of Shakespeare's Caliban, who, at the end of act II, scene II, of *The Tempest,* sings " 'Ban, 'ban, Cacaliban/Has a new master.—Get a new man" before shouting "Freedom."

The irony of this, of freedom often simply being a change of masters, was not lost on the proponents of individualism. So, over the years, the idea of individualism as an aspect of societal cooperation fell away for a part of society (if it had ever held such a belief in the first place) until Rand's conception was able to emerge from writings like Antin's and from movements like the "New Thought" of the late 19th and early 20th centuries. North America, in its abundance, had proved to offer too much for restriction to apply to the imagination:

> A virgin continent, immeasurable rich in land and resources, sang its song of infinite promise. How could a man fail in such an environment, except through laziness or vice? Those who carried this view to the extreme of insisting that the poor and unfortunate deserved their sufferings were probably few, but faith in America made it a commonplace that a man could become rich if he worked at it.[42]

John Cawelti, a pioneer of popular-culture studies, is actually writing here about the early years of the 19th century, a time of hope and high expectation that would last, with significant drops (the Civil War, the Great Depression, and so on), well into the later part of the next century. The periods of disappointment, though deep and sometimes long, always contained the idea of their end: So much more was out there in the limitless land that the bad times *had* to end, new possibilities and progress becoming manifest. Americans of all cultures believed that.

* * * * *

Restriction only chaffs. Failure happens only when people are not "allowed" to succeed—or so many Americans believe. The less government interference or restriction, the better.

More than a century ago, Frederick Jackson Turner wrote that "the frontier is productive of individualism. Complex society is precipitated by the wilderness into a kind of primitive organization based on the family. The tendency is anti-social. It produces antipathy to control, and particularly to any direct control. The tax-gatherer is viewed as a representative of oppression."[43] This grew into the contemporary stereotype of one of the American cultures—the Borderer one, of course.

Historian and social critic of the 1960s and 1970s Christopher Lasch, who, along with Marin and others, saw America growing into a new narcissism at that time, connected this new movement to the old stereotype:

The contemporary narcissist bears a superficial resemblance, in his self-absorption and delusions of grandeur, to the "imperial self" so often celebrated in nineteenth-century American literature. The American Adam, like his descendants today, sought to free himself from the past and to establish what Emerson called "an original relation to the universe."[44]

Though that may be overstating the case, the 19th century really was the time of the growth of the *idea* of a single American character, something of an irony considering that this generalization is based on the sanctity of the individual, itself something of a contradiction to the assumption of an American universal. It is a conceit, growing out of writings of the years surrounding the Revolution, of a secular-liberal cultural consensus, something that never really was there (witness the Civil War) and that never even existed as cultural unity even in New England or in the South. The fact is that the "real" individual (in either of its basic American conceptions) has never existed in European-based American society. There has always been a submerged state, family, ethnicity, and culture behind any "independent" individual.

There have always been, of course, many American cultures, but the two I have been focusing on here have always been at the heart of the particularly American illusion of individualism, and these, once more, are the cultures growing from those Scots-Irish Borderers and from the English Enlightenment. In addition to the four "folkways" of David Hackett Fischer, of which the Borderer is one, there have been (and are), of course, Native American and African American cultures; a variety of Jewish, Italian, Latino, and Asian American cultures; and more. Strangely, in more ways than we generally imagine, in these days of ethnic pride, these have all consolidated (though significant cultural differences do remain, not to mention overt cultural markers) around Borderer or secular-liberal attitudes—in the political arena, at least.

Unlike the situation today, when what seem to be ethnic differences are celebrated, a century ago, these separate identities within the "whole" were seen as a potential or even an actual problem. Horace Kallen once observed that "the natural hyphenation of the American citizen may become the basis for disruptive action, and as a consequence, the term 'hyphenated American' has become a term of reproach."[45] In other words, this diversity scared some of those who did believe in a melting pot, in the idea that all the hyphenations would become one single "American." Indeed, often, people coming out of these heritages *have* taken on the trappings of an American "ideal," but, like other Americans, they have also kept with them,

intentionally or not, a great deal of what their ancestors had provided—
especially if they came to this country as families or members of larger groups
and not simply as individuals. Today, though, the pendulum of attitudes has
swung far the other way, accenting difference at the expense of very real
similarities, a state of affairs that is itself a result of American focus on
individualism.

* * * * *

As we have seen, any discussion of the individual or the family clearly tails off
into discussion of culture, of heritage, of ethnicity. Just as the individual is for
the family, family, of course, is the glue and the center of culture and ethnicity
and the means of their perpetuation. Working the other way, ethnicity has a
great deal to do with American conceptions of individualism, contributing
to them even within the greater developing American cultures. Here again,
we have what might seem a paradox, but it is one with a great deal of power
and continuity. It concerns the forgotten ethnicity of immigrants from the
British Isles, the four folkways described by Fischer, and a suppression of ethnicity in favor of perception of class by American writers of the 19th century
and scholars of the 20th.

Bourne wrote, almost a century ago, that "America shall be what the
immigrant will have a hand in making it, and not what a ruling class, descendant of those British stocks which were the first permanent immigrants,
decide that America shall be made."[46] This was not completely true, not even
at the beginning. For one thing, it ignores the Borderers completely—they
were never part of the ruling class Bourne imagined. One of the effects of
such attitudes, today, has been a low-level sense of frustration on the part of
the spiritual and physical descendants of these Borderers in particular, a frustration that now manifests itself as one of the factors that has led to the "red
state"/"blue state" split that has solidified over the past generation. This
can be seen in the Electoral College results of the last six elections. Since
1992, the map has looked basically the same (taking into account Bill
Clinton's regional appeal). New England, the upper Midwest, and the West
Coast have gone one way, the rest of the country another. Though this
pattern, speaking loosely, is much older, now it seems set in stone.

It had certainly always been there—as can be seen through a quick look at
the Electoral College results of presidential elections almost since the founding of the nation. The change toward what appeared to be a more nationally
unified electorate shown in Franklin Pierce's 1852 victory disappeared in
1856, the contentious issue of slavery joining a deepening divide between a

rapidly industrializing Northeast and an agrarian South and West. James Buchanan won as a southern and western candidate, though he fell well short of half of the popular vote, though that was indeed a higher percentage than Lincoln would get four years later. Lincoln, like Buchanan, won with only a plurality, succeeding due to a divided opposition. It was the Electoral College margin that mattered, however, and it is also the Electoral College that shows best the splits in American culture.

Because of the Civil War and the disruption in voting and voting patterns it engendered, we do not see the older patterns reemerging until 1876, when Rutherford Hayes's election showed a North/South split that also certainly reflected the war but that just as certainly reflected the prewar past and foretold the broader divisions that would devil the country for the next century and more. With James Garfield's election four years later, the split was even more apparent and more concrete. Grover Cleveland's election in 1884 simply confirmed the pattern, though this time it was the southerners who succeeded. His defeat in the Electoral College, not the popular vote, four years later showed only how narrow the divide was—as did his election in a three-way race in 1892, when he succeeded with less than half of the popular vote.

In 1896, we see a pattern of division almost identical to the one of the early 21st century, McKinley winning with California and Oregon, the northern Midwest, and those eastern states outside of the old Confederacy At that time, it was the Republican Party that represented the industrialized states. The year 1900 showed much the same result, but with some gains by McKinley in the West.

The most stark North/South split came in 1904, when Theodore Roosevelt swept everything outside of the Confederacy except for two states, Kentucky and Maryland, contiguous to it. Four years later, Taft lost the new state of Oklahoma (also contiguous to the Confederacy) and also saw erosion in the West, losing Nebraska, Colorado, and Nevada.

In one of the rare national coalitions, Woodrow Wilson took almost the entire country except for a rump remainder of the North that went to Roosevelt running on the Progressive ticket. Taft won only one state, Utah. Even so, Wilson earned far from half of the popular vote, succeeding only because of the split opposition. When he was reelected, the North reemerged as an almost solid opposition. In 1920, only one of the states of the Confederacy went for Warren Harding, Tennessee, and only one outside state, Kentucky, went against him. In 1924, the South was solid again but expanded only to Oklahoma, the rest of the nation going to Calvin Coolidge.

In 1928, Alfred Smith was solidly trounced by Herbert Hoover winning, outside of a rump South, only Massachusetts. Hoover himself, however, lost all but part of the Northeast four years later. And the Northeast, again, four years after that, was the only place Franklin Roosevelt did not sweep. Roosevelt lost ground in the Midwest in 1940 and a little more in 1944 but won with sweeping Electoral College majorities.

The frustration that is solidifying this split in the 21st century stems in part from a feeling of disenfranchisement on the part of many whites that began as a reaction to the civil rights successes of the 1960s. It has settled into what, so far, has been a permanent national cultural and political rift on the heels of the Reagan era, a rift that can be identified by differing visions of the place and role of the individual.

* * * * *

In the aftermath of the civil rights movement, according to Herbert Gans, panethnic coalitions formed not so much from a racist base but as a result of threats perceived by the "ethnic" whites, threats they felt "as homeowners and jobholders, by black demands."[47] This "backlash," coming primarily from urban whites in media-saturated areas and not so much from the more rural Borderers, gathered a great deal of publicity, bringing new attention to the various newly powerful ethnic groups, attention that filtered into entertainment media, helping make the "ethnic American" the new stereotype of the American, in popular media, at least, and further disenfranchising the Borderer (who, in many ways, had been on the outside in American since arriving in the 18th century)—though also bridging the gap between the Borderers and the "ethnics" in terms of racial concerns, among other issues.

The popularity, in the 1960s and early 1970s, of former Alabama governor George Wallace crossed between the groups: "Many, though certainly not all ... ethnic voters saw in Wallace a kindred spirit; a man despised and dismissed by distant social planners all too ready to sacrifice working-class families on the altar of upper-middle-class convictions."[48] Nathan Glazer sees this as the end of a peculiar (given racial prejudice) 1930s coalition between "ethnic" whites, African Americans and other minorities, and southerners, one that started fraying when the Democratic Party began to commit itself to civil rights in the late 1940s.

Cultural affinities and cross-cultural alliances are ill defined and often changing. According to Matthew Frye Jacobson, one of the significant political developments in America over the past 50 years has been the increasing "centrality of ethnic and racial differences to our conception of the nation, the tenacity of ethnic identity among the descendants of earlier European immigrants, and the evolution of ... 'multiculturalism.' "[49] At the same time, racial tensions have led to a "move to distance oneself or one's group from monolithic white privilege [which] gave way in some cases to a politics of white grievance that pitted itself against unfair *black* privilege (as in the ensuing affirmative action debates), often, ironically, couched in a Civil Rights language poached from blacks themselves."[50] This has also had the effect of increasing alienation from the putative greater American culture by Borderer descendants, who were now seeing themselves as outsiders, as I have said, in what they had believed their own land. Their alienation led to an increased focus on the individual and individualism as the greater societal structures, in their minds, were failing them more and more often.

What was going on to cause this? In keeping with Gans, Jacobson claims that "in the years beyond the melting pot there arose a new national myth of origins whose touchstone was Ellis Island, whose heroic central figure was the downtrodden but determined greenhorn, whose preferred modes of narration were the epic and the ode, and whose most far-reaching political conceit was the 'nation of immigrants.' "[51] This left out the Borderers and the other British folkways, the actual dominant cultures, almost completely. They had no ethnicity, in many eyes, and no culture beyond the much-derided American "norm" of the 1950s. On the other hand, "in their loving recovery of an immigrant past, white Americans reinvented the 'America' to which their ancestors had journeyed. The ethnic revival recast American nationality, and it continues to color our judgment about who 'we' Americans are, and who 'they' consider outside the circle of 'we the people' are, too."[52] It also silently spoke volumes about whom Americans are not, this new "displacement of Plymouth Rock by Ellis Island in our national myth of origins"[53] undercutting long-held and cherished ideas of place and belonging of those Americans without ability to tie themselves in with the new sort of ethnic identity. After all, the new immigrants, no matter what was imagined, "invented no new social framework. Rather they brought over bodily the old ways to which they had been accustomed."[54] Ultimately, they joined hands with one or the other of the older cultures while maintaining, symbolically for the most part, their ancestral ethnicity.

*****

It even seemed at times as though the ethnics were assimilating completely:

> The urban ethnic families of early television's *The Goldbergs, Life with Luigi,* and *Mama* had yielded in the assimilationist 1950s to the whitebread pedigrees of *Father Knows Best* and *Ozzie and Harriet* (the Goldbergs themselves became "de-Judaized" and moved to a

homogenized suburb called Haverville). In American television from about 1954 to 1968, "ethnicity" was the exclusive preserve of a handful of culturally isolated—if lovable—oddballs: Lucy's husband, Ricky Ricardo; Danny Thomas's uncle, Tonoose; Rob Petrie's cowriter, Buddy Sorrell.[55]

But it soon became apparent that the "ethnic" was not the oddball in post-WWII America; the rural American was. Shows like *The Beverly Hillbillies*, *Green Acres*, *Petticoat Junction*, and more made it clear that it was now the Borderer who was the comic outsider, not the "ethnic."

To make matters worse, the entertainment media trumpeted ethnicity even louder each passing year. This could now be seen in myriad popular genres, including, to pick just one example, the musical, both in film and onstage. Jacobson writes of a

tight alignment between ethnic film and the musical [that] was partly due to the tradition that remained intact within the musical even as the genre began to fade. The folk musical, for example, whose earlier exemplars include *Hallelujah*, *Annie Get Your Gun*, *Oklahoma*, and *The Music Man*, continued to emphasize the communal ethos of a bounded regional or cultural universe—often portrayed as a backwater —but now shifted its attentions toward a different version of the romanticized "folk."[56]

These new "folk" might be the Puerto Ricans of *West Side* Story, the Highlanders of *Brigadoon*, or the Jews of *Fiddler on the Roof*. For all that he was a caricature demeaning the Borderer, L'il Abner had been replaced by Tevye—and the loss was felt if not understood.

Given that, as Jacobson later argues, "ethnicity *is* the assimilated norm,"[57] Gans posited that ethnicity, starting even in the second generation, loses its real meaning, its demands on the individual, becoming "symbolic ethnicity." Gans characterizes this as "a nostalgic allegiance to the culture of the immigrant generation, or that of the old country; a love for and a pride in a tradition that can be felt without having to be incorporated into everyday behavior."[58] The symbols involved become an easy way for the "ethnics" to distinguish themselves from "nonethnics," from those Americans who cannot dredge up a symbolic connection to a European (or, later, Asian, African, or South American) heritage—which would be the Borderers, in particular, but also the rest of the descendants of early settlers. However, the "Anglo-Saxon was merely the first immigrant, the first to found a colony. He has never really ceased to be the descendant of immigrants, nor has he ever succeeded in transforming that colony into a real nation, with a tenacious, richly woven fabric of native culture."[59] This fact, generally, is forgotten. Though the "ethnics" may have assimilated in all substantive particulars with the "mainstream" culture, the symbols of ethnicity allow them to retain pride of distinction without having to live a life apart from most of America, as Hasidic Jews or the Amish do. Unfortunately, "symbolic ethnicity," in this sense, can seem like traditional Jewish cooking—but without the kosher part.

✶✶✶✶✶

There is more to it than that, of course. "Symbolic ethnicity" may *seem* simply window dressing, but there is something behind it, and something that may be much broader, and that is what Robert Merton calls "group-based truth," a source of comfort and cohesion. That this exists was clearly evident (if anyone needed to see it proven) in the aftermath of the 2012 presidential election—when it became apparent that, in the days leading *up* to the election, the Romney campaign and its supporters had developed a vision of reality that was confirmed within the group but that had little relation to what was going on outside. So powerful was the insider "truth" that Romney would win that the candidate did not even bother to pen a concession speech in case things went wrong. Of course, group-based thinking is at the heart of any cult, not excluding the cult of individualism.

Given that his article appeared in 1972, some of Merton's comments are a little eerie in light of the 2012 election, where an essentially white-male group convinced itself that it knew best about what was happening in an increasingly diversified nation. Though he was writing specifically about the field of sociology, Merton's words can be as easily applied to Republican politics:

> Although Insider doctrines have been intermittently set forth by white elitists through the centuries, white male Insiderism in American sociology during the past generations has largely been of the tacit or de facto rather than doctrinal or principled variety. It has simply taken the form of patterned expectations about the appropriate selection of specialties and of problems for investigation.[60]

In terms of contemporary American politics, however, the principle expands to other groups of people who claim that, based on their Insider positions, they have special knowledge that Outsiders cannot share:

> It would thus seem to follow that only women can understand women— and men, men. On the same principle, youth alone is capable of understanding youth just as, presumably, only the middle aged are able to

understand their age peers. Furthermore, as we shift to the hybrid cases of ascribed and acquired statuses in varying mix, on the Insider principle, proletarians alone can understand proletarians and presumably capitalists, capitalists; only Catholics, Catholics; Jews, Jews, and to halt the inventory of socially atomized claims to knowledge with a limiting case that on its face would seem to have some merit, it would then plainly follow that only sociologists are able to understand their fellow sociologists.[61]

The identity politics of the early 21st century are based on acceptance of the truth of this notion—and the fate of the Romney campaign (or Republican understanding of what that fate would be) seems to have hinged on it. But is this the whole of it? Merton makes the point that all of us are at various times both Insiders and Outsiders, and he argues that a there can be "a transition from social conflict to intellectually controversy ... when the perspectives of each group are taken seriously enough to be carefully examined rather than rejected out of hand."[62] Knowledge, even Insider knowledge, does not end with identity (Merton writes about de Tocqueville as an Outsider able to shed light on Insiders in a way that Insiders could not)—but it seems to, in American politics.

The point is that we must be careful when we make judgments about identity, even about "symbolic ethnicity" or cultural affiliation. Identity can hide things from Outsiders, just as there are things Outsiders can see that Insiders might, for one reason or another, ignore. The goal is to not ignore *any* claim of identity, no matter how frivolous it may seem, for there may be things behind it that we outside of it may not understand. That a nonkosher Jew chooses to cook using traditional Jewish recipes does not necessarily mean that he or she is simply attempting to throw a Jewish patina over an assimilated lifestyle. There may be serious connections involved.

That said, it is worth noting that a number of scholars of ethnicity have pointed out that many of the behavioral traits associated with ethnicity are

> working-class behavior, which differs only slightly among various ethnic groups, and then largely because of variations in the structure of opportunities open to people in America, and in the peasant traditions their ancestors brought over from the old country, which were themselves responses to European opportunity structures. In other words, ethnicity is largely a working-class style.[63]

Strangely enough, this, by default, leaves the Borderers as the original standard for American working-class behavior—or even for behavior outside of the working class, of which many Borderer descendants certainly are not members (the tradition is a rural, farming one). "In sharp contrast to the stubborn, biological, fixed inheritances of 'race,' 'ethnicity' stressed culture: it represented an outlook rather than a condition of birth; a cultural affiliation rather than a bloodline; a set of sensibilities and associational habits that, however tenacious, were subject to the forces of assimilation and change."[64] For many Americans, even those of immigrant roots, the underlying culture they adhere to is now one that stems from basic Scots-Irish Borderer outlooks of hundreds of years ago. In many ways, the veneer of ethnicity *has* become, as Gans argues, merely symbolic (or expressive of a cultural duality), the stronger and older culture in America having won out simply by being able to embrace a certain amount of surface difference. This is true not just of the Borderer-based culture but of the secular-liberal side, too.

* * * * *

Both American cultures, like feuding children, are close to each other in language and in many other aspects but are distinct enough for the fissure between them to have been apparent for a long time. The differences between the two, often mistaken as differences in class, are subtle but none-theless real. The secular-liberals have retained a stronger interest in the cultures of Western Europe, for example, particularly of England. The learning of the Enlightenment was much more important to them than to the Borderers—just look at their early colleges, almost all of which focused their curricula on European models with Latin and Greek language study an important part of student learning. There are plenty of other differences, some of which will be explored in subsequent chapters but all of which add up to two cultures that look and sound much the same but that are, at heart, quite distinct.

In *Groundwork of the Metaphysics of Morals*, Kant provides a "categorical imperative": Act only on the maxim that, at the same time, you can imagine should become a universal law. Move, in other words, from the personal to the universal in consideration of all your actions. Asma writes,

> Systematizing human societies along scientific principles (in this case, using sentiments or feelings) was the beginning of the end of favoritism in the West. The seeds of our opposition to bias and partiality are sown in this Enlightenment era. ... How you *feel* about someone will not, according to Kant, help you do the right thing. Feelings, sentiments, attachments, and emotions are surefire paths to bias, favoritism, partiality, and self interest. ... The way to purify and perfect ourselves as

impartial spectators—who can best judge right from wrong—is to make us into better logicians.[65]

The categorical imperative is as important a marker as is Rand in distinguishing the patterns of thought in the two largest American cultures. A major part of Enlightenment and liberal ideology, it never caught hold, certainly not with the same fervor, amongst Borderer descendants who continue to see obligation to family and friends as trumping fairness to outsiders. On one side of this cultural divide we have a tradition of rationality that suppresses emotions and connections. On the other we have recognition that humans can never operate simply on a basis of rationality—that attempting to do so is simply a denial of the reality of what makes us human in the first place. Each has a different impact on myths and visions of individualism. Asma continues,

> Well-educated liberal secular Westerners see morality exclusively as the respecting of individual rights. Fairness between autonomous individual agents is the defining feature of our morality. ... [In] other cultures, immigrant groups, and even rural cultures in the United States [people] thing of morality as more than fairness and rights. They think of it as relating to loyalty and patriotism, sacred/profane issues of purity, temperance, obedience to authority, and other values.[66]

As Asma sees it, the two approaches are incompatible. In American politics, we see this to be apparently true as the split between the two cultures becomes broader and deeper, understanding across the divide becoming less and less possible. We also see it in divergent political vocabularies and in distinct definitions of key concepts such as "individualism."

✶✶✶✶✶

The assumption of a national shared character that ignores very real cultural distinctions continues to push discussions of contemporary American culture or cultures into certain directions while others, probably more fruitful, are ignored. This assumption is convenient and easy, but it does turn away from the complexities of reality.

Like many others, the liberal political commentator E. J. Dionne simplifies the divides of today by assuming a "we" even as he writes of division:

> Underlying our political impasse is a lost sense of national balance that in turn reflects a loss of historical memory. *Americans disagree about who we are because we can't agree about who we've been.* We are at odds

over the meaning of our own history, over the sources of our national strength, and over what it is, philosophically and spiritually, that makes us "Americans." The consensus that guided our politics through nearly all of the twentieth century is broken. In the absence of a new consensus, we will continue to fight—and to founder.[67]

Though he does start off in the right direction here, Dionne allows himself to be diverted by the myth of consensus. Furthermore, by completely eliding family (ethnic) differences and assuming a "we" that has never been there in the first place, he is able to make the dubious assumption that Americans are all one family, that the dispute he refers to is, in fact, a family squabble. As we have seen, it can certainly seem that way. If it is, the siblings are close to becoming permanently estranged.

Not only that, but the "consensus" Dionne imagines having been in place through the 20th century was only a consensus (if it was one at all) among the urban "elites" of the East Coast and the West Coast and a few other major metropolitan areas. The pattern of the last six presidential elections, as we have seen, is actually much older, just resurgent, and it is not one pointing to any basis agreement. Regional differences appear intractable. As a result, the noble purpose Dionne sets out for his book *Our Divided Political Heart* is doomed for failure from the start. Americans are not one family with a single family identity any more than they are one ethnicity. Again, if they are any sort of family, they are one where communication may no longer be possible.

Later in his book, groping to grasp the distinctions I present here as being between Borderers and the secular-liberal "elite," Dionne tries to lay the failure of the late 19th-century populist movement personified by William Jennings Bryan at the feet of a simplistic rural/urban split:

> Bryan worried many in the cities by embracing his role as the champion of the countryside so passionately. "Burn down your cities and leave our farms, and your cities will spring up again as if by magic," Bryan had declared in his "Cross of Gold" speech. "But destroy our farms and the grass will grow in the streets of every city in the country." The line brought cheers in the vast open spaces of Kansas and Nebraska. It fell flat among many on the teeming sidewalks of New York or Pittsburgh. And the voters were moving, in droves, to the cities. Many of the urban newcomers were immigrants from southern and eastern Europe who brought with them their own traditions and, in the case of Catholics and Jews, religious faiths quite distant from the evangelical Protestantism that inspired Bryan and many among the Populist rank and file.[68]

Bryan was using the rural/urban split as much more of a metaphor than Dionne, who (again) assumes one umbrella American culture, recognizes. The split, as Bryan certainly knew, is cultural as well as geographic and economic as, ironically, Dionne's own comment about the immigrants—who entered into the coastal, urban culture—indicates. This "urban" culture, newly invigorated by immigration, had little substantive contact with the Borderer-based culture of much of the rest of the country. Its political unity with the Borderers stems from convergent cultural ideas, not from substantial personal contact. These ideas have led to a marriage of convenience only, not a merging that creates a single family or, ultimately, culture.

There are other dichotomies and contradictions involved with American individualism as well, one of which has been made manifest by two of the great successes of the first decade of the digital age, Wikipedia and Craigslist. Both Wikipedia's founder, Jimmy Wales, and Craigslist's Craig Newmark, longtime fans of Ayn Rand, tried to incorporate her "selfishness" into the entities they created. As Jennifer Burns writes,

> At the root of Wikipedia are warring sensibilities that seem to both embody and defy Rand's beliefs. The website's emphasis on individual empowerment and the value of knowledge, and its own risky organizational model reflects Rand's sensibility. But its trust in the wisdom of crowds, celebration of the social nature of knowledge, and faith that many working together will produce something of enduring value contradict Rand's adage "All creation is individual."[69]

Newmark also created a website that relies both on community and on individual action, feeding "on a Randian iconoclasm against established ways of doing business and her faith in human rationality, [but] it also undercuts Rand's individualism through its emphasis on collaboration and mutuality."[70]

★★★★★

Since the 1970s, limits have appeared around America's once boundless optimism, widening cultural distinctions that were easily avoided when the future seemed limitless and with room for all. The United States has begun to struggle with the idea that there is not always a bigger and better tomorrow; problems must be faced instead of moved away from in a flight further west. Compounding that, as Lasch says, "we are fast losing the sense of historical continuity, the sense of belonging to a succession of generations originating in the past and stretching into the future."[71] Some have adjusted to the new paradigm, turning away from the material desires that had driven many of their forefathers. Others, though, react in frustration, angry and confused by a situation that does not offer them what they had been raised to think should be theirs. They refuse to reject the idea of an America great enough to offer success to all of its citizens and so begin to find excuses, nefarious influences and even conspiracies striving to bring down righteous citizens. These influences and conspiracies include immigrants, especially illegal immigrants, and also the people who "take advantage," who use government programs that the "good" people have to pay for.

Since the 1970s, as well, we have seen a quickening in the shift in what is too often considered the American shared character, a shift that has left a large part of the population, the part that I gather together as Borderers, once more on the outside. Not only were African Americans gaining new respect within the American media landscape, but so were others. "After decades of striving to conform to the Anglo-Saxon standard, descendants of earlier European immigrants quit the melting pot. Italianness, Jewishness, Greekness, and Irishness had become badges of pride, not shame."[72] They were now what Richard Alba names as a distinct group, "European Americans."[73] Though the Borderers, too, were descended from Europeans, their ancestry was so shrouded in the mists of time and so at variance with other European particulars (the Scottish lowlands, not surprisingly having been about the poorest area of the continent) that it could no longer be identified with any single European ethnicity. Besides, even if it could, the Scots-Irish had very little they could call their own, no distinct cuisine or language, no religion ever unusual to America, no particular tradition of art. What they did—and do—have are much more intangible features that are generally ignored in discussions of ethnicity. Included in these is their staunch individualism, a trait they also give gladly to those who come into their midst.

*****

For the last 40 years in academia, the field of Ethnic Studies has been devoted primarily to African American, Asian American, Latino American, and Native American concerns. Studies of *European* American ethnicities are generally housed in departments also devoted to the studies of their languages. It would seem, then, that American Studies would be the only place left to house Scots-Irish Studies, for there is no such nation for the latter and no such language. As a subordinate culture (not even a culture, to many, but a "class") in the eyes of traditional academics and a culture without many of the external markers used to define a particular ethnicity or culture, it is generally relegated to Appalachian Studies, a regional-studies field, if it is recognized as a distinct field at all.

One of the reasons there has been little attention paid to the Borderer culture is that it does seem so similar to the assimilated "ethnic" cultures in America—even more so than to the dominant media and intellectual culture. And, indeed, many have used the immigrant experience—or, rather, the myth of the immigrant experience to provide validity to extant American myths. Jacobson writes, "A major lesson from the 'immigrant experience' that recurs again and again in conservative writing is that in America, discrimination can and will be overcome with hard work and the passage of time—a conviction whose corollaries include myriad assertions about bootstrap self-help and the impropriety of state intervention in correcting for the injustices of racial stratification."[74] This is not just part of the experience of more recent immigrant groups: It has been a basic part of Borderer beliefs for a long time. A major part of Borderer bitterness today, in fact, comes from realization that the myth has not panned out. Rather than reexamining the myth, however, and seeing if the fault may lie there, many people simply try to locate blame in outside, unknowable forces.

* * * * *

The American individualist is facing other problems today, too, ones far beyond ethnic or cultural ancestry or even of definition. Marin cites Claude Lévi-Strauss as making a critical anti-individualist statement: "For Lévi-Strauss the crucial human moment is not the moment of separate awareness; it is the moment of human meeting, in which the other's existence creates for us a sense of the depth and complexity of the world."[75] Not only is the individualist faced with the fact that it is in human reaction and interaction that real achievement occurs, but the very environment militates against the individualist as survivalist. As Lasch, again, notes, "Having surrendered most of his technical skills to the corporations, he [the individual] can no longer provide for his material needs."[76] No longer is it possible to *actually* be self-sufficient—or even a necessary cog in the system: Everyone can be replaced. The only real hope for the individualist depends, as Marin says, "directly upon the ways we act individually and in community."[77] This, unfortunately for the Borderer individualist, is exactly the ideal of individualism that grew up through the secular-liberal culture of the coasts—and it is not what the Borderers are used to imagining. So it is understandable why unwillingness to accept this alternate view has become another important reason Mettler's "submerged state" has developed and it is also the reason that "going Galt,"* though often threatened over the past few years, is a meaningless gesture.

Individualism, for all 21st-century Americans, has become an abstraction and, in its purest form, an unattainable ideal. That has not reduced its impact, however, or the necessity of trying to understand the genesis of American faith in individualism, no matter how it is defined.

---

*"Going Galt" is a reference to John Galt, the main character of Ayn Rand's *Atlas Shrugged*. Galt organizes a secret strike by movers and shakers, with the idea that they are the real force behind economic success. The phrase refers to those who, feeling oppressed by an increasingly collectivist society, refuse to use their talents in its service.

CHAPTER 3

From the Borderlands to Ulster to the Western Colonies to Be American

Where did the almost obsessive focus on individualism in America come from? It certainly has been around for a long time. Still, it is not a question easily answered, at least not from examination only of histories of 17th- and 18th-century immigration from the British Isles, from the Netherlands, from France, or from any other European sources of early American settlers. Many of those immigrants came as parts of idealistic religious movements like that of the Pilgrims or, later, the Quakers. Others came to get rich through the largesse of kings to whom they and their descendants remained loyal for a century or more. None of these seem to represent the cultural breeding ground one would expect for the type of in-your-face individualism that would soon arise in parts of the British colonies and the new nation that followed.

Still other immigrants, however, and in huge numbers, came as slaves and indentured servants. Many of the latter group came from among those fleeing Ulster Plantation in what is now Northern Ireland, where they had hoped to make a go of things but instead had found strife there as dramatic as that they had left behind back home on the border between Scotland and England. In a better situation than the African slaves, the indentured servants were still at the lowest level of white colonial society—their "free" fellow Scots-Irish Borderer countrymen, also immigrating in droves, only slightly better off. Together, they were considered the dregs of colonial society. Where others had come to America from Europe *for* something, be it fortune or freedom from religious persecution, many of these people had agreed to articles of indenture only out of desperation or had managed to scrape together money for passage but little else. Treated poorly by just about every other European in the colonies, they turned their own anger on those even lower on the ladder than they were (the African slaves), on those whose place "above" them they had learned to resent, and even on the Native Americans with whom, once they had finished their servitude or had decided they could not settle among the established communities, many competed for domination on the frontier.

Unlike most of the other European colonists in America, the Scots-Irish, or Borderers, were predominantly uneducated, even by the English standards of the time. Some could read enough to slowly make out their Bibles, but that was about it. As a result, few of them left a record of their experiences. This left their story almost completely unknown. Over a century after the Revolution, in 1890, at the first of a short-lived series of Scotch-Irish "congresses," the lack of knowledge of the process of immigration from Ulster Plantation to the American colonies was described and attempts were made to explain it:

> A good deal of surprise was expressed at the Congress that a history of the Scotch-Irish had never been attempted; but we do not have to seek far for the reason. There is ample material from which to speak in a general way of their origin and of their existence in Ireland, but when we come to their emigration to America, excepting the causes which led to it, it is meager in the extreme. Coming from one part of Great Britain to another, no record has been preserved of their arrivals as would have been the case had they been of alien origin; and all we know is that while a large majority came to Pennsylvania, others settled in Virginia and the Carolinas. The country along the Atlantic coast was then comparatively thickly settled, and the Scotch-Irish took up their abodes on the outskirts of civilization. This was not because the Quakers sent them there, as has been asserted, to protect their own settlements from the Indians, or because the Scotch-Irish did not wish to live near the Quakers, who were continually finding fault with them, but for the same reason that now takes the emigrants to the West,—*i.e.*, because there good land is cheap and large families can be supporter at a small expense.[1]

This was not the whole of it, nor is it particularly accurate. As we will see in the next chapter, the good and cheap land was not so easily available as the myths of the West, established even before 1900, supposed. But it is true that the Scots-Irish were pretty well ignored in the histories. They should not have been. Just by their numbers, they should not have been.

*****

In *A Population History of the United States*, Herbert Klein presents a graph of the mean centers of population for the United States, 1790–2000.[2] It shows that the 1790 center was not far from Baltimore, Maryland. By 1810, the center had moved west, to the northernmost part of what is now Virginia (remembering that the Virginia of the time included all of West Virginia). By 1860, a steady due-west progression had taken it across into Ohio, not far from the Ohio River. In a steady movement across the southern portions of Indiana and Illinois, the center finally had crossed the Mississippi River into Missouri by 1980. All of these areas save the first had had a strong Scots-Irish Borderer presence from initial settlement on and still do. The argument that the Borderers are at the heart of the "real" America does, as can be seen from this progression, have a certain validity. But it did not make the Borderers famous.

Still, with this movement began a shift of political power away from the East Coast, a shift culminating in the election of Andrew Jackson in 1828 as the first Borderer president. The change, as we know, was dramatic: "By the census of 1860, the original thirteen seaboard states of 1790, which initially contained 97% of the national population, now held only just over half of the total."[3] Though political power was falling into Borderer hands, American intellectual and financial strength remained in the Northeast, an area with, for the most part, cultural identities and beliefs quite removed from those of the Borderers settling behind and even beyond the expanding frontier.

From the crucible of the Scottish Lowlands, tempered in Ulster, the Borderers came to the colonies already hardened and set in their ways. Seeing antagonism, real or imagined, on the faces of just about everyone they came across, they only wanted to be left alone—something that rarely happened to them and that happens just as rarely to their descendants, both physical and spiritual, in the America of today. One of the most important groups in the shaping of the American character, they are, paradoxically, also one of the most ignored (which is different from "left alone")—for America's histories were written elsewhere than in the backcountry or on the frontier. American history has been written largely in the Northeast or in areas culturally descended from that region.

Even today, the descendants of the Borderers can claim a singular distinction in politically correct America: They are the only ethnic group that can be derided at will anywhere in the country. Even in the great Borderer stronghold, the mountains of Appalachia, it is fine to make jokes about "hillbillies" and "rednecks." The people there, at least, know a little of what they are talking about and often are embarked on irony when they joke—elsewhere, not so much.

A few years ago, at a university reception, I found myself in conversation with a group of colleagues, all of whom were either African American, Hispanic, or native New Yorkers (or a combination thereof). One of them made a comment about "devolved" "red state" culture, about hillbillies. Everyone laughed but me. As gently as I could, I told the group that the people they were disparaging were my people. No one believed me. Not only, I discovered, had none of them ever met anyone with family in the hills, but they refused to believe that a college professor could have that sort of background, even remotely. They also refused to accept Appalachians as having any sort of ethnic identity worth protecting or respecting. That is reserved, of course, for African Americans, Hispanics and, today, Italians, Russians, Chinese, South Asians, and the rest.

Borderers have gotten used to this. Many have learned how to skewer both disdainful easterners and their ethnic fellows. One of these was Joe Bageant, whose opening to one of his blog posts reminds me of my thoughts during that conversation with my colleagues:

> You may not meet them among your circle of friends, but there are millions of Americans who fiercely believe we should nuke North Korea and Iran, seize the Middle East's oil, and replace the U.S. Constitution with the Christian Bible. They believe the United States will conquer the entire world and convert it to our notions of democracy and fundamentalist Christian religion. . . . You may not believe me, and if you don't I cannot blame you for never having been exposed to such folks. Only an idiot or a masochistic observer of the American scene would subject himself or herself to these Americans. I like to think I am the latter, but the jury is still out.[4]

This is the way Borderer descendants, more often than not, feel they have to talk about themselves today, especially to "blue state" Americans whose understanding of the reality of the lives of many of their fellow Americans is woefully small. Bageant, still tongue in cheek, goes on to describe the Borderers as descended from "a group of Celtic cattle thieves killing one another in the mud along Hadrian's Wall":

> The homeland of the original Borderers was a squalid place. Denuded of forests and incapable of growing enough food to support its inhabitants, much less produce enough to sell within the traditional English culture of commerce, the natives survived by and gloried in "reiving" [cattle rustling]. It was a land of alternating famine and overpopulation, the only constant being warfare between England and Scotland along

the fluctuating border. Rooted in centuries of national fighting—and in those rare times of peace, inter-clan warfare among themselves—they maintained their fierce ways, clan loyalties and holdings. The right to hold any turf they occupied was determined by their ability to defend it. Holding such miserable land was a worthwhile effort mainly in as far as it created clan proximity so it could be held. It was a vicious, near pointless circle. Given the unceasing looting, burning and moving, the Borderers built impermanent earth and log dwellings called "cabbins." Within their smoky cabins they lived a quick-tempered, hard drinking, volatile lifestyle, one that anthropologists say can still be seen in American trailer courts today.[5]

Mixing truth and sarcasm, Bageant presents, as well as anyone can, both the stereotype and the truth of Borderer life.

Even "serious" journalists fall into the ages-old trap of believing the worst of Borderers. Colin Woodard, in his book *American Nations: A History of the Eleven Regional Cultures of North America*, can see only the downside of Borderer culture, writing, "Proud, independent, and disturbingly violent, the Borderlanders of Greater Appalachia have remained a volatile insurgent force within North American society to the present day."[6] He goes on to write that, in America, they

> fell back on their old-country practice of taking the law into their own hands. Justice was meted out not by courts but by the aggrieved individuals and their kin via personal retaliation. "Every man is a sheriff in his own hearth" was a Borderlander creed that informed the Scottish practices of "blackmail" (as protection money), the blood feud (most famously practiced by the Hatfields and McCoys) and "Lynch's law," named for Appalachian Borderlander William Lynch, who advocated vigilante justice in the lawless Virginia backcountry.[7]

This sort of description makes it difficult for many Americans to take seriously Borderer culture, for it does little more than confirm long-held prejudices. And, by the way, one West Virginia Hatfield, called "Sid," made famous in the John Sayles film *Matewan*, was a *real* sheriff, a dedicated lawman who was gunned down on a courthouse steps not in a feud but because he stood against coal-mining interests and for the common people.

It is only today that we Americans as a whole are beginning to understand the mistake of ignoring the Borderers, for they have become the dominant force on the conservative side of the broader American culture, they are the "red staters" who elected Ronald Reagan and George W. Bush, the suspicious right wing pandered to by Grover Norquist and his antitax crusade, the fundamentalists who see religion in a light entirely foreign to the Massachusetts and Pennsylvania believers of the 17th and 18th centuries, the anti-immigrant crusaders who cannot abide anyone not willing to live like themselves. So influential are they that they have pulled the entire American political discourse toward them, creating a "center" far to the right of what it was under Richard Nixon, just 40 years ago.

* * * * *

But who are these people, really? What makes them appear so mean and closed minded to outside observers? Part of the answer lies in that torturous path from the Scottish Lowlands through Northern Ireland and on to the American frontier starting in the 17th century. The root cause, though, is much older, stemming from the difficulties of eking a life from weak, hilly fields in an area beset by antagonists both north and south. Like their Irish cousins, the Borderers were a "problem" to England from the time the country coalesced and they continued to be a "problem" even when England and Scotland united, on the death of Queen Elizabeth, under her nephew James Stuart.

From the point of view of the new King James I of England (also James VI of Scotland), the idea and value of creation of "plantations" in the Irish counties of Down and Antrim on the Irish Sea closest to Scotland, plantations where English and Scots settlers could quickly and easily establish new communities, must have seemed a no-brainer and a problem solver. Just three years into his reign, in 1606, two Scottish "entrepreneurs," Hugh Montgomery and James Hamilton (who had made a deal for Irish land with an imprisoned Irish lord), induced "tenants and other Scots from the south-western regions to come over as farmer-settlers. Since the distance was only twenty or thirty miles and the inducements were great, the risk was worth taking."[8] Thousands of others thought so, too, at least. After all, Scotland at that time "had never known orderly government or a rule of law instead of by men, nor had the country ever, for many years at a time, known peace. Life everywhere was insecure, not only because of recurrent wars with the English, but even more because of abominable economic methods, a niggardly soil, and constant cattle raiding and feuds."[9] Even when no actual war was going on, fighting was common between clans as revenge and even as protection against the omnipresent cattle thieves. "Life on the border was notoriously unsafe. At least until the Reformation, travel was dangerous anywhere in Scotland unless one went accompanied by armed men."[10] It is no wonder that, given the chance, thousands of Borderers jumped toward the unknown rather than staying with the misery of home.

The king, wanting to please populations in both of his new kingdoms (English settlers would soon come over to Ireland, too), wishing to reduce the Irish "problem" that had bedeviled his predecessors by establishing a population more loyal to him, and, finally, wanting to fill his coffers, believed rightly that the Borderers would immigrate, given minimal incentives. "With the example of Montgomery and others and with his courtiers looking with hungry eyes upon the thousands of ownerless acres in the attractive Ulster countryside, James now decided upon an ambitious scheme of colonization of that region."[11]

Senator Jim Webb, in his own book about his Scots-Irish heritage, describes how the Plantation was laid out:

> Characteristic of traditional Anglo-Norman precision, the 500,000 acres of the original Ulster Plantation were laid out with exactitude. Half would be divided between "Undertakers"—lords and gentry of England and Scotland who would agree to "plant" Protestant farmers and also provide fortifications behind which their planters might defend the allotted areas, and "Servitors"—proven soldiers who could be used in further military operations in Ulster. One-tenth (50,000 acres) would be allotted to the twelve municipal corporations that comprised the government of London and would be responsible for developing trade.[12]

Though the story of this colonization rarely appears in American textbooks, the colonization of Ulster would prove every bit as important as Jamestown or Plymouth Rock to the history of the United States. Millions of Americans (including me) can claim as ancestors people who passed through Ulster Plantation—and their cultural impact can be felt to this day. After all, it was those now called the Scots-Irish who were at the forefront of western expansion, changing the backwoods into the frontier and establishing new European-based communities from the Alleghenies and Appalachians all the way to the West Coast. Their influence, as a result, is out of all proportion to their numbers.

Yet, so unknown is the division between the Scots-Irish Borderers and other American cultural traditions that scholars find it easy to assume that they mixed easily and naturally with the other colonists, creating one broad American culture. A generally astute Princeton professor, Nell Irwin Painter, for example, claims mistakenly that the "first alien wave" of immigrants to North America was that of the Catholic Irish after about 1830. She writes that before "about 1820, most Irish immigrants had been Protestants from the north of Ireland, fairly easily incorporated into American society as simply 'Irish.' "[13] Presumably not aware of the acid reception the Scots-Irish received (and the cultural pride that reception helped engender), she even goes so far as to argue that they styled themselves "Scotch Irish" after the Revolution simply to distinguish themselves from Catholic Irish—in keeping with the anti-Catholic sentiments that had grown within the other folkways.

The very old distinctions between the English and the Borderers were higher than might be imagined. This would even have been true once the English language dominated the island. There was, for example, a lot less dependence on grain and cereal crops and a lot more on livestock among the Borderers than farther south in England. The idea of a "commons" that had become central to English agriculture by the end of the Middle Ages was not found so much in the borderlands, so there were fewer well-established villages with traditions tied to the land, certainly not ones grouped around a commons. Partly as a result, there was little manorial control or loyalty, and many of the houses of the poorer people were considered to be little more than temporary residences, thrown up quickly and easily abandoned (or rebuilt after destruction in one of the recurring wars). Fealty remained with family and not with a lord, and what inheritance there was relied not on a system of primogeniture but was partible. All in all, there was less of a commitment to place than one would find among the English. If important at all, place and place-bound tradition was significant and prized for what it might lack— control from faraway central authority and the safety of being far from the beaten track.

*****

Though I may use "Scots-Irish" or "Borderer" as a shorthand for the people who moved from the border region to Ulster Plantation and then to (most often) the Delaware Valley before proceeding into the Appalachian Mountains, it is important to remember that this group in no sense constituted either a "race" or a religion: "Lowlanders who left Scotland for Ireland between 1610 and 1690 were biologically compounded of many ancestral strains. ... Even if the theory of 'racial' inheritance of character were sound, the Lowlander had long since become a biological mixture, in which at least nine strains had met and mingled in different proportions."[14] Though they are descended from Gaelic tribes, recent study shows, as might be expected, that the

> Scottish population seems genetically more similar to the English than to the Irish population. . . . This result is in keeping with the geographical proximity between Scotland and England and the sharing, therefore, of more historical and prehistorical influences than with Ireland. The degree of sharing between Scotland and Ireland or England is probably structured according to geography.[15]

If this is the case, all of the nine strains are likely present to some extent in pretty well the entire population of the British Isles. There are, according to James Leyburn, three strains from antiquity: the Stone Age aborigines who inhabited the islands and two Celtic groups, the Gaels and the Britons, who pushed the Gaels toward Ireland, Scotland, and Wales. Added to these are four from the millennium after the Roman conquest: the Romans themselves (though they did not colonize), the Angles and the Saxons, the Scots (another Celtic, or Gaelic, group), and the Norse, who both raided and settled along the coasts. The final two (much smaller in influence) are the Normans and the Flemish. None of these, even if ancestors of the Lowland Scots alone, makes them significantly genetically distinct from any of the other peoples of the British Isles.[16]

In terms of religion, the Scots-Irish were mixed, too—and reasonably accepting of religious differences. Though the majority of those who migrated from Scotland to Ulster Plantation were likely to have been Presbyterian, a surprising number (including some of my own ancestors) married into Irish-Catholic families. In America, they mixed freely with the Irish, the Huguenots, and the Germans, few of whom shared their own religion but all of whom were, like the Borderers, somewhat out of place in the English colonies. Most of the Scots-Irish believed that religious belief and activity rested with the individual and that, therefore, no individual should try to force belief on another.

Whatever unique characteristics there are that can be attributed to the Lowland Scots, genetics clearly had little or nothing to do with them. To Leyburn, unlike those who see the Scots-Irish as primarily mean and clannish, the "most obvious" trait of theirs is "dourness":

> This word, derived from the Latin *durus* and the French *dur*, literally means hardness and durability, having the qualities of iron. Men who survive centuries of living in a hard environment, both physical and

social, learn how to endure the worst that life can send them. The Scot
knew famine and plague, thin soil, insecurity of life and property, raids,
and aggression. He early learned to fight back, to give blow for blow,
and then, when he had done his best, to endure.[17]

These were not easy people to like or to know. When I read the passage
above, I think of a picture I have of my Appalachian grandfather, his brothers,
and their father taken in the 1930s or 1940s. They do not scowl, but none of
the faces looks like it ever hosted a smile—they make Grant Wood's *American
Gothic* look a frolic. And they were not unusual.

＊＊＊＊＊

Two of the many families from the central border Lowlands to go to Ireland
were the Huggins and the Carruths, both from Dumbartonshire, both settling in Antrim, Ireland, toward the end of the migration from the Lowlands
to Ireland. The son of those Huggins would eventually marry the grand-
daughter of those Carruths and would migrate to Cecil County, Maryland,
where a son, James, was born in 1715. He eventually married the grand-
daughter of a French (probably Huguenot) immigrant whose son had
married the daughter of Ulster Scots. After what appears to have been a stop
in Lancaster County, Pennsylvania, they made their way down what became
known as the Great Wagon Road (perhaps the first great nonriver and
noncoastal European migration route of North America) with thousands of
others through the Shenandoah Valley, ending up in Rowan County, North
Carolina. They went this way, partly, to skirt the settled areas of Virginia so
that they could avoid the English. Though they are ancestors of mine, family
tradition has long forgotten them as anything but names, and histories were
rarely written about such folk. They do provide an outline, however, of the
path of thousands upon thousands of those who passed through Northern
Ireland from the Scottish Lowlands on their way to, though they probably
did not know it at the time, what was then the American backwoods.

Why did they leave the settled area of the Delaware Valley? Frankly, though
the statement of that Scots-Irish congress is to the contrary, they were not
wanted. Woodard writes that "Philadelphia newspapers accused them of a litany
of misdeeds, counterfeiting of currency, murder, the rape of a six-year-old child,
and making 'threatening words against authority.' . . . Officials did their best to
get them out of town and onto the frontier."[18] And the Borderers obliged.

Writing about the establishment of the town of Carlisle in Pennsylvania's
Cumberland County in the 18th century, Judith Ridner makes an important

point about the Scots-Irish who were among the first European settlers of the area:

> Although their geographic mobility and cultural flexibility in Ireland and America earned them a reputation as a "people with no name," this was mostly a misnomer. For the Scots-Irish, however adaptable they were as a people, nonetheless expressed a distinct cultural identity in America through their shared experiences as immigrants, Protestants, and British citizens. In Pennsylvania, their identity was also intimately connected to their experiences as inhabitants of the colony's interior.[19]

They were not simply the lowest class of whites or the poorest. Theirs was a distinct culture, one growing and changing on the frontier. Removal to America provided them no more peace than they had found in the Scottish Lowlands or on Ulster Plantation, but it did have an impact on them, hardening them even further, though that hardly seems possible. As Ridner points out, "During the Seven Years' War and Pontiac's Uprising, Cumberland County's Scots-Irish colonists were among the first to suffer the violent consequences. Likewise, during these wars and then the American Revolution, British and American leaders called on many of these same colonists to assist them in defending the borders of the empire or nation."[20] And they did assist.

The homes of these settlers were not much more permanent than those they had built for generations back in Ireland and on the Scottish/English border, for the success of their settlements was always questionable, at best:

> Populated mostly by humble squatters, these settlements depended on Indian goodwill for their existence. Moreover, because these mostly Scots-Irish colonists possessed little more than linen and liquor, they had to live much like Indians to survive. They practiced subsistence agriculture and hunted. They drank, caroused, and sometimes fought with each other and their Indian and trader neighbors. And because markets were distant, they relied on bartering with the local Native peoples for needed goods in a frontier exchange economy. This was a harsh world, one marked by hard work and considerable brutality.[21]

We shall see, in the next chapter, that theirs really was not a subsistence economy, and I will explain why. Other than that, Ridner's depiction seems accurate. She further notes that they were called "idle trash"[22] by surveyor Samuel Blunston, one of the people sent to the area by Thomas Penn (son of Pennsylvania founder William Penn) to bring order and set up a town.

His attitude, like the lifestyle Ridner depicts, was not local to Cumberland County. Anywhere they were in contact with the older colonists, the Scots-Irish were generally looked down upon. Anywhere they settled, they had to make do with what they found, having brought little with them.

The character of the Scots-Irish became the character of much of America, though the attention of cultural historians has focused much more closely on the influence of what David Hackett Fischer describes as the first three waves of immigrants from the British Isles. The first of these was that of the Puritans, occurring mostly in the 1630s or shortly thereafter. The second was of "a small Royalist elite and large numbers of indentured servants from the south of England to Virginia"[23] over the next three decades or so. The third, loosely associated with the Quakers, saw movement of people from the North Midlands into the Delaware Valley over the following half century. The Scots-Irish, the last major English-speaking wave before the Revolution, arrived also over half a century, large-scale migration (possibly about 250,000 people[24]) ending with the start of hostilities in 1775. The Borderers had to move through the established coastal colonies, setting themselves at the "back" of the still English-focused colonies, and their lives and needs were interesting to very few of the establishing American elites. In fact, the concept of "East Coast elites" in the minds of Borderer descendants can be traced back to this time.

Exacerbating antipathy toward the older colonists on the coast is the fact that many on the 18th-century arrivals, as I have said, were indentured laborers. Indeed, of what Herbert Klein estimates was 307,000 European immigrants arriving between 1700 and 1775, about half, or over 150,000, were indentured. As soon as these immigrants had worked off their debts, many of them high-tailed it to the hills, "progressively moving to the western parishes of the coastal states and beyond the colonial frontier into new territory"[25] and, though Klein does not say it, as far away as they could get from their former masters.

According to Henry Gemery[26] and David Galenson,[27] the vast majority of the indentured servants (upwards of three-quarters; perhaps even 9 out of 10 during the decades before the Revolution) were male. Given the heavy competition for wives that surely resulted, it is likely that many of these men left the settled coastal areas as soon as they could for another reason, eventually integrating into the Borderer culture they joined on the western frontier if they managed to find wives there, whatever their home culture had been.

The move of young men to the frontier in the 18th century was not restricted to men who had completed their indenture. Native-born colonists joined them and also eventually integrated into the Borderer culture. Gemery outlines the pattern:

(1) Five colonies—Massachusetts, Connecticut, Pennsylvania, Maryland, and Virginia—experienced net out-migration of American-born men of militia age. Three of those—Massachusetts, Connecticut, and Virginia—probably incurred net losses even with foreign immigration. Pennsylvania and Maryland, however, experienced net gains because of the counterbalancing foreign inflows.

(2) The colonies with the greatest in-migration of the native-born were the Carolinas and New York.

(3) Migration across regions occurred in two distinct patterns. Internal migration from the New England region was to the middle colonies, but New York and Pennsylvania defined the outer limits of New Englanders' movement. The second pattern from was from the middle colonies to the south. ... Virtually no New Englanders moved to the South and, New York aside, few middle colony or Southern males of militia age moved North.

(4) Mobility was greater in the South, and the distances moved were greater as well.

(5) Internal migration was uniformly out of the cities, to rural areas.[28]

The "South" here includes the Appalachian region, which was probably the destination of many of these men (aside from the New Englanders).

The use of indentured labor had been falling even before the Revolution, replaced by slave labor in the South and "free" labor farther north resulting from the quick growth of the domestic population:

The declining relative importance of indentured servitude in the labor forces of both the Chesapeake and Pennsylvania in the third quarter of the eighteenth century is reflected in the generally low estimated levels of net white immigration to both of these regions in the decades after 1750, decades in which rapid growth of the domestic population of the two regions was also tending to diminish the relative importance of immigrant labor in their work forces.[29]

Americans outside of the South no longer needed to import labor. Enough was being grown at home. Partly as a result of that, it would be a long time before another group—those potato-famine Irish—would come in anywhere near the numbers of the Borderers.

*****

Two points about the pattern of immigration are worth emphasizing. First, as I have said, the majority who arrived in the 18th century were single males. Second, immigration split immediately into two groups, those who headed directly to the frontier (where they were joined by those internal migrants already mentioned) and those who stayed in the "settled" areas, particularly in the cities.

In terms of cultural and ethnic continuation, young single men are probably the weakest link. Not part of a new family unit and removed from their childhood families, they care for and carry less heritage than any other demographic. This makes them more adaptable to the group they end up among—marrying into or settling with—as many of the young men from other ethnic groups did when they came upon the Scots-Irish as they moved toward the frontier to make new lives for themselves. The fact is that single young men are more easily assimilated into a culture than are families or other larger groups, especially as they have to marry into that culture if they are going to have wives at all. This gave an added boost to the expansion of Borderer culture.

The pattern of westward movement would continue, of course, through the 19th century:

> In contrast [to the enslaved African-Americans], all other elements of the American population proved to be highly mobile. Noted by all contemporaries as well as later demographers was the long-term movement of the population of the United States toward the West. The older seaboard states, although containing the majority of the large cities and the bulk of the population, were losing population at a steady rate to the ever-expanding frontier throughout the late 18th and all of the 19th century. This movement in the pre-1860 period was primarily into the Northwest territory, those territories to the north and west of the Ohio River (Ohio, Indiana, Illinois, Michigan, Wisconsin, and parts of Minnesota and North Dakota) and was dominated by young adults, primarily men.[30]

The American experience of those replacing urban populations from abroad would be quite distinct from that of earlier immigrants, though they later would find they shared certain sympathies, providing another ingredient of the mix and the separation leading to the political-cultural divide dominating the early 21st century.

Fischer does not seem to like the "borderers" (the name is taken, of course, from their early home on the English/Scottish border, but it befitted their new role on the backwoods border between the English colonies and the Native Americans), reflecting the sentiments of the earliest setters since soon after the time of their first arrival. Relying on stereotypes and sweeping generalization, Fischer argues that, unlike those earlier immigrants, the Borderers came with no idealistic vision: "Among the North Britons, there was no talk of holy experiments, or cities on a hill."[31] These people came only for the better chance or to escape from penury and, like their parents or grandparents who had moved to Ulster, just "to find a new life and to live it on their own terms."[32] Through this movement by necessity, not choice, they were planting the seeds, of course, of one strong strain of American individualism. Their "simple" goal of economic survival, however, seems to have lowered them, in Fischer's eyes and in those of many others from the 18th century on. Already, by the time of the Revolution, there was a fractious cultural divide within the colonies, much more acrimonious than our history books usually tell.

One problem, of course, was that the Scots-Irish did not know that they should respect their "betters." Fischer observes, "Border emigrants demanded to be treated with respect even when dressed in rags. Their humble origins did not create the spirit of subordination which others expected of 'lower ranks.' This fierce and stubborn pride would be a cultural fact of high importance in the American region which they came to dominate."[33]

In reaching his conclusions about Borderers, Fischer seems to rely heavily on what members of the other three groups wrote about the Borderers, including Charles Woodmason, whose journals were published as *The Carolina Backcountry on the Eve of the Revolution* and who was extremely frustrated by the people he found in the South Carolina hills. Fischer characterizes him as having learned that the backcountry "golden rule" was do to others what they threaten to do to you—before they manage it.[34] He also quotes folklorist Cecil Sharp, writing more than a century later, saying in a letter that the Borderers came from the least developed part of England[35] (which was certainly true), and he notes that the English/Scottish border had not seen a 50-year period of peace before 1745.[36] He describes that culture of feuds and of cattle rustling and "reiving," stealing from neighbors,[37] that has become the most common Borderer stereotype. Ultimately, he says, the "so-called Scotch-Irish who came to America thus included a double-distilled selection of some of the most disorderly inhabitants of a deeply disorderly land."[38] They were the "other," the side of the British "personality" that no one (that is, no *proper* one) wanted to acknowledge. They were backward; they were ignorant. Worst of all, they were poor.

Fischer does quote at least one Borderer, a Lieutenant James MacMichael, who says that, in the American colonies, he had been seen only as a barbarian.[39] As Fischer describes them, the Borderers came from the lower ranks of society, below that of earlier immigrants. They were "farmers and farm laborers who owned no land of their own, but worked as tenants and undertenants. A large minority were semiskilled craftsmen and petty traders. In northern Ireland, many had worked in the linen trade—impoverished handloom weavers, unemployed agents, traders and entrepreneurs."[40] Yet, even so, they seemed unable to recognize that their betters were better. What other colonists saw as unwarranted pride proved a constant irritant.

Through the centuries since, the movement westward apparently integrated many of the cultural descendants of the Scots-Irish into what was often presented as a broader and cohesive American culture. The Appalachian Mountains region alone remained relatively free of that later commingling, retaining its distinct cultural stance through dialect, in particular, but also through lifestyle. What seemed a dilution of the culture through expansion and inclusion of Europeans from other backgrounds, however, was less a cultural broadening than might be expected, as 21st-century political divisions continue to show.

*****

While migrants moving west were often following tracks into territory whose first European settlers were Scots-Irish Borderers, a different progression was happening in the urban areas of the East, further dividing America. Though New York City reached a population of half a million before the Civil War,[41] the growth was not internal but was fueled by immigration from Europe. As we have seen, these new Americans were somewhat different from those moving west, for that group included a large number of native-born colonists, people *leaving* the cities and towns whose growth was now accounted for by the newcomers from Europe. "The growth of both urban and total population was increasingly fueled by that other major population movement in pre–Civil War America—the arrival of foreign immigrants who paid for their own passage across the Atlantic."[42] These people were coming into cultures very different from that in the West, cultures descended from the other three of Fischer's folkways. Those who stayed in the East assimilated (to some degree, at least) into one of those cultures (which were different North and South and, before the Civil War, different North, Middle, and South). Some of them, of course, joined those American-born in the movement west, but many never really directly encountered the Borderer culture of America at all.

*****

Not all agree that the split in American culture comes from a Borderer ethnic base and following immigration into different geographic cultures. In writing about individualism in America, Stephanie Walls argues that the split between Americans comes not culturally but within Enlightenment-descended liberals in America themselves, leaving the Borderers completely out of the history of influences on the political divides that continue into the early 21st century:

> It was not until the Industrial Revolution that classical liberals began to divide into two distinct groups. ... The Lockean acknowledgment of the importance of society and the surrender of some individual autonomy is similar to those positions held by the Progressives and ultimately by advocates of the modern welfare state: those whom we call "liberals" today. These people wanted governmental and social policies to help raise the standard of living for a segment of society that had not benefited from the Industrial Revolution. Other liberals, in response, took a hard-line individualist approach, arguing that the government was a "necessary evil" that should not be given more power than necessary.[43]

I argue instead that the split *was* much more culturally based than this model admits, going back to a time generations before the Industrial Revolution.

To recap, though ignored by the histories taking their starting points in the East that the Borderers had skipped over in the first place, much of American culture is indeed of Scots-Irish descent, that "folkway" showing as much influence today as Quaker, Cavalier, and Puritan combined. Yet, over the centuries, the Appalachian culture and, to a lesser degree, its descendants throughout the Midwest and West have been consistently portrayed in negative lights. Is it any wonder, then, that the cultural descendants of the backcountry harbor resentments against the East Coast cultural descendants of Quakers, Cavaliers, and Puritans?

Taking away the stereotypes created by these other groups, what were the borderers *really* like? And what did *their* culture provide to modern America?

* * * * *

Just who were these people actually, these Borderers who have been so often dismissed with stereotypes by the likes of Fischer or simply ignored in the story of the United States as most often told? There is no easy answer to that, certainly without utilizing stereotypes oneself, but we can say, as Rodger Cunningham tells us, that "the core of the Appalachian people was essentially formed by events which took place in the twelfth and thirteenth centuries,

and which to some extent were prepared for by repeated patterns of events
going back to the earliest agricultural settlement of Britain, five thousand
years earlier."[44] These were not people who came to North America to leave
their culture and past behind but, rather, people already used to carrying
it with them—for often they had nothing else. Fischer quotes the 16th-
century writer John Major:

> In Scotland, the houses of the country people are small, as it were, cot-
> tages, and the reason is this: they have no permanent holdings, but
> hired only, or in lease for four or five years, at the pleasure of the lord
> of the soil; therefore do they not dare to build good houses, though
> stone abound, neither do they plant trees or hedges for their orchards,
> nor do they dung their land; and this is no small loss and damage to
> the whole realm.[45]

With a war a generation, furthermore, one did not collect "things." Whatever
one had, one had to be able to carry it away at a moment's notice. Roots,
then, were in family and in relationships, not in land or ruler—or even in history. For the Scots-Irish, it has been that way for over a thousand years. This,
clearly, is the root of the inclusion of family and friends in the concept of the
individual as understood in that part of modern American society descended
from them, and it is what makes clan loyalty (or, today, patriotism) so important to them.

We know less about the history of the Scots-Irish than about most other
European cultures, especially those with a closer connection to the Roman
Empire. This is true for several reasons. First, the continuity of power over the
past two millennia on the continent and in the British Isles has stemmed from
Rome—and, as the cliché has it, history is written by the victors. Second, history
is *written*. Having no great tradition of the written word, being primarily an
"orality" culture (to use Walter Ong's term[46]), the Scots-Irish have had little
say about the contents of the documents that have come down to us. Just look
at Fischer's descriptions of them in America: As I have said, few descriptions
come from the Scots-Irish themselves. Even the people known today from
Scots-Irish history are people who were known to outsiders. Most of the
culture's own heroes have long been forgotten.

Webb, whose *Born Fighting* has been one of the most successful stories of
the Scots-Irish in America, depicts his ancestors as "a warlike culture that
indulged in little trade and left few tangible records, other than the observa-
tions from the more learned peoples who observed them."[47] With typical

understated Scots-Irish irony, Webb uses the bias of the observers, who clearly felt that they *were* the more learned ("more lettered" would probably be closer to the truth) to make the point that the Scots-Irish have almost always been defined by others.

Like most actual historians, as well as Bageant, Webb anchors his distinctions between the English and the Scottish in Hadrian's Wall, one of Rome's attempts to provide safety for the lands it ruled. The people around it, of course, neither completely Scot nor completely Irish, let alone English, are exactly those who came to be known as "Borderers." Though the feudalism brought to England by the Normans in 1066 was imposed on them along with the Norman/English culture, it did not take. The top-down manorial system did not flourish in the tougher hills where control was harder to maintain and the older tribal relationship structures remained in place. The blows to individualism and bottoms-up initiative landed by feudalism were not nearly so effective as they were farther south after the Norman Conquest. Imposition of the pyramid structure culminating in the kind of English social hierarchy that came to be so identified with that country was never completely successful—one of the reasons that, as Webb comments, "the story of the rise of Scotland cannot be told through a simple enumeration of kings and royal houses."[48] Another, of course, was the nearly constant wars.

One reason for the frequency of the wars was, as with the failure of feudalism, the landscape itself. As Webb writes,

> Not unlike Appalachia, Scotland is a land of difficult water barriers, sharp mountains and deep hollows, soggy moors and rough pastures, and of thin, uncultivable soil that lies like a blanket over wide reaches of granite. Armies such as the Roman legions described by Cassius Dio tended literally to become bogged down as they advanced into Scotland's interior. And (again not unlike Appalachia), a central government that wished to impose its will on the tough, weapons-wielding folks who dwelled back in the hollows would be guaranteed a hostile reception unless it had the full cooperation of local leaders.[49]

One of the impacts of the wars—and of poor soil that made crops for export difficult to cultivate—was that the border region never became a real part of the growing pattern of European trade economies, economies that brought not only riches but integration into the knowledge base growing through the new "literacy" (again, using the term as Ong would) cultures. As a result, the border region was a real backwater, one of the poorest and least "educated" areas of all of Europe.

Though the Borderers are often conflated with the Scots, they were never the same. Thomas Sowell writes,

> People of Scottish ancestry have long been among the more prosperous groups in the United States, but people of the same ancestry in the Appalachian region have also constituted one of the most enduring pockets of poverty among white Americans. As long as our view is confined to American society, it may be plausible to believe that "objective conditions" in Appalachia, or the way people were "treated" there, accounts for the anomaly. Indeed, prevailing social doctrines all but require that approach. Yet, if the history of the Scots is viewed internationally, then it becomes clear that the subgroup which settled in Appalachia differed culturally from other Scots before either boarded the ships to cross the Atlantic.[50]

Though I could quibble that the Scots-Irish are no "subgroup," Sowell's point is well taken. The Highland Scots had little to do with the culture of the border.

Still, the two were long considered part of one nation. Whatever the truth may be, it is interesting that it was Robert the Bruce through the victory at Brannochburn in 1314 who established Scotland (though not the disputed border region) as an independent kingdom and himself as the father of a nation (though a nation constantly beset from the south). In many respects, Robert the Bruce was a particularly appropriate ruler for a nation whose leaders in both the Highlands and the Lowlands traditionally came from the people rather than through imposition from the state as in the feudal model. Understanding this, Bruce ruled through the consent of the governed (through the consent, at least, of the heads of the clans) and not simply through might. As Webb writes,

> Neither Bruce nor any other Scottish leader could fight or rule without the consent—and the unique notion of kinship—of those who had brought him victory. . . . [This was] an entire people born largely through resistance to the yoke of Rome and hardened through centuries of warfare. Nor was it simply the attempted rule of the English that would spur Scottish defiance. A people had been formed, from the bottom up. Later centuries would scatter them across the globe. And wherever they traveled, they would bring with them an insistent independence, a willingness to fight on behalf of strong men who properly led them, and a stern populism that refused to bend a knee, or bow a head, to anyone but their God.[51]

Webb's romantic notion of the Scots-Irish is certainly as much myth as reality, but it is myth, I argue, that forms a people.

Michael Hechter, in *Internal Colonialism: The Celtic Fringe in British National Development, 1536–1966*, uses a model based on a duality of "(1) the *core*, or dominant cultural group which occupies territory extending from the political center of the society (e.g. the locus of the central government) outward to those territories largely occupied by the subordinate, or (2) *peripheral* cultural group."[52] Cunningham expands on this, identifying *three* regions or regional identities as significant to the development of Appalachian culture from England and into North America. The first is the "civilized" Roman, English, then American East Coast culture (the core). The second, the one Hechter did not need to address, is the culture "outside" of those others, often seen as savage or barbarous—the Celts (for the Romans), the Highlanders and Irish (for the English), and the "Indians" (for the East Coast). Between them, in the Scottish Lowlands, in Ulster, and in the backcountry of Appalachia, is the third, an intermediate culture, the periphery to the metropolitan core, acting both as a buffer against the "outside" and as a political and cultural force for expansion.[53]

To the list of "outside" peoples, I would add the African Americans, even though they are not represented by a particular physical place (though they come close, with their concentration today in urban areas in much of the United States). Since slavery (a different model, obviously), they have also taken on the role played by the other outsiders of the past—and, even with an African American in the White House, they continue to play that role today. Latinos should also be added on as another outsider group, especially in light of contemporary anti-immigrant feelings.

What we have here is, basically, a cultural progression based on a paradigm of discovery, conquest, and colonialism—a parallel to what Wayne Franklin calls discoverers, explorers, and settlers[54] but with its darker side exposed (explorers becoming conquerors or even exterminators). Perhaps, though, it is actually even closer to Octave Mannoni's colonizer-colonial-native model described in his book *Prospero and Caliban* about colonization in Africa. The Guyanese political economist Walter Rodney, in *How Europe Underdeveloped Africa*, also describes the tensions between the metropole and the periphery in colonization of Africa in a way that certainly reminds one of the internal colonialism of Hechter. In applying a similar model to the situation of the Borderers, Cunningham pushes further, writing that

> the metropole . . . encourages them to take out this violence on the ones next in line, the "savages." Thus they are manipulated into carrying out the metropole's genocidal program while being culturally and socially destroyed themselves. They are encouraged to see themselves as the

representatives of "civilization" against "savagery," while the metropolitan in fact looks on them as little, if at all, better than savages
themselves.[55]

What has resulted from this, Cunningham goes on to say, is "the fundamental
social and cultural trauma undergone by what was to become the Scotch-
Irish and Appalachian peoples."[56] As it does for all people on a colonial
periphery, this trauma shaped not only Borderer cultures but a large part of
the greater culture as well, in this case, American culture, certainly influencing
the attitudes toward central authority that are played on by America's right-
wing activists today and the narrow, prescriptive feelings toward individual
initiative and responsibility that are now so prevalent.

One of the myths that Rodney tries to counter concerns the idea of "developing" colonial or postcolonial areas. Instead, he argues, such places are
being actively "underdeveloped." The same was true on the English/Scottish
border, in Ulster Plantation, and in the mountains of Appalachia and the
pattern can be seen even in the exploitation of the newly settling West. The
problems of such areas are not, as Cunningham also points out, the "growing
pains" of development but rather result from maintaining the periphery as
periphery, never letting it become part of the metropole, exploiting its resources and its people for the metropole, but always keeping it at a distance.[57]
This fact is critical to any understanding of the resentments today toward the
"mainstream media" and the "eastern liberal establishment," toward the
people that Nixon's Vice President Spiro Agnew, a generation ago, called "an
effete corps of impudent snobs who characterize themselves as intellectuals"
as they gathered to protest the Vietnam War. With some justification, those
on the old peripheries of the United States still feel they have long been
exploited by an uncaring metropole.

* * * * *

Perhaps it is true that those on any periphery are paranoid, but this is understandable, particularly for the Borderers, for they were caught between two
forces, one defined for them as "savage" and the other as "civilized." They
felt that they were allowed to be neither, nor to make choices for themselves,
deciding which is which, for example, civilized or savage. But the real disaster
of the metropole-periphery-savagery model is that it leaves nobody unaf-
fected, not even those of the metropole who see themselves as "above" both
the Borderers and the so-called savages. "It is plain how this essentially paranoid mentality dehumanizes and destroys those beyond the frontier, but the

dwellers inside the frontier are themselves victimized in a more subtle but also deadly way."[58] No one survives any type of colonialism unscathed.

To better understand the position of the people at the periphery, it is worth taking a short look at what Mannoni calls the "colonials," people who naturally share many traits with the Borderers. He writes that

> the personality of the colonial is made up, not of characteristics acquired during and through experience of the colonies, but of traits, very often in the nature of a complex, already in existence in a latent and repressed form in the European's psyche, traits which the colonial experience has simply brought to the surface and made manifest.[59]

The colonials, unleashed from the restraints of their home societies, react in ways that are detrimental, to say the very least, to the "natives" they encounter, to the putative savages. To place the blame, then, on the Scots-Irish for the near extermination of Native Americans (under the leadership of Andrew Jackson, one of their own), is a little disingenuous. In Mannoni's view, it could have been—and would have been—any "Europeans" who did it. The entire culture, the entire United States, in this particular case, shares responsibility for what amounts to attempted genocide at the very least. Responsibility cannot simply be passed off onto those relegated to the periphery. The very nature of the "colonial" existence leads to just that sort of activity, no matter the origin of the "colonial" himself or even herself. In addition, just as with slavery, even those not directly involved often profit even while decrying it.

* * * * *

Contrary to popular impressions, the Scots-Irish were never quite the inward-looking people of legend, never wanting to deal with outsiders. Still, "the tendency to respond to the existence of others as a threat to its own being, is a fundamental part of American consciousness and of that of the West as a whole,"[60] and much of that does come from Borderer influence on the culture of the new settlements. The Borderers have always been suspicious but suspicious of real or possible (and certainly not imaginary) representatives of outside power—of the colonial powers, be they of king or congress. But, as I have claimed and as Cunningham, again, says,

> The "Scotch-Irish" themselves experienced many admixtures of immigrants, especially English ones, both in Scotland and later in Ireland. And finally, of course, a goodly portion of Appalachians themselves are not of "Scotch-Irish" origin at all but are derived from the original

natives; from German, Welsh, English, Highland Scottish, and Black settlers; or from later arrivals.[61]

By assimilating so many others, the Scots-Irish culture remained dominant even as actual Scots-Irish numbers dwindled in relation to the whole, even as it took on aspects (the German-style barns, for example, seen so often in Appalachia) of the other cultures and embraced their children. This is another key fact in any attempt to understand the contemporary American culture that emerged from Scots-Irish backgrounds: It may seem racist and clannish to outsiders, but the culture continues to embrace those outsiders willing to accept its norms.

Genealogical studies of Scots-Irish families puts the lie to their insularity. The Scots-Irish frequently intermarried with outsider ethnic groups and religions. What I found in simply looking at my own family is completely consistent with Cunningham's statement that "once in Ireland, the settlers seem to have converted and/or intermarried with the subject race to some appreciable degree."[62] A surprising number of my Scottish ancestors who passed through Ulster Plantation left there (generally several generations later) with Irish spouses or left behind Irish parents or grandparents on one side. My typical Scots-Irish ancestry includes Highland Scots, Irish, Welsh, English, French, and Germans. Others have much the same, but might include Italian or Native American ancestry—or even African American.

* * * * *

Once they got to America, the Borderers did not stay long on the East Coast. Carrying with them what Fischer simplistically and incorrectly calls "the ancient border habit of belligerence toward other ethnic groups,"[63] they moved west and southwest, completely with the blessings of the earlier settlers of Pennsylvania and Maryland, some of whom, as we can imagine, saw them as a useful buffer between "civilization" and the even more savage Native Americans. As a result,

> it was the Scotch-Irish ... who settled closest to the frontier, and it was primarily the Scotch-Irish who moved in successive waves down the Great Valley between the Blue Ridge and the Alleghenies, spilling back eastward out of the gaps where the valley is pinched behind Roanoke, and the colonizing henceforward the Piedmont region of the Carolinas.[64]

They took the Great Wagon Road (though wagons, early on, could only make it halfway through the Shenandoah Valley) often ending up in the

Piedmont areas of the Carolinas or in the hills above them. According to Fischer, they had simply "drifted south and west along the mountains of Maryland, Virginia and the Carolinas."[65] His use of "drifted" is a telling mark of his own disdain for the Borderers. For they didn't "drift."

Unwelcome in the Delaware Valley and unwilling to come under the sway of the English of Virginia, they skirted the lands where they were unwanted, seeking areas where they could establish their own communities. They really could not, at that time, strike out directly west—the mountains were still a generally unexplored barrier, and the Native Americans were not weak enough, relatively, for that direct an incursion to be successful. The Scots-Irish felt they were being pushed or would soon be pushed and were moving as far as they could in response or as preemption: "You can't kick us out; we're already leaving."

It is for this reason that the Scots-Irish and those who joined them and took on their culture were so important to later movements west. Their homes *were* the western frontier at the time of the Revolution. Not only did this make them best prepared for the push into "savage" territory (for they were the ones who had already dealt most directly with the "savages," the Native Americans), but they also retained the sorts of skills that an individual family would need in settling far from the resources of the metropole. As Cunningham says, "Frontier mountain dwellers from the beginning had different tendencies from lowland dwellers in some fundamental attitudes; ... this difference predated and underlay, though it was accentuated by, the differential effects of nineteenth-century 'progress.'"[66] "Civilized" attributes did not help on the frontier.

The irony of this is that, though they were themselves seen as close to the "savages" (I am using the word as the "civilized" colonials might, not as any sort of accurate description of Native Americans) by those of the other "folkways," the Borderers were also the advanced guard of "civilization," making safe room for the very people who so looked down on them—but also, in many respects, making it possible for these new settlers to join *them*, to take on more of the Borderer culture than managing to do the reverse.

It has long been accepted that the frontier, the "manifest destiny" of the American people that pushed the country across the continent, created a nation and not just a state. Frederick Jackson Turner, perhaps the first significant historian writing about that frontier, wrote,

> We note that the frontier promoted the formation of a composite nationality for the American people. The coast was preponderantly

English, but the later tides of continental immigration flowed across to the free lands. This was the case from the early colonial days. The Scotch-Irish and the Palatine Germans, or "Pennsylvania Dutch," furnished the dominant element in the stock of the colonial frontier. With these peoples were also the freed indentured servants, or redemptioners, who at the expiration of their time of service passed to the frontier. Governor Spotswood of Virginia writes in 1717, "The inhabitants of our frontiers are composed generally of such as have been transported hither as servants, and, being out of their time, settle themselves where land is to be taken up and that will produce the necessarys of life with little labour." Very generally these redemptioners were of non-English stock. In the crucible of the frontier the immigrants were Americanized, liberated, and fused into a mixed race, English in neither nationality nor characteristics. The process has gone on from the early days to our own. Burke and other writers in the middle of the eighteenth century believed that Pennsylvania was "threatened with the danger of being wholly foreign in language, manners, and perhaps even inclinations." The German and Scotch-Irish elements in the frontier of the South were only less great.[67]

Turner, we see today, was wrong: The frontier Scots-Irish people were not "Americanized" in the way he means. In fact, they were in the process of assimilating the other settlers into their own culture, one that did, indeed, come to be known as "American" but one that is quite distinct from the coastal (and, by Turner's time, northern) secular-liberal American culture that is often conflated with the Borderer one to produce an imagined American culture of the whole. Not a single, mixed "race" or culture was formed. *Two* came out of European immigration, two that look so alike that the historians of the dominant one have long ignored the other, seeing it as only a debased part of their own culture.

This realization goes against the myth of American culture that has prevailed for over two centuries. Horace Kallen, for example, writes of Americans of English descent after the Revolution as "a homogeneous people, all in all like-minded, inevitably self-conscious, regardful of their roots in the mother country, and speaking of her, even after the signing of the Declaration of Independence, as 'home.' "[68] Twice, sometimes three-times displaced from mother-country roots, the Borderers had no such illusions and claimed no such roots.

The slighting of Borderer culture continues today, of course, even if unconsciously (when looking at history). One of the more startling things, for example, about Matthew Frye Jacobson's *Roots Too: White Ethnic*

Revival in Post–Civil Rights America, a study of the quest for roots among white immigrant Americans, is not just that it almost completely ignores internal migration: The Borderers and their descendants get no mention at all. There is nary a word of Appalachia in the book or of "Scots-Irish" or "Ulster." Yet the experiences of the Appalachian immigrants are not so different from that of the European (or Asian) ones. "Hansen's Law," the idea that what the first generation of immigrants wants to forget their grandchildren will want to remember, has worked as well for them as for the grandchildren of people from much farther away. Too well, perhaps, for each generation, in reclaiming the past, finds less than its grandparents forgot—and today's Borderers are the grandchildren of the grandchildren of the grandchildren of the grandchildren of their immigrant ancestors.

Among those who have most fervently supported the myth of an American identity have been, oddly enough, the Borderers. They saw (and see) the coasts, the cities, and the far north of the country as not reflecting the "real" American experience of their own ancestors and themselves. They still see America as their own, even after centuries within a country whose national conversations have long been dominated by a secular-liberal establishment that reflects a culture quite different from the one that really is their own.

Alone in the Wilderness: The Myth of Daniel Boone, the Reality of the Border, the Rise of Jackson, and the Background of John Brown

In seeking to understand the American mythology of individualism, there is no better place to start than with Daniel Boone. As biographer Robert Morgan writes, "Boone would embody in his actions and attitude the aspirations and character of a whole era."[1] Morgan might be correct in more ways than many of us, looking back on Boone centuries later, may realize. Though not of Scots-Irish descent and born to a Pennsylvania Quaker family, Boone's attitudes (and those of his father and brothers) proved to be in closer keeping with those of the Borderers who were trekking down the Shenandoah Valley during his early years than they were with the staid and, now, often stay-at-home coastal colonists. Also, Boone's life is emblematic of the problems of the frontier, not just those of the developing "need" for defeating native inhabitants and of settling a new land but even of those created by tensions between the poor of the backwoods and the richer East, problems that amounted to what could best be described as "internal colonialism."

When Boone was 16, his family started a long process of movement along with that continual stream of Borderers down the Great Wagon Road, first west from their eastern Pennsylvania home to about where the town of Carlisle would soon be laid out and then south through the Shenandoah. The Boones eventually settled on a spot in the Yadkin River valley near Mocksville, North Carolina, perhaps 15 or 20 miles from where Salisbury, to be the seat of Rowan County and the nearest town of any substance, would soon be established.

So many others went the same route during that period (including many of my own ancestors) that the population of the area of the Carolinas that became known as the Piedmont "grew from a few hundred in the 1740s to more than 39,000 European Americans and 3,000 African Americans by 1767."[2] The region the Piedmont is a part of, "Greater Appalachia," which, according to Colin Woodard, had "started as a civilization without a government. The Borderlanders were not really colonists, brought to the New World to provide some lord or shareholding company with the man-power for a specific colonial project. They were immigrants seeking sanctuary from a devastated homeland, refugees who generally arrived without the encouragement or direction of officials and often against their wishes."[3] But, as we will see, they *were* soon as good as colonized themselves.

Before the massive crossing of the Appalachians and Alleghenies starting a generation later, this Piedmont region was part of the "Wild West," an unstable area dominated by scoundrels as much as by the prevalent hardscrabble settlers and the remnants of Native American nations. Henry Nash Smith points out "the contrast between civilization and savagery that lay at the root of the distinc-tion between the Wild West and the domesticated or agricultural West. The frontier of agricultural settlement was universally recognized as the line separat-ing civilization from savagery."[4] In the 1750s, the Piedmont was on the wrong side of that line, which was quite a bit closer to the coast or to the banks of the great navigable rivers of the East, including the Potomac, the Susquehanna, the Delaware, and the Hudson. That would change quickly, of course: "Two-thirds of the American population of 3.9 million lived within fifty miles of the ocean in 1790. In the next half-century 4.5 million Americans crossed the Appalachians, one of the great migrations in world history."[5] In the meantime, places like the Yadkin River valley would become major jumping-off points for those, like Boone, who would make their way through the Cumberland Gap to explore the new West of Kentucky and even farther, laying out pathways for the settlers who would follow.

The experience of the settlers in the Piedmont did more than prepare them to move farther west. What happened to them provides an example of pressures that lead me to include them with the many cultures that have experienced "internal colonialism." In fact, it was often these pressures that led people already on the frontier to go farther into the West. Not only were they seeking a new life, but many of them were also fleeing situations of exploitation.

Like the residents of the western settlements of Pennsylvania and the people who were trying to establish farms in the hilly west of Virginia, the Scots-Irish Borderers—and people such as Boone who had joined them—of the Carolinas certainly were poised to be the leaders of the movement west, establishing trails through the mountains and even laying out towns for the millions who would follow them over the next century. Not only were they geographically in the right place, but they knew more about the nearly subsistence farming necessary on the frontier than did any other group of European settlers and so could show the way in agriculture, too. Not only that, but they had assimilated a great deal of knowledge of hunting and means of survival in North America from the Native Americans they were in more frequent contact with than were any other group of colonial-era settlers. As a result of their leadership in the westward expansion, they would become one of the most influential of all of the European immigrant groups, out of all proportion to their numbers. Yet they were also probably the poorest, forced to take risks just to survive. But they were hardy: Toughened by generations of strife and privation, they were able to withstand just about anything the new continent could throw in their way.

The Borderers understood self-reliance and they resented it when they had to depend on others. Often fervent Calvinists or devotees of New Light descendants of Calvinism, they believed in a personal relationship with God and wanted nothing to do with churches, like the Anglican and Catholic, with centralized dictates. In addition, many of them moved on because they soon found that they were no longer able to stay where they had settled in the colonial backwoods of the Piedmont, Virginia and Pennsylvania. Their land often proved not even to be theirs but belonging to speculators first in England and then in the coastal states.

These people on the frontier were unlike anyone else in the colonies, most of whom, by the mid-18th century, had settled into towns or onto farms cultivated for generations (or almost within sight of the established ones). Unlike those solid citizens, these Borderers were people who, often, had nothing. But, like the urban poor of today, they *did* know how to survive—by whatever means were necessary. If nothing else, they were tough. Charles Woodmason, an Anglican ministering to them, described these hardscrabble people as "a Sett of the most lowest vilest Crew breathing—Scotch Irish Presbyterians from the North of Ireland."[6] They were all of that, too—in the eyes of outsiders.

Not surprisingly, and showing just how little people change, we hear the same about certain groups today and more often than we should. We hear it about African Americans and even Latinos, Russians, and Chinese. It is a description of poor immigrants who do not know the rules of behavior for the culture—or whose place within the broader culture is so low that they have nothing to lose by acting without restraint, having nothing to protect. Though commonplace, it has little to do with the reality of *any* culture.

* * * * *

The Piedmont was fast filling not only with Scots-Irish Borderers but with Germans, English, and others who, perhaps having finished their indenture, had been loathe to stay in the settled areas of the colonies or, perhaps, simply could not afford to or who, quite simply, were men who had been unable to find wives and work in the coastal communities. It can almost seem, through a quick look, as though the newcomers to the region were gathering for the express purpose of moving on over the mountains, but most of them would probably have preferred to settle in the Piedmont or the foothills permanently. Few of them had much of anything in the way of possessions to tie them down, however, and eventually found they had no land to hold them. So, they were free to move on when pushed.

They had arrived with little more than simply the hope that they could find land to farm without interference due to prior claims of ownership and with, perhaps, a gun and an ax, and the few supplies that could fit on a packhorse or on their backs. If they were lucky, they had a bit of money for buying a cow, a pig, a few chickens, and seed corn. When they moved on farther west, they rarely had much more, their attempts to work their ways out of poverty in the Piedmont generally having failed.

Though some came as families, many others were single men dreaming of setting up homesteads where they could eventually bring wives—if they could find them. So poor were they that Woodmason, when he traveled among them, felt "obliged to carry my own Necessaries with me—As Bisket—Cheese—A Pint of Rum—Some Sugar—Chocolate—Tea, or Coffee—With Cups Knife Spoon Plate Towels and Linen."[7] Hospitality he sometimes found, but he wanted a little bit more, and it was rarely available. When you come from the well-to-do into situations of poverty, as Woodmason and many travelers from the East discovered when they traveled in the backwoods, you have to carry your own comforts. The people there would have shared had they anything to share. But they had next to nothing.

The problem, even back then, was that it gets easy to start blaming the poor for their lacks. Woodmason struggled with that—as the middle classes in America have ever since. Like all impoverished people everywhere, the Borderers recognized these attitudes on the part of those who styled themselves their "betters"—and became more determined than ever (if that were possible) to get out of poverty on their own, without the help of these condescending strangers. Furthermore, they believed that their poverty was at least partially the fault of those same people, certainly of the bankers and speculators from the East—and wanted to get as far away from them as possible. Their individualism, grown in reaction and from generations of struggle,

was also a result of confidence in their own abilities to survive and even pros-
per and of the belief that they were being held back only by others attempting
to exploit their own hard work.

*****

John Mack Faragher, another biographer of Boone, comes tantalizingly close
to understanding the place of Boone within this culture of the backwoods,
but, unfortunately, he also does so without recognition that there were,
even then, two white American cultures (more actually, but only the major
two, the Borderer and secular-humanist or secular-liberal concern us here).
Though common, this is a little strange, for the split becomes evident in even
cursory looks at the War of the Regulation in the Piedmont, at the political
divisions of the early Federalist period, at the rancor of the Whiskey
Rebellion, and, of course, at the growing rift between those still looking to
England for guidance and those now looking west to what they imagined as
a blank slate for them to fill with their own drawings.

During George Washington's administration, this split was papered over
by the fact that one of the leaders who seemed to be representing the interests
of the Borderers, Thomas Jefferson, leader of what were seen in some quarters
as Americans Jacobins (those who seemed overly influenced by the French
Revolution), was a tried-and-true son of the elite and no Borderer himself.
Faragher writes that Boone, on the other hand, "was a hero, but a hero of a
new, democratic type, a man who did not tower above the people but rather
exemplified their longings and, yes, their limitations."[8] Jefferson, certainly,
was no leader like that. Also, the type of leadership Boone represented was
not "new" to Borderers. William Wallace comes through legend from the
13th century as much the same sort of hero, as do many more recent
Borderer heroes. Jefferson was a hero both of democracy and independence.
These others were heroes of independence alone—a different thing.

Boone, whatever allegiance he may have developed for the United States
during and after the Revolution, spent many of the later years of his life moving away from its power. If anything, he was not a hero of the United States
but of freedom and of a developing American sort of individualism and desire
for self-sufficiency—again, much as Wallace became in his older legend.
Certainly, he was no hero of the secular-liberalism and American democracy
held dear by the likes of Jefferson. That was a liberalism of the East, quite distinct, as we have seen, from the individualism of the frontier.

What Faragher does point out, correctly, is that Boone is one of those
heroes who really did rise in legend from the people of the frontier

themselves. Though raised a Quaker, he had the real spirit of a Borderer and lived as one, even collecting debts as one. He was literate enough to read the Bible and *Gulliver's Travels* and maybe even *Robinson Crusoe*, but his was not a concern for scholarship. He could survey and plan, but he was not really that interested in sticking around to see the results (partly because he was constantly in legal trouble over debts but partly because the real action, in his mind, was always moving a bit farther west). Like any Borderer, he preferred (legendarily) to keep away from neighbors moving too close, choosing rural or woods life over that of the town.

The towns, in Boone's eyes as in those of many of the Borderer settlers, were rife with legal entrapments and predatory businessmen. Necessary optimists, the Borderers were always betting on a better day coming—specifically betting on a successful harvest or hunting trip, both requiring supplies acquired in advance and generally on credit. The debts they incurred each spring before planting or each winter before setting out on the hunt ensnared them when luck did not go their way—and many of them surely felt that the lenders and the law merely waited for something untoward to happen at harvest or for Indians or scoundrels to abscond with their pelts while taking none of the risks themselves. Boone, certainly, "ignored business, forgot business"[9] and returned to the woods as quickly as he could after each trip to town, going back to those occupations that he and most Borderers believed to be of greater importance: hunting, farming, and caring for the family.

The debt of the Borderers was not always simply the result of needing money at the start of a hunt or a planting. Sometimes the debt came as a result of exploitation by suppliers and landowners and even by those who provided the market for Borderer crops and pelts. With very little legal or political clout, the people of the backwoods were open to exploitation by those backed by the legal and economic powers of the coast, an exploitation (given the cultural distinctions involved) that amounted to the same thing as colonialism, something only the Borderers, of the white population in America, continued to experience after the Revolution.

Life in the backwoods, though sometimes hellishly difficult, was certainly organizationally simple in comparison to that of the older European settlements of the coastal areas. The people who stayed and tried to make a go of it in the Piedmont tried to learn to make do with what they could produce themselves if at all possible—but it was not always as completely possible as the idea of the simple life could make it seem. In fact, it was rarely even partially possible, but not because the resources and other necessities could not be found. Certainly, away from navigable waterways, goods from England not only were prohibitively expensive but also, often, could not even be transported in. People had to make what they could from what was at hand or pay exorbitant prices, especially for those things they were finding they absolutely needed, like seed for planting. So they bought only what they had to, engaging in commercial agriculture to make money to pay for these necessities, taxes and mortgages and little else, only *dreaming* of a self-sufficiency away from a monetary economy.

Talking of the physical state of a group of people who had gathered to hear him preach, Woodmason wrote, "It would be ... a Great Novelty to a Londoner to see one of these Congregations—The Men with only a thin Shirt and pair of Breeches or Trousers on—barelegged and barefooted—The Women bareheaded, barelegged and barefoot with only a thin Shift under Petticoat."[10] They could not afford anything else—not from their own inability to economize but at least in part because much of the profit from their activity alit in the metropoles of the coast and not in their own pockets.

Corn was the primary initial crop of the new settlers, and not just for their own consumption. It was cheap and comparatively easy to grow and sell, if need be. Woodmason frequently mentions it as about the only food to be found in the settler cabins he describes. It also proved extremely versatile. Not only was it a ready nourishment, but it was easily dried, ground (with a mortar and pestle, if no mill were yet established nearby) and stored for meal and grits for consumption over the winter. The cob, the shuck, and the stalk also proved useful, feeding animals, filling mattresses, and acting as ready kindling. It also was the basis for the ubiquitous alcoholic beverages (for sale as well as for home consumption), especially the whiskey that would later become famous as "moonshine." Corn could be successfully planted even by scattering seed over cleared but unplowed ground. Later, because of the need for cash, commercial crops, such as wheat and, sometimes, tobacco would be added but corn remained central.

By 1750, Rowan County, with Salisbury becoming its seat on the founding of the town five years later, was already known as a rough-and-tumble though fast-growing area. Already, the coastal government was eyeing the Piedmont as it filled up with Borderers, but it still had not made its influence consistently felt. That would come a decade later, culminating in the late 1760s in what came to be known as the War of the Regulation which brought the fractious backwoods under greater government control. In the meantime, people got along as best they could, living not far removed from the way many of their ancestors had back on the border of Scotland and England, responsible for themselves, their families, and no one else. The main differences lay in the facts that, first, they now had to clear much of the land

and, second, they used new survival skills they had managed to learn from the Native Americans whose land they were, quite frankly, commandeering.

One thing that was not different was that exploitation they quickly fell under. The land they were farming, even when they were the first Europeans to settle on it, was not theirs. Nor was it land of the Native Americans who had, in many cases, abandoned it. The land "belonged" to grantees from the English Crown (Earl Granville being the most important of these in the North Carolina of the time before the Revolution), to other English and Scottish speculators, or to coastal bigwigs who had established claims. Few of these had ever even seen the land, but as soon as it was profitable to do so, they began exploiting their claims at the expense of the poor settlers, people who sometimes had no idea the land was "owned" at all—making them "squatters" on land that had never before been worked by Europeans. These settlers, because of the debt incurred to absentee owners, never could be true subsistence farmers, though many (including Woodard, who writes that, instead of "trying to produce cash crops for export, the Borderlanders embraced a woodlands subsistence economy"[11]) have imagined they were just that.

The absentee landlords and mortgage holders controlled the backwoods economy in a number of ways, all of which forced the farmers either into a monetary economy or into a flouting of colonial law, a precarious situation for families living on the edge of subsistence. They now found themselves needing cash to pay mortgages and quitrents and taxes imposed by distant overlords—or dodging the law. The farmers knew they could make it on their own, but, because of the current system of landownership, they needed a stake to get started and at least a small cash flow to repay any mortgage, the taxes, and any loans for supplies. If they could only get ahead on these, they would need no other help—or so they believed. Their hard work and individual initiative would be enough, allowing them to make or buy what little they needed. "What they were after was not self-sufficiency, but rather family continuity and economic independence, or 'competency,' "[12] writes Marjoleine Kars, a historian of the region. She continues, "People squatted and improved land in expectation of applying for title as soon as circumstances permitted. When that time came, however, some found that the land they had been working, now quite valuable because they had cultivated it, was no longer available,"[13] "owned," as it were, by distant speculators. This helped keep them in poverty.

If not that, a drought year would come, or the family hunters would return in the spring empty handed, and they would be right back in debt again, their dreams of individual independence dashed. To make matters worse, their lenders were often also their buyers and their suppliers—so they had to sell at prices set by those they had borrowed from and to buy at their prices, too. There was no real free market in operation—and there would not be, for farmers, for generations, if ever. This was another means, in Borderer eyes, for keeping them in poverty.

The farms of the backwoods made money—but, again, that money did not stay on the farm. It headed elsewhere in the classic pattern of colonialism. In the American colonies, it headed to the coast and to England. Land speculators, including some who would soon be leaders of the American Revolution, got rich while the poor Borderers and those who had joined them got poorer. As Kars writes, "The majority of people came to the Piedmont expecting to patent land from the crown or Granville for reasonable prices. Instead, many ended up paying dearly for their own farms, due to the speculative ventures"[14] of people often far away from the Piedmont.

Their situation was compounded by a corrupt system of county courts soon established, with justices appointed by coastal cronies to help protect their investments while building their own fortunes. These justices

> set local tax rates to finance public works, oversaw tax collection, ordered the sale of property for debts, and had it in their power to release the desperate poor from their debts and tax burdens. Justices oversaw the morality of the community by punishing swearing and sexual transgressions. They ordered the apprenticeships of poor, illegitimate or mixed-race children, handled guardianships for orphans, and regulated the treatment of servants and slaves.[15]

And more. They were aided by sheriffs and court clerks whose only legitimate income came through fines and fees—and who were also on the make, looking for any way to take advantage of the defenseless. Seized property and land would be auctioned. Is there any doubt who would likely buy? Is there any doubt that these "entrepreneurs" were engaging in classic colonialist activity?

Kars argues against the too-usual depiction of the rural Borderer farmers as stupid, that their resistance to the debt burdens they found themselves under was a "misguided response of simple people caught between traditional attitudes and a commercial culture they did not fully understand."[16] She is right: Such attitudes toward the Borderers are generally nothing more than an unthinking acceptance of colonial attitudes or of middle- and upper-class attitudes toward the lower economic classes in general. As she claims,

> When people insulted the local magistrates who increased their debts by charging high court fees, when they threatened the personal safety of

their creditors, when they recaptured their possessions from the sheriff preparing to sell them at public auction to satisfy taxes or debts, or when they freed themselves or their neighbors from jail, they were not acting out of ignorance or backwardness.[17]

They were acting from outrage, just as contemporary "Tea Party" activists do. Yes, they could sometimes be mistaken (and today's Tea Partiers often are), but their grievances had—and have—a real basis in personal experience, something people looking in from afar often fail to understand.

One thing the Borderer farmers were certainly aware of was that they were paying an unfair share of taxes. *Their* land was taxed, and they had to pay poll taxes, excise, fees for court services, and more—while those paid little or nothing who owned the vast acreages they had "squatted" upon and wanted to buy. The difference, today, is that the Tea Partiers believe it is the people *below* them on the social scale who are benefiting, getting government largess paid for through Tea Partier taxes and not those above. For the Borderer farmers, there was no one below them anyway—except the few black slaves in the area, slaves owned not by them but by the people they were paying money to, the already rich.

As I have said, Boone, that paragon of American spirit and virtue, also got caught up in the debt cycle that ruined so many of his contemporaries. It happened a number of times during his life. Apparently, he went west not only to get away from people but also to get away from debt, land speculators, and the corruption that was, more often than not, the law. He knew, like the farmers around him, that he could make it on his own—if only he would be allowed to—but that human circumstances were against him. He had the individual talent, but society was structured against him.

*****

The equivalent of today's Tea Party movement in the late 1760s in what was then the west of South Carolina and North Carolina grew out of Borderer desperation in the face of corrupt officials taking what the settlers saw as their own livelihood. Those who protested are the ones who came to be known as the "Regulators." Their Regulator movement—often couched today as a class conflict between the poor small farmers in the central Piedmont and the more established slave-owning planters from the coast (the people who controlled the colonial government) or between people of dissident churches emphasizing the personal relationship to god against the powerful anti-individualistic Church of England—was also a clash of cultures. Many of the Borderers, after all, had come down to North Carolina through the Shenandoah to *avoid* the

English in Virginia and to escape the Pennsylvania Quakers. Here were the English again, encroaching upon them with their lawyers and bankers, almost all of whom seemed corrupt and anxious to profit from the hard work of the settlers.

The Regulators resisted what they saw as corrupt courts rigging judgments almost always in favor of those with connection to the coastal government. The goal was simply honesty in government and a withdrawal of punitive intrusion into personal lives. The weakness of the movement was that it was relatively leaderless, the idea of individualism having already taken strong hold among the mainly Scots-Irish settlers, no one wanting to tell others what to do.

The Regulator agitation lasted in fits and starts from 1765 until 1771 when frustration spread widely and resulted in what looked like more organized resistance. At a "battle" at Alamance, North Carolina, a large force of several thousand Regulators was routed by a substantially smaller (but disciplined) coastal militia. At least six Regulators were eventually hanged, others fading into the backwoods.

Though it is popular to see the War of the Regulation as a precursor to the American Revolution, it is more appropriately the precursor to the Whiskey Rebellion of the 1790s. After all, the Regulators were in rebellion not against British rule but against American colonial government. This was not a quest for independence as much as resistance to what was seen as an overreaching by local or colonial corrupt authority. The distinction may seem slight, but it is quite real and resonates to this day. The Regulators did not want to replace one government with another but simply wanted government to go away or, at least, restrict its role. It is in this that they set the stage for the American individualism behind the Tea Party movement of the early 21st century.

Woodmason, of all people, eventually became something of a champion of the Regulators, even though he was not comfortable with the backwoods population, generally. He wrote,

> You were without any Representatives in the Legislature—Not a Road established—Not a Church, Minister, or any Divine Ordinances. You liv'd as without God in the World with out Law, Justice, Religion, or the least Security of Property. The Protection of Government was not extended to You—So far from it, that it was deny'd. . . . Instead of being counted Free Men, who had serv'd their King—brav'd Dangers—and on Credit of the Public Faith, settled this inhospitable Wilderness to make it a land flowing with Milk and Honey, and the Glory of all

Lands (as it soon will be) You were thrown under ev'ry possible Discouragement. Ev'ry Obstacle laid in Your Way, to keep You as a Distinct People from the Lower Settlers and only as a Barrier between them and the Indians for Security of their Negroes and Plantations.[18]

From barrier between the English and the Scottish to barrier between the colonists and the Native Americans. Borderers, indeed!

In that essay of his that changed the way American historians viewed the western frontier at the end of the 19th century, Frederick Jackson Turner romanticized the relationship between the wilderness and the westward-moving colonists. He remarked on the difference between the coastal Americans and those moving west, though he did not recognize that many of the differences between the two groups were not simply the result of contact with the frontier but rather stemmed from the differences in cultural background going back to Europe, those between the Borderers and the others of the British folkways. Turner was not always wrong in his conclusion, just incomplete. He wrote,

> The wilderness masters the colonist. It finds him a European in dress, industries, tools, modes of travel, and thought. It takes him from the railroad car and puts him in the birch canoe. It strips off the garments of civilization and arrays him in the hunting shirt and the moccasin. It puts him in the log cabin of the Cherokee and Iroquois and runs an Indian palisade around him. Before long he has gone to planting Indian corn and plowing with a sharp stick, he shouts the war cry and takes the scalp in orthodox Indian fashion. In short, at the frontier the environment is at first too strong for the man. He must accept the conditions which it furnishes, or perish, and so he fits himself into the Indian clearings and follows the Indian trails. Little by little he transforms the wilderness, but the outcome is not the old Europe, not simply the development of Germanic germs, any more than the first phenomenon was a case of reversion to the Germanic mark. The fact is, that here is a new product that is American. At first, the frontier was the Atlantic coast. It was the frontier of Europe in a very real sense. Moving westward, the frontier became more and more American.[19]

The new frontiersperson was not really a "new product" but a Borderer often with strong Scots-Irish roots, someone who brought to the West survival skills developed over centuries in the Lowlands and honed in the conflicts of Ulster Plantation—or who had learned from such people. The new frontiersperson was someone unlike most of the settlers of the coastal regions, poorer and oppressed in different ways. The new frontiersperson was someone, yes, who could adapt what "he" found into "his" own arsenal but who was changing the West much more than "he" was changed (for he and she were already different from the earlier colonists). The new frontiersperson was someone rejected by the solid citizens of the coastal communities but ready to learn all that he or she could as they made their way west—learning from earlier European arrivals and from the Native Americans. The new frontiersperson was instrumental in pushing ever farther west, generating what would amount to genocide of Native Americans under the later direction of that president of their own, Andrew Jackson. Yet there was even more to it, especially during the 18th century: "The frailty of existence and the violence of everyday life continued to make frontiersmen different from easterners, and contributed to the alien perspectives of the two districts. The cultures and interests of East and West were so contrary during those years that both sides predicted violent conflict."[20] To make matters worse, even "those easterners who had experienced the trials of wilderness living found it difficult to sympathize with the perspectives, the culture, and the violence of frontiersmen. Knowledge of back country conditions and settlers bred contempt more often than empathy."[21] At the time of the Revolution, the real American divide was not North/South with slavery as the touchstone but rather East/West, with economic independence vying with class and cultural differences as the dominant split.

The Borderers were hemmed in. On one side was the East, imposing taxes and claiming oversight and ownership. On the other were the Native Americans, fighting as hard as the Borderers to preserve their own autonomy.

The American Revolution did not change the situation. Though the people of the backwoods bought into the words and actions of the Revolution, they were not treated as an equal part of it by eastern leaders. Their petitions for their own self-governance were rejected or ignored by the state legislatures and the Continental Congress. Their grievances went unaddressed.

*****

The Scots-Irish must have found the ideas of the Revolution, especially concerning taxation, particularly satisfying. The excise taxes of England had grated on their parents and grandparents: Back on the Scotland/England border in the early years of the 18th century, it had taken years for the Crown to break down resistance to the taxes. The Borderers there knew how poor they were and knew that never before, "within memory, had the poor, the propertyless, and the disenfranchised been taxed for support of the government."[22] This was in the British Isles. Generations before the American Revolution, Borderers had already been fighting against what they saw as unfair taxation.

Beyond that, the situation among American whites was complicated by very real cultural differences. Just as they had been cultural and political outsiders back in Ireland and on the Scottish/English border, so were the Scots-Irish during the Revolution. Though they supported it, many came to believe "that state officials sought to deny them the fruits of independence—to exclude them from the 'all men' of the Declaration of Independence."[23] They turned their hopes to the Continental Congress for backing for new, Borderer-run states but found little support there, either.

The divide that would dominate American politics through the next two and a quarter centuries was already in place. Recognizing this, political historian Michael Rogin, writing in the second half of the 20th century, saw the interplay of Native American and European settler somewhat differently than did Turner almost a century earlier:

> We may respect modern historians who insist that the meeting of red man and white was a "culture conflict" not to be judged by standards outside the cultures. But white culture was deeply riven within. White men encountered not merely another culture in Indians, but their own fantasies, longings, and fears. Self-proclaimed liberal values cracked under this pressure. The culture conflict overwhelmed liberal values of individual responsibility.[24]

This may be a little bit closer to the truth, if "liberal values" are taken in an Enlightenment vein, but I do not think it fair to say that the wilderness was something of a "heart of darkness" for the settlers, many of whom came from backgrounds the Enlightenment had hardly dented and who were used to extremely difficult lives in the first place. Their "individual responsibility" had never extended further than family and friends. It is more likely that, instead of being overwhelmed, Enlightenment sensibilities were simply ignored—except where they dovetailed with the ingrained individualism and mistrust of authority already present. It is not surprising, therefore, to discover that "the problem of the West, some easterners believed, was one of education or, if need be, suppression of nonacculturated immigrants."[25] As it had long been for the Borderers, personal survival, along with that of family and friends, was the entire agenda.

The first of the attempts by the backwoods at self-government was the proposal to create a state called Transylvania, whose sponsor, Richard Henderson, had hired Boone to explore the proposed region for him. Boonesborough would have been its capital, and the state would have covered a good part of what is now Kentucky. The quest to become a 14th member state of the

Continental Congress was unsuccessful, of course, meeting resistance from the likes of New Englander John Adams. Transylvania was followed by attempts to form Westsylvania and, established by Regulator veterans, Watauga—the first in the west of Pennsylvania and the second in what is now northeastern Tennessee. That latter area would be part of the proposed state of Franklin after the Revolution, another state that never managed to make its way.

Many on the frontier, certainly, were uncomfortable with government control from the East. They hoped that, as citizens of new states in a loose federal system, they would have more control over their own destinies than they had ever maintained in their past of oppression.

*****

Of course, one of those destinies, as in the Revolution itself, was (the Borderers hoped) control over their own systems of taxation and revenue. But this was not going to happen, not as long as the power remained in the East. In 1791, the new American government imposed a "sin tax" on whiskey, an attempt to balance a federal budget severely out of alignment. What resulted is perhaps the only widely remembered violent split between the coastal "elite" and the growing "backwoods" culture, a conflict that has become known as the Whiskey Rebellion. Ron Chernow, in his biography of Alexander Hamilton (who was instrumental in imposing the tax), describes the situation the tax was meant to take advantage of:

> The mostly Scotch-Irish frontiersmen of western Pennsylvania, who regarded liquor as a beloved refreshment, had the highest per-capital concentration of home-made stills in America. In places, whiskey was so ubiquitous that it doubled as money. The rough-hewn backwoods farmers grew abundant wheat that they couldn't transport over the Allegheny Mountains, which were crossed only by narrow horse paths. They solved the problem by distilling the grain into whiskey, pouring it into kegs, and toting them on horseback across the mountains to eastern markets.[26]

Though a show of force in 1794 dispelled overt resistance, the frontier farmers remained unwilling to cooperate. This was the start of a tradition of alcohol-tax avoidance that would become legendary in the 20th century as bootleggers like Junior Johnson "ran" liquor, in his case from Wilkes County in the west of North Carolina down to Charlotte, becoming expert drivers and the first NASCAR stars—and inspiration for films such as Robert Mitchum's *Thunder Road* (Arthur Ripley, 1958) and a even variety of Burt Reynolds movies in the 1970s.

In the eyes of the government in the East, the resistance to the tax did not seem quite so simple as it probably did to the farmers. The farmers, after all, were part of "a truly desperate populace, a growing body of frustrated men with little to lose."[27] They were, they had discovered, no better off than before the Revolution. If anything, they were poorer. This was also the time of the French Revolution turning sour—in terms of blood running in the streets (quite literally) in what became known as the Reign of Terror. The term "Jacobin" was already being borrowed from the French by Americans to describe their more populist brethren, one of whom, according to Chernow, extolled Robespierre and wanted to construct a guillotine.[28] The responsibility for the divide, then, and the resistance to the tax was placed, in many secular-liberal minds, on forces outside of the United States and not on cultural difference within: "Changing attitudes toward the French Revolution during the 1790s would ... help eastern nationalists to explain the causes of political violence among what they identified as a frontier rabble of foreign anarchists."[29] The backwoods population certainly was, in cultural terms, "foreign" to the eastern elite, but the situation was much more complicated. Richard Hofstadter's presentation of it in the 1960s would have us believe that "the men who with notable character and courage led the way through the Revolution and with remarkable prescience and skill organized a new national government in 1787–88 had by 1796 become hopelessly divided in their interests and sadly affected by the snarling and hysterical differences which were aroused by the French Revolution."[30] The situation, as evidenced by the earlier War of the Regulation, was a great deal more complicated than even that—and much older.

Certainly, those on the populist side of the growing divide did use the French Revolution as a rallying point. After all, the English, on whom the Northeast still looked with affection, had never been friends to the Borderers and were enemies to the French. A treaty with England, the Jay Treaty, negotiated in 1794 and put into effect two years later, became a major point of contention and even became a convenient peg for marking the start of a two-party political system in America:

> The popular fury that swept city after city again disclosed the chasm separating the two main political factions. On the Fourth of July, [John] Jay was burned in effigy in so many cities that he said he could have walked the length of America by the glow from his own flaming figure. For Hamilton, these protests confirmed his premonition that Jeffersonians were really Jacobin fanatics in disguise.[31]

Though part of this new-seeming divide was ideological, just as much of it was cultural and was even based in religion. As Smith observes, "The belief in the Western farmer's social inferiority was . . . strengthened by certain ideas derived from the New England theocratic tradition. From this standpoint, all emigrants were actually or potentially criminal because of their flight from an orderly municipal life into frontier areas that were remote from centers of control."[32] The growing West was dominated by Scots-Irish, Irish, Germans, and even some French Huguenots, none of whom, unlike New Englanders and the Virginia planters, had traditions of cultural or political allegiance to England or a religious tradition analogous to that of New England.

The West was a place, as we have seen, quite different from the now-settled East:

> It was wild and very violent. It was a place where humans prided themselves on their inhumanity and gouged each other's eyes in recreational contests. The frontier had a logic of its own and brooked no instruction from the East. Inhabitants cared little for outsiders. They were independent actors on the American scene, beyond the pale of some eastern values and many eastern laws.[33]

Historian of the Whiskey Rebellion Thomas Slaughter continues to describe the situation of the residents of western Pennsylvania:

> The statistics of land-ownership and population growth reveal a society in extreme social and economic turmoil. They describe a place where poverty was the standard in 1780 and where living conditions declined over the next fifteen years. The tiny mud-floored and often chimneyless cabin was the common abode of these pioneers, and outside the towns these flea- and lice-infested hovels sprouted up and an increasing rate over time. The percentage of rural landowners declined by about 59 percent over the same period. Wealth became concentrated in the hands of fewer men residing in the West, while absentee-owners from the East enhanced their holdings. A majority of residents experienced a sharp decline in all economic categories even as they pushed back the edge of the wilderness.[34]

The West may have seemed a land of promise in the East; the reality, in the decades after the Revolution, was often quite different. Rather than independent yeomen, the settlers were seen as nothing more than, in Hofstadter's words, "poor Western squatters."[35] They "were alone and resigned to it.

They were a fiercely independent people who accepted the labor, the lice, and the landscape of the wilderness with a stoic, often stupendous, fortitude."[36] They expected nothing from the coastal governments, either state or federal, and

> they denounced the remoteness of the new institutions and the inadequate representation they would have there. The perspective of these pioneers was different from those who wrote and voted to ratify the Constitution, but similar to that of colonists who had opposed the Stamp Act. They had much in common with Englishmen who had resisted the intrusion of a national government empowered to collect excises and otherwise usurp local rights and control.[37]

When the excise passed Congress early in 1791, it was opposed by "virtually all the men who could be considered representatives of frontier districts."[38] Like the people they represented, they felt that having to "fight off barbarous savages with one hand and rapacious tax-gatherers with the other would be a hardship even for those hardy pioneers, inured though they were against trauma and suffering."[39] They saw the imposition of the tax as an "ideologically offensive excise [laid] on top of the other ordeals."[40] Meeting at Redstone, Pennsylvania, later in the year, protesters agreed "that their needs had been ignored yet again by a remote central government overly influenced by wealthy eastern merchant, speculators in western lands and public securities, and other 'moneyed-men.' ... To these men, the issues raised by the excised seemed precisely analogous to those of the Stamp Act."[41] In some of their more violent actions, some factions deliberately imitated the Boston Tea Party, dressing as women or Indians. The resistance was not localized: "The frontier of every state south of New York experienced unrest."[42] No excise was collected at all in Kentucky. On the coast, there was little problem. "Only on the frontier was resistance widespread and effective."[43]

Three years later, a large group of frontiersmen attacked the home of a tax inspector, leading President Washington to respond through a show of force, a militia raised in the East that he led personally. Getting wind of this, the backwoodsmen once more faded away. Unlike with the Regulators, the few who were captured were not hanged but were pardoned or acquitted. Slaughter writes,

> Like the Stamp Act, the whiskey excise produced a simultaneous challenge to ideology and interest and thus created a truly volatile situation. It served to divide East against West, city against country, settled versus wilderness societies, mercantile versus agricultural interests, in a way

few other issues could. These divisions already existed; the excise debate revealed long-festering wounds from past and continuing controversies. They were disagreements of importance to people on either side—to their politics, their morals, their purses, and their ways of life.[44]

It was a difficult life the Borderers found on the frontier, but, again, it was not unfamiliar. The houses they built were small, sometimes only several hundred square feet in size. One son of Abraham Lincoln, Robert Todd Lincoln, had an outline created of the dimensions of his father's birthplace, a home similar to those that would have been found not just in Kentucky but also in early Rowan County and in western Pennsylvania and anywhere else on the frontier. It was placed in stone before the front entrance to his palatial home Hildene in Vermont as a reminder of how far his family had come. It is a startling sight today, at the steps of a mansion, but this, hardly as big as a small room in an American home of the 21st century, was the size of house many of the new backcountry settlers, especially the Borderers, whose homes in Ireland and on the English/Scottish border had not been much fancier, were used to—even if they had their dreams of something better.

*****

Small as the homes were, people rarely lived alone. A man might want to build his own cabin, but he would wait until he was married and his wife pregnant, living with relatives or friends in the meantime—another one of the reasons for the importance of family and friends to American individualism. If there was a bed, it was not the realm solely of an individual or a couple but generally of children, too, and perhaps as many other adults as could fit. Visitors, never turned away, arranged themselves as well as they could, perhaps among the older children on a pallet on the floor. There were advantages to this: In a place where the only heat was from a rude fireplace, a small house meant less work cutting wood for keeping warm, and, as the fire died down during the night, a larger number of bodies close together kept the temperature higher. Morgan writes that "a kind of privacy was created by everyone ignoring each other. And even if you woke in the night and heard the sounds of lovemaking nearby, you pretended not to notice. That the crowding in the cabins and little houses was no hindrance to lovemaking is proved by the number of children born on the frontier."[45] Woodmason tells of "Cabbins quite open and exposed. Little or no Bedding, or anything to cover them."[46]

These cabins were often far apart. Morgan finds it paradoxical "that settlers did not congregate in villages, as most of their ancestors had in Britain and on the Continent, but moved into the woods and cleared an isolated place."[47] Rogin would likely agree but probably would not find a paradox, arguing instead that the family, not the village, was the glue keeping together colonial culture, writing that "eighteenth-century America was organized around families. In European societies, other long-established institutions—church, state, standing army—stood alongside the household and shared social functions with it. . . . American society, lacking deep historic roots and developed social institutions, made the family supreme."[48] Neither scholar seems to have been paying attention to the distinction between the life on the English/Scottish border and that of most of the rest of Europe. As we saw in the previous chapter, the Borderers were not nearly so centered on village life as were the English and did not have the same type of community roots. Because of the centuries of displacements through wars and unstable land tenure, they were used to moving into new areas for work as tenant farmers and did not feel quite the same need to rely on established villages. About all they desired from a village was a market for what they would not need for their own sustenance—and a source for the few manufactured items they could not produce themselves. The villages, furthermore, were the sources of oversight by government, anathema to the Borderers from way back— again as we have seen. The family, on the other hand, did not tie one down, but could move with the individual, be it from hovel to hovel for work in the lowlands, to Ulster Plantation, or into and then out of the Delaware Valley.

While waiting for his own family either to arrive or to start, a man might live in a cave or a simple lean-to, clearing land and constructing rude livestock pens, fencing a garden area, and marking the sources of clean water so that waste disposal would take place elsewhere—and downstream. Preparing acreage for home and for farming was backbreaking, and the hours were long— and it had to get done before winter set in and hunting and trapping began. The next spring, a crop could be planted on the cleared ground by simply spreading seed or, if one were lucky, sowing fields tilled by oxen, if the family owned a team or could borrow one. Borderers knew how to do all this. Lore from the branch of my family that settled on the Ohio River in 1804 has it that the first people of their village of Gallipolis had been Frenchmen fleeing the Revolution there. So little did they know of clearing land, the story goes, that they buried on the spot the trees they cut down. After a year of near starvation, most of those who had survived packed up and left. They were replaced, for the most part, by Borderers who knew what they were doing, even if they were not quite so educated or refined.

Even though the settlers who did understand how to eke out a livelihood on the frontier were living primarily on their own and by their own resources, the cycle of debt, ensnaring them in a society they thought they had left behind, started early. As we have seen, farmers, with rarely a reserve built from past years, often needed loans for seed and equipment or even to pay for rights to the land. They had to hope for a good harvest and to bet on it with borrowed money. For many of them, the bets would fail at some point or another, inducing them to move once more, heading farther west in a process that only reached its limits almost two centuries later when the "Okies" (many of whom were also Scots-Irish and German) piled up against the coast in California. In the meantime, the lure of the West persisted: "The West meant free land and independence from feudal rule and quitrents, from debt and debtor's prison, from censures of the church and the class system, from servitude and poverty. The West was the place to rise, to become better, larger"[49]—or so they believed, even when their experience was to the contrary.

The West of myth, even in the early 19th century, even when Boone was still alive but already legendary, was a place where people could regulate their own affairs, free of governments and banks breathing down their necks, looking to take whatever they could even before a person had managed to really get things going. These institutions were *stifling* then just as, in the eyes of the 21st-century Tea Party movement, they are now. Left alone, given room, they believed, people could do better.

* * * * *

Though he knew little of the roots of Borderer culture, James Fenimore Cooper did manage to capture some Borderer attitudes in the first of his novels featuring Natty Bumppo, *The Pioneers*, published in 1823. Smith connects Bumppo with Boone, writing that "although Boone was not exactly the prototype of Cooper's Leatherstocking, there is a haunting similarity between the two figures."[50] Cooper's novel divides into features of class a number of things that are really also cultural distinctions. In a sense, that is no matter, for Cooper was trying to follow the model of the rising British novel of the era where class was an essential component of the story, heroes and heroines climbing from the middle or starting in the upper. Given the American settings of his Leatherstocking tales, Cooper felt he had to imitate at least that part of the formula to gain commercial success. He imposed on the American cultures, as they appeared in his tales, a class structure that was really not in keeping with the actual situations of the time. This is evident in words spoken early in *The Pioneers* by patriarch Marmaduke Temple to his cousin Richard Jones about an apparent backwoodsman:

> I found him on the mountain hunting in company with the Leather-Stocking, as if they were of the same family; but there is a manifest difference in their manners. The youth delivers himself in chosen language, such as is seldom heard in these hills, and such as occasions great surprise to me, how one so meanly clad, and following so lowly a pursuit, could attain.[51]

Though Cooper's upper classes come off as idealized and even a little ridiculous (in terms of American actualities) in their unreality, his backwoodsman Bumppo carries more than a little bit of Borderer truth. The differences Cooper shows were deeper than class, though he never manages to address that fact directly. Still, in his first encounter (in the book) with Temple, Bumppo expresses a quintessential Borderer sentiment through what can almost be read as an echo of Boone:

> "... although I am a poor man I can live without the venison, but I don't love to give up my lawful dues in a free country. Though, for the matter of that, might often makes right here, as well as in the old country for what I can see."
>   An air of sullen dissatisfaction pervaded the manner of the hunter during the whole of his speech; yet he thought it prudent to utter the close of the sentence in such an undertone as to leave nothing audible but the grumbling sounds of his voice.[52]

Bitter experience of might making right had been around the backwoodsmen throughout their lives, whether before or after the American Revolution, as the War of the Regulation and the Whiskey Rebellion make clear. For the Scots-Irish Borderer, coming from Ulster and the Scottish Lowlands, there would be a clear family memory of much the same thing even before arrival in North America. There was probably a great deal of retained bitterness and anger in their decisions to forgo the settled areas of the East for the much harsher life in the backwoods. Yet, rich and unwelcomed, the power of the East followed them, reaching far into the frontier, controlling much of the new land and almost all of the power.

Late in *The Pioneers*, rather than have his home entered by despised officials who are looking to arrest him, Bumppo has burned it—an extreme though typically Borderer reaction. He then turns himself in voluntarily to the authorities:

"What would ye with an old and helpless man?" he said, "You've driven God's creatur's from the wilderness, where His providence had put them for His own pleasure; and you've brought in the troubles and deviltries of the law, where no man was ever known to disturb another. You have driven me, that have lived forty long years of my appointed time in this very spot, from my home and the shelter of my head, lest you should put your wicked feet and wasty ways in my cabin. You've driven me to burn these logs, under which I've eaten and drunk—the first of Heaven's gifts, and the other of the pure springs—for the half of a hundred years; and to mourn the ashes under my feet, as a man would weep and mourn for the children of his body. You've rankled the heart of an old man, that has never harmed you or your'n, with bitter feelings toward his kind, at a time when his thoughts should be on a better world; and you've driven him to wish that the beasts of the forest, who never feast on the blood of their own families, was his kindred and race; and now, when he has come to see the last brand of his hut, before it is incited into ashes, you follow him up, at midnight, like hungry hounds on the track of a worn-out and dying deer. What more would ye have? For I am here—one too many. I come to mourn, not to fight; and, if it is God's pleasure, work your will on me."[53]

This plaint comes from the heart of a long-despised and benighted people with a recognition of the greater power of others but also with an unwillingness to bow to it. This actually comes not from a noble sentiment, though it seems to, in Cooper, but from the simple will to survive with at least a little self-respect intact, a will that had pushed the Lowlands Scots through centuries of deprivation—and sometimes even into violence of a sort that Bumppo, here, eschews.

* * * * *

Trying to place attitudes like Bumppo's—and the violence generated against Native Americans—within a broader cultural context, one including all Americans, Christopher Lasch writes that the

> violence they turned against the Indians and against nature originated not in unrestrained impulse but in the white Angle-Saxon superego, which feared the wildness of the West because it objictified the wildness within each individual. While celebrating the romance of the frontier in their popular literature, in practice Americans imposed on the wilderness a new order designed to keep impulse in check while giving free rein to acquisitiveness.[54]

He is conflating the two cultures, of course. The Borderers did not fear the West or even the Native Americans nearly as much as they feared the East.

The "romance of the frontier" was not theirs at all. To the East, it was Borderer impulse that needed to be kept in check, just as the authorities in *The Pioneers* try to keep Bumppo in check. And the acquisitiveness, of course, was also a trait of the East, not so much of the Borderers who were the first into the West.

Smith, in *Virgin Land*, sees Cooper as a part of the secular-liberal culture and not, though the passage quoted above may seem otherwise, a defender of Borderer sensibilities. He was

> a consistent and explicit conservative in social theory despite his care-fully limited endorsement of political democracy, was quite willing to acknowledge that refinement and gentility were conceivable only in members of an upper class with enough wealth to guarantee its leisure, and a sufficiently secure social status to give it poise and assurance. The form of the sentimental novel suggested exactly these assumptions. But other novelists who tried to deal with the agricultural West felt them-selves under some compulsion to extend the application of the sound-ing platitudes of democracy and equality from politics to social and economic life. They therefore faced a continual struggle to reconcile their almost instinctive regard for refinement with their democratic the-ories and their desire to find some values in the unrefined West.[55]

Cooper, in other words, was at the forefront of a tradition of seeing America's cultural divisions simply in terms of class. "Whatever the orators might say in glittering abstractions about the virtues of the yeoman, the novelists found themselves unable to control the emotions aroused by the Western farmer's degraded rank in the class system."[56] Not only writers of fiction fell into this tradition. Francis Parkman, one of 19th-century America's most prominent historians, also saw cultural divisions in terms of class:

> On his vacation try of 1842 about Lake George, he could write in his diary such a passage as this:
>
> > "There could be no finer place for gentlemen's seats than this, but now, for the most part, it is occupied by a race of boors about as uncouth, mean, and stupid as the hogs they seem chiefly to delight in."
>
> And even in his full maturity in 1878 he called the working classes "the barbarians of civilization."[57]

By the time of his early vacation (Parkman was not 20 at the time), America's "upper classes" had seen an ascension of the Borderer to political power on the national stage, a scary turn of events for them. Parkman, in fact, grew up with this new political reality: Andrew Jackson, that first Borderer president, had won 12 of the 24 states of the union and a plurality of the popular vote in 1824, over 40 percent—the rest being split between three other candidates, John Quincy Adams being elected only when the election was thrown to the House of Representatives. Four years later, Jackson would win outright.

"The contests in 1824 and 1828 between Jackson and John Quincy Adams provided a perfect study in contrasting political ideals. Adams's administration was the test case for the unsuitability of the intellectual temperament for political leadership in early nineteenth-century America."[58] The cultural divisions within the United States highlighted by those elections have actually been evident in its presidential elections since the end of Washington's second term. Generally, we tend to sweep them into a North/South split, but it really is quite a bit more complex than that. When John Adams was elected in 1796, New England supported him solidly, the rest of the country going pretty much for Jefferson—but it was not, at that point, enough to offset Adams's support. Of course, Adams was a New Englander and Jefferson was from the height of Virginia's "cavalier" culture, but regional pride was not the only difference. The split between the Federalist and the Democratic-Republican attitudes went beyond geography, but Jefferson did manage to bring together the more established white southerners and the new westerners, the people of the backwoods, in a coalition that would survive for two centuries, though party affiliation would certainly change. In 1800, with help from New York, Jefferson took the presidency away from Adams, making it look like a new national consensus might be possible.

Hofstadter sees the split the election widened as the Federalists' own fault, the result of their mishandling of a political situation, their loss being not the start of a new majority but what should have been a temporary setback:

> The shabby campaign against Jefferson, and then the Alien and Sedition Acts, manifested the treason of many wealthy and educated Federalists against the cultural values of tolerance and freedom. Unfortunately, it did not follow that more popular parties under Jeffersonian or Jacksonian leadership could be counted on to espouse these values. The popular parties themselves eventually became the vehicles of a kind of primitivist and anti-intellectualist populism hostile to the specialist, the expert, the gentleman, and the scholar.[59]

Completely unable to see the Borderer culture as having any value at all, Hofstadter becomes an advocate solely for the secular-liberal tradition and the expense of the other. His own attitude confirms that there certainly was a widening cultural split that survived far into the 20th century, with "the specialist, the expert, the gentleman, and the scholar" defined by one side in ways that excluded almost anyone from the other. "Popular writers, understandably proud of the political competence of the free man, were on the whole justifiably suspicious of the efforts of the cultivated and wealthy to assume an exclusive or excessively dominant role in government. Their suspicions did not stop there, however, but led many of them into hostility to all forms of learning."[60] As much as anything else, the hostility was to what was seen as a kind of cultural cudgel, not to learning itself. The truth of this would be observed over the 19th and 20th century as public schools became critical parts of American communities, both new and old, and on each side of the cultural divide. Still, Hofstadter could claim that

> The first truly powerful and widespread impulse to anti-intellectualism in American politics was, in fact, given by the Jacksonian movement. Its distrust of expertise, its dislike for centralization, its desire to uproot the entrenched classes, and its doctrine that important functions were simple enough to be performed by anyone, amounted to a repudiation not only of the system of government by gentlemen which the nation had inherited from the eighteenth century, but also of the special value of the educated classes in civic life.[61]

The cultural split had begun to really appear in presidential politics in 1808, when it was only in New England (and Delaware) that James Madison did not succeed, a pattern that was repeated, but with DeWitt Clinton, the Federalist candidate, picking up ground in the Northeast in 1812. In 1816, only Massachusetts, Connecticut, and Delaware did not go for James Monroe in the Electoral College, who swept the states four years later.

In 1824, John Quincy Adams took all of New England (with New York adding a great deal of support), and Jackson and Henry Clay divided almost all of the rest of the country. Without Clay in the race four years later, Jackson won handily in a country that had expanded extensively to the west while New England, of course, had remained as it had been. Jackson's reelection was something of a rout, with Massachusetts, Connecticut, and Delaware (once more) providing a large part of the opposition. This election marked a real change in American attitudes toward just who should govern. Hofstadter writes that "the Jacksonian conviction that the duties of government were so simple that almost anyone could execute them downgraded the functions of the expert and the trained man to a degree which turned insidious when the functions of government became complex."[62] Many on the secular-liberal side of the divide today would agree, but the "anyones" keep getting elected, and the United States continues along.

Martin Van Buren was able to put together a national coalition in 1836, in terms of Electoral College votes, at least, handily defeating the three regional Whig candidates. In 1840, however, one of those three, William Henry Harrison, turned the tables on him, also managing to gather Electoral College votes from across the country. When James Polk, another Borderer, was elected four years later, it may have seemed once more that the days of regional politics were over, for once more there was no "solid" region anywhere in the country. The same was true when Zachary Taylor was elected in 1848. In 1852, taking all but four states and gathering in over three-quarters of the Electoral College votes, Franklin Pierce seemed to be once again showing the way for a united electorate. But that, as we know, was not to last: The Civil War was less than a decade away. Of note, both James Buchanan, president on the eve of the Civil War, and Abraham Lincoln were from Borderer backgrounds.

*****

The impact of Jackson, given the huge historical events a generation before his presidency and a generation later, can sometimes be minimalized. He was not really the inheritor of Jefferson but the start of a new political reality, one that scared many New Englanders through the uncouth (in their terms) manners of many of the new politicians. Political scientist Michael Rogin puts his finger on one of the major roots of the cultural splits of the time that Jackson represented one side of:

> Liberal America transformed itself while Jackson lived from a family-based, eighteenth-century, household order to the market society of the Age of Jackson. Family ties, unmediated by traditional social institutions, played a greater role in eighteenth-century America than in Europe; and the family-based order provided revolutionaries with a model of America virtue. But the household order could not sustain itself, in bourgeois society, against internecine conflict and market expansion. The rise of market society threatened the achievement of the fathers—an independent, virtuous American identity—as it destroyed family-based society.[63]

Though Rogin makes temporal a split that was cultural, he is pointing out one of the significant cultural changes of the 19th century. It was not, however, a destruction of "family-based society" but a rise of the economic power in the region dominated by the secular-liberal tradition. What we were beginning to see was a split between cultures with extremely different ideals and goals, not the destruction of one of them or its absorption into the other. Yes, economic power allowed the secular-liberal Northeast establishment to hold parity with the growing power of the Borderer culture of individualism and the family, but it could not destroy it. Though it certainly is true that "from 1815 to 1845, the years in which Jacksonian Democracy emerged and flourished, America transformed itself from a household to a market society,"[64] this would ultimately prove a tremendous, though temporary, defeat for Borderer culture and one that made it even more invisible in American culture than it had been before but not one that made it go away. If they had been forced into the commercial economy from even before the Revolution, they were now finding themselves crushed by a market society even more removed from Borderer individualistic and family-oriented society. Though he sees a change more dramatic than I do (not recognizing that the frontier culture never was able to be one of self-sufficiency), Rogin does recognize the impact on the Borderers of this economic change: "The mass of people, no longer primarily supporting themselves, suffered [from market-driven depressions] as they had not under subsistence conditions. Even in good times, large external economic institutions—bank, factory, and market itself—gained increasing control over the conditions of existence."[65]

It was Jackson's administration that introduced the Borderers to Washington, D.C. Revulsion at what they found there led to the start of a Borderer attitude toward the capital that continues to be strong today. Rogin describes it: "Jackson located republican simplicity in the countryside; pomp, intrigue, hidden motives, and conspiracy dominated Washington."[66] "Inside the Beltway," obviously, was a concept long before the D.C. Beltway itself was ever imagined.

The impact of the Borderers continued to be just as strong even when submerged. Even John Brown, one of the seminal figures of the Civil War, was a product of Borderer culture. Whatever one may think of him, the early life of the abolitionist, as presented by W. E. B. Du Bois, provides a clear picture of the trials of the Borderer life during the first half of the 19th century. Du Bois describes an individualist of strong convictions struggling in a system defined and controlled from afar:

> The vast physical fact in the life of John Brown was the Alleghany Mountains—that beautiful mass of hill and crag which guards the somber majesty of the Maine coast, crumples the rivers on the rocky soil of New England, and rolls and leaps down through busy Pennsylvania to the misty peaks of Carolina and the red foothills of Georgia. In the Alleghanies John Brown was all but born; their forests were his boyhood

wonderland; in their villages he married his wives and begot his clan. On the sides of the Alleghanies he tended his sheep and dreamed his terrible dream. It was the mystic, awful voice of the mountains that lured him to liberty, death and martyrdom within their wildest fastness, and in their bosom he sleeps his last sleep.[67]

Though he had tried to earn a New England education, Brown never managed it (eye problems stopped him), returning to complete his education on his own in the expanding West: "He undertook to study by himself, mastering common arithmetic and becoming in time an expert surveyor."[68] He was, ultimately, no child of the East, and certainly not of the South. He was one of a new type of American, iconoclastic (there were people in the West as passionately proslavery, of course, as Brown was passionate for abolition), and self-reliant. Though he was a descendant of Puritans, Brown (like Boone) exemplifies that other culture he joined, the one established through the Scots-Irish Borderers:

He knew nothing of games and sports; he had few or no companions, but, "to be sent off through the wilderness alone to very considerable distances was particularly his delight. . . . By the time he was twelve years old he was sent off more than a hundred miles with companies of cattle." So his soul grew apart and alone and yet untrammeled and unconfined, knowing all the depths of secret self-abasement, and the heights of confident self-will.[69]

This description could be of one of any of thousands of the new residents of the western lands. Brown, for all his fanaticism, was no unusual person in this regard.

Again like Boone, Brown, for all his independent character, was tied to an economic system that had little regard for any people in the West—for those not already part of the financial elite, at least. His early "prosperity, like that of his neighbors, and indeed, of the whole country, was partly fictitious, and built on a fast expanding credit which was far outstretching the rapid industrial development."[70] As has happened so many times since, an overheated economy crashed, taking much of Brown's new wealth with it:

Probably after the crash of 1837, Brown hoped to extricate enough to buy land in Virginia and move there, but things went from bad to worse. Through endorsing a note for a friend, one of his best pieces of farm property was attached, put up at auction and bought by a neighbor. Brown, on legal advice, sought to retain possession, but was arrested and placed in the Akron jail. The property was lost.[71]

This crash, though it was brought on by Jacksonian policies, probably made the split between East and West as wide as it had ever been, though that other divide, North and South, would soon be getting all the attention—in part because of Brown's own future actions.

*****

In writing on success myths in America, Richard Weiss claims that

> until that time [the 1830s], the United States, to all appearances, was developing a society chiefly of industrious yeomen of middling circumstances, and therefore untroubled by extreme inequalities of wealth, a nation the latter-day Puritan might approve. The triumph of Jackson introduced a disturbing element into this picture. The ordered liberty so precious to the heirs of Puritan moderation was being relegated to oblivion by marauders who styled themselves "natural" men. The religion of the Puritans had dictated a social as well as an individual ideal.[72]

This reflects the myths of American history as they have been presented for generations now, myths of yeomen farms lettered and familiar with the Enlightenment traditions of an overarching secular-liberal culture. It relegates the Borderers to "marauder" status at best, stripping them of any cultural heritage or even learning. The weaknesses of this viewpoint should be readily apparent through the discussions of this chapter. That the Borderers did not possess the particular types of knowledge or focus of the secular-liberal culture did not make them stupid or barbarians. That their differences went unrecognized as anything beside the "natural" devolution of the lower classes has been an egregious oversight in the evolving American political dialogue, one that has made the divides of the 21st century wider than they should ever have become and that also allowed Borderer individualism to evolve from what had been merely a cultural trait into something with the power of a cult.

CHAPTER 5

How the Other Half Lives

The American identity, as it began to develop in the new nation at the end of the 18th century, was imagined and written in New England, imagined and crafted separately by the southern white elite, and endured in the West. The great debates of the country in the 19th century centered on the conflicting views of North and South, reaching their peak with the outbreak of the Civil War. The West, in the context of this divide, either continued to be seen as grounds for extension of the North/South conflict or was ignored. Ignored, that is, until toward the end of the century when it became the new symbol of a grand American unity, myths concerning it even then crafted by the intellectual elite of New England and by East Coast writers generally.

In addition, while New England and New York were developing the first real American intellectual and artistic culture and the South was building its antebellum "paradise" on the backs of slaves, the Borderers of the West were busily engaged in a genocide that no one wanted to praise or even admit was happening. At the same time, they were eking out a living on land that often, as soon as they tried to lay claim to it, already seemed to be "owned" by someone from the East. The Borderers had no time for the "fully articulated pastoral idea of America"[1] that had emerged on the back of the Enlightenment and that was popular as an ideal in the East. Whatever garden they could find or create or conquer or defend was not often even *theirs* for very long. More frequently than we imagine, they were forced once again to move farther west and start from scratch—again. Poverty breathed down their necks; little of their lives would ever qualify as "pastoral."

Given the romantic vision that had grown up even then concerning the frontier, it must have been quite a shock for many from the coast during the 19th century when they encountered the reality of the west instead. Any sense of the "pastoral ideal" that, according to Leo Marx, had been building for so long in New England would have been quickly smashed. Easterners from areas that had been home to established European-based communities for more than a century must have felt that they had found a completely alien culture when they met the real frontier. Expecting to find Americans of a familiar type, they would certainly have been confused—if not scared half to death, creating an image that later would become the basis for the Eastern "dude" in tales of the West.

* * * * *

If, as some of those in the East had argued, the landscape makes the man, then why were the backwoods folk so "devolved," so unlike their eastern countrymen? The land, after all, was abundant, filled with possibility. Why had the white people on the frontier not become, if they needed to change at all, more like the "noble" Native Americans? Such questions must have bedeviled any observant easterner as he or she traveled west. Writing about Robert Beverley's *History of the Present State of Virginia*, which was first published at the beginning of the 18th century, Marx says, "The new garden of the world, which Beverley has celebrated as the cause of all that is most admirable in the joyous Indian culture, now appears to have had a bad effect upon the English."[2] Beverley was not seeing the progress he had expected or a new and growing "society" (in the English sense of the word, almost one of class) on the frontier. All he found were people just as "base" as their ancestors had been back on the England/Scotland border—people a lot less sophisticated (in English terms) than those in the older, coastal colonies. Travelers for the next three centuries found much the same.

Numerous theories were put forward to explain the differences between the uncouth of the frontier and then settled "interior" of America and the civilized of the coast. Some writers actually blamed the land that had seemed so promising (as Beverley was coming to conclude at the end of his book), others blamed class distinctions, and still others saw the lack of civilizing government as the problem. Unfortunately, as all the writers were from the East (or from Europe) until well into the 19th century, those actually from the frontier culture had no voice in the discussion, no ability to ground the debate in the actual facts of the matter. As they would remain for generations more, they had been made mute. Few outsiders understood either their perspective or their background, allowing erroneous conceptions to be put forward unchallenged and then to become received wisdom.

Because his own opinions were so rarely heard, it proved easy to romanticize the frontier farmer, transforming him "into a cult figure. Instead of striving for wealth, status, and power, he may be said to live a good life in a rural retreat: he rests content with a few simple possessions, enjoys freedom from envying others, fells little or no anxiety about his property, and, above all, he does what he likes to do."[3] It was only when the fans of the pastoral actually came into contact with backwoods folk (which was rare, admittedly) that such views were challenged—and the blame, then, was placed not on the ideas but on the people who were not living up to standards others had imagined for them. It was the farmers' fault; they must have allowed themselves to become debased. So disillusioning was this to the East that, according to Henry Nash Smith, "in the early nineteenth century ... the farmer could be depicted in fiction only as a member of a low social class."[4]

To account for the cultural slide that they thought they were seeing (or hearing about) on the frontier, many writers came to promote a

> theory of social stages which places the West below the East in a sequence to which both belong. The West has no meaning in itself because the only value recognized by the theory of civilization is the refinement which is believed to increase steadily as one moves from primitive simplicity and coarseness toward the complexity and polish of urban life. The values that are occasionally found in the West are anomalous instances of conformity to a standard that is actually foreign to the region.[5]

In other words, the frontier had no culture—and it was the duty of the East to impose one. Here again, we have one of the classic patterns of colonialism, the metropole putatively bringing "civilization" for the benefit of the local population of the periphery—while lining its own pockets, of course. Furthermore, "the notion that the lore and the mores of the backwoodsman might be interesting without reference to his function as a standard-bearer of progress and civilization, or his alarming and exciting barbarism, or his embodiment of a natural goodness, was quite late in appearing."[6] The resulting newer myth was created once the idea of the debased frontiersman had outlived its usefulness, the greater myth of an inclusive "manifest destiny" making it seem out of keeping with the newer ideas of American progress. Reflecting the views popular as the 19th century progressed to its end, Andrew Carnegie, an immigrant himself (from Scotland), saw the Americans as one culture, writing that "they are essentially British."[7] Those who could not live up to that, again, were ignored or seen as debased anomalies.

One of the only differences between traditional conceptions of colonialism and the colonialism going on as the American West was settled by Europeans was that many of the people being colonized, the Borderers who had already arrived, were little different in language and bodily appearance from their "saviors." Almost all of them were white. What was going on, we find when we step away from the traditional myths of westward expansion in America, was a pattern little different from that of the internal colonialism that Michael Hechter explores, colonialism that occurred back in the British Isles themselves. One significant difference, of course, was that this colonial activity came fast on the heels of an earlier type of colonization but by a different group (the Borderers themselves) that was one of conquest and displacement. What remains clear, however, is that a much greater percentage of Americans than is generally admitted come from traditions where they have felt the brunt of colonialism even after the Revolution rather than simply having been the colonizers. For many of us from both cultures, our ancestors have been both colonizer and colonized, but the experience of the Borderers lasted long after real independence came to the secular-liberal culture of the coast.

Aside from (or in addition to) the English Enlightenment tradition that bypassed, for the most part, Borderers and Borderer-based communities, coastal American thinkers were developing their own ideas of community and individual interaction, ideas quite different from what was growing on the frontiers, growing with little notice in the East. After all, the coast looked to the West primarily in commercial terms and as an outlet for excess population. It did not expect to find independent intellectual activity there.

* * * * *

Though today's Tea Partiers and fundamentalist Christians (both descendants of Borderer culture) try to gainsay it, the United States *was* founded on Enlightenment principles that excluded religion, for example, from the public political sphere and made science and "rational thought" the pillars for what was hoped would be a new type of society. Though the secular-liberal founders of the country themselves tried to deny it—even going so far as to construct the Constitution in both a populist and an elitist fashion (witness the distinct structures of the House of Representatives and the Senate)—most of them were elitists in terms of both class and culture. They believed that most of their fellow Americans were not as "enlightened" as they were and that the vast majority needed instruction as well as learned guidance. Take Benjamin Franklin: As John Cawelti claims, his "conception of self-improvement was closely related to his belief in the necessity of a self-selecting and self-disciplining elite, men of virtue voluntarily assuming the leadership of society."[8] Like many of today's elitists, he skipped over cultural distinctions by substituting this idea of self-selection for success and leadership—something that was as much a fiction in the 18th century as it is in the 21st.

Franklin himself followed a long tradition of Americans who have felt they could best tell others how to manage their lives. In fact, according to Richard Weiss, even the later

> success literature bears much resemblance to the prescriptive writings of the divines of seventeenth-century New England. These Puritan guides gave advice on the achievement of material success, but always in the context of a larger framework of values. More than lists of commercial maxims, these writings were essays on the general conduct of life.[9]

At first, the Borderers fled this sort of admonition, especially when it came from those who saw Borderer culture only as a degraded form of their own. However, by the end of the 19th century, Borderers, like many other Americans, were embracing it as their own—as can be seen in the popularity across the cultures of such phenomena as the Lyceum movement, New Thought, Chautauqua, and others that sparked what Weiss calls "success literature" and that promoted a new conception of self-reliance. The impact of these, however, was somewhat different on the Borderers than it was on secular-liberal Americans.

Franklin, as we can easily imagine, probably would have been reluctant to put the distinctions between what he saw as classes of Americans into cultural terms. "Human happiness and social welfare were, in Franklin's view, dependent on two things: teaching prudence and self-restraint to the mass of men and encouraging the development of a new self-made leadership composed of men of practical ability and disinterested benevolence."[10] The elite would assist those rising to join them from the masses, no matter their backgrounds—something that anyone who watches societies in practice (not in the ideal) knows is not going to happen. In reality, we assist those who are "like us" much more than we help others. Sometimes we actually impede the progress of those furthest from us in similarity. Ability and drive are much lower on the list of criteria we look out for.

As time went on and at least some people began to see the limits of Franklin's ideals, presentation of the vision that Franklin tried to promote became more and more restrained. As Cawelti, again, explains, "Later philosophers of success followed Franklin in the assumption that the new elite would select itself, but they narrowed Franklin's ideal of intellectual, moral, and economic improvement to a conception of individual economic achievement."[11] This did not have the result of slowing the growth of the idea that anyone can make it on their own, if only they are willing to put in the right effort. If anything, by narrowing the focus to economic success only, such writers fertilized it. No longer did you have to be good to be successful, though many began to believe that if you were successful, you were good.

At the same time, in the eyes of people from the secular-liberal tradition growing out of the English Enlightenment, there was indeed another criterion for success, a social one. There was only one "right" way to the cultural top, and that did not include either financial success alone or what Borderer culture might feel its members might be able to do for themselves. Conforming to the secular-liberal norm was required. Borderers could rarely cross that bar.

★ ★ ★ ★ ★

Though attitudes toward the Borderers as uncouth and unlearned were seconded by coastal Americans, they could be seen most clearly through the eyes of the British who, paradoxically, often saw only one American whole, an essentially Borderer one:

> The contrast between nineteenth-century English and American attitudes toward self-improvement appeared often in the comments of English travelers in America. Mrs. Trollope, who visited America in the 1830's, was stupefied by the pride that leading Americans took in the fact that they were self-taught and self-made, which, as she acidly remarked, meant to her only that they were badly taught and badly made.[12]

Mrs. Frances Trollope was a delightful writer (one can see where her son Anthony gained his talent), but she was the product of a society of rigid class lines, where learning was defined from the top, as were fashion and style. She recounts a conversation she had while on the road:

> For the great part of this day we had the good fortune to have a gentleman and his daughter for our fellow-travellers, who were extremely intelligent and agreeable; but I nearly got myself into a scrape by venturing to remark upon a phrase used by the gentleman, and which had met me at every corner from the time I first entered the country. We had been talking of pictures, and I had endeavoured to adhere to

the rule I had laid down for myself, of saying very little, where I could say nothing agreeable. At length he named an American artist, with whose works I was very familiar, and after having declared him equal to Lawrence (judging by his portrait of West, now at New York), he added, "and what is more, madam, he is perfectly *self-taught*."

I prudently took a few moments before I answered; for the equalling our immortal Lawrence to a most vile dauber stuck in my throat; I could not say Amen; so for some time I said nothing; but, at last, I remarked on the frequency with which I had heard this phrase of *self-taught* used, not as an apology, but as positive praise.

"Well, madam, can there be a higher praise?"

"Certainly not, if spoken of the individual merits of a person, without the means of instruction, but I do not understand it when applied as praise to his works."

"Not understand it, madam? Is it not attributing genius to the author, and what is teaching compared to that?"

I do not wish to repeat all my own *bons mots* in praise of study, and on the disadvantages of profound ignorance, but I would, willingly, if I could, give an idea of the mixed indignation and contempt expressed by our companion at the idea that study was necessary to the formation of taste, and to the development of genius. At last, however, he closed the discussion thus,—"There is no use in disputing a point that is already settled, madam; the best judges declare that Mr. H—g's portraits are equal to that of Lawrence."

"Who is it who has passed this judgement, sir?"

"The men of taste of America, madam."

I then asked him, if he thought it was going to rain?[13]

Amusing, but Mrs. Trollope is completely unwilling to contemplate that there might be other aesthetics equal to her own from the English gentry—or that there might be other forms of "study" than those with which she was familiar. At another point, she writes,

The social system of Mr. Jefferson, if carried into effect, would make of mankind an unamalgamated mass of grating atoms, where the darling "I'm as good as you," would soon take place of the law and the Gospel. As it is, his principles, though happily not fully put in action, have yet produced most lamentable results. The assumption of equality, however empty, is sufficient to tincture the manners of the poor with brutal insolence, and subjects the rich to the paltry expediency of sanctioning the falsehood, however deep their conviction that it is such. It cannot, I think, be denied that the great men of America attain to power and to fame, by eternally uttering what they know to be untrue.

American citizens are not equal. Did Washington feel them to be so, when his word outweighed (so happily for them) the votes of thousands? Did Franklin think that all were equal when he shouldered his way from the printing press to the cabinet? True, he looked back in high good humour, and with his kindest smile told the poor devils whom he left behind, that they were all his equals; but Franklin did not speak the truth, and he knew it. The great, the immortal Jefferson himself, he who when past the three score years and ten, still taught young females to obey his nod, and so became the father of unnumbered generations of groaning slaves, what was his matin and his vesper hymn? "All men are born free and equal." Did the venerable father of the gang believe it? Or did he too purchase his immortality by a lie?[14]

Mrs. Trollope puts her finger on one of the core problems with the American myth—and it is no wonder her book caused such disapprobation in America. But she remains chained to her own biases. Like many East Coast Americans and other English visitors, she is unable to see beyond her *own* conceptions of class and culture—and of whom one counts as a "man"—in *her* vision of the American West.

* * * * *

Though the two great American cultures, the Borderer and the secular-liberal, continued to grow side by side, never quite melding, there was still a great deal of influence, one upon the other. Quite a few from the coast joined the movement west, many of them integrating into Borderer culture. Some Borderer figures, such as Abraham Lincoln and Samuel Clemens, were able to learn to negotiate the coastal culture well enough to operate in it extremely successfully despite their roots. Others also proved influential on both sides of the divide though they came from the East. Perhaps the most important of these during the 19th century (and beyond) was Ralph Waldo Emerson. Lines of his, like "A great soul will be strong to live, as well as strong to think,"[15] resonated as much with Borderers and their growing myth of self-sufficiency as with easterners who, for the most part, could only dream of a self-reliance that those on the frontier actually struggled to attain (but rarely did) on a daily basis. "The American Scholar" and "Self-Reliance" in particular are replete with phrases that rang true, though for different reasons of course, with 19th-century Americans of almost every sort.

In many ways, Emerson is an earlier and deeper Ayn Rand, a real scholar and thinker instead of a simpler manipulator of words and stories who is attempting to find ways to suit her extant predilections and to remake a solitary point. He believed quite as strongly in the individual as she would, a century later, but expressed his belief in a much more accommodating and encompassing framework and upon careful consideration of the alternatives —and as part of a broader and fuller philosophical exploration. In "The American Scholar," he writes, "In self-trust, all the virtues are comprehended. Free should the scholar be,—free and brave. Free even to the definition of freedom, 'without any hindrance that does not arise out of his own constitution.' Brave; for fear is a thing, which a scholar by his very function puts behind him. Fear always springs from ignorance."[16] Like Franklin, Emerson would ideally like to bring every person to this point or would, at least, allow it. Rand would not even bother; it is all up to each individual— even to discover the possibility. There is an expansiveness to Emerson that rings true to many people but particularly to Americans raised up in the individualist traditions of both the Borderers and the secular-liberals:

Another sign of our times, also marked by an analogous political movement, is, the new importance given to the single person. Every thing that tends to insulate the individual,—to surround him with barriers of natural respect, so that each man shall feel the world is his, and man shall treat with man as a sovereign state with a sovereign state;—tends to true union as well as greatness. "I learned," said the melancholy Pestalozzi, "that no man in God's wide earth is either willing or able to help any other man." Help must come from the bosom alone. The scholar is that man who must take up into himself all the ability of the time, all the contributions of the past, all the hopes of the future. He must be an university of knowledges. If there be one lesson more than another, which should pierce his ear, it is, The world is nothing, the man is all; in yourself is the law of all nature, and you know not yet how a globule of sap ascends; in yourself slumbers the whole of Reason; it is for you to know all, it is for you to dare all.[17]

Again, this is an expansive vision, one open to all—quite different from the parsimonious dreams of Rand and of those in the 21st century who follow her.

In "Self-Reliance," Emerson makes clear that he sees a difference between individualism and selfishness, with individualism the more noble:

I must be myself. I cannot break myself any longer for you, or you. If you can love me for what I am, we shall be the happier. If you cannot, I will still seek to deserve that you should. I will not hide my tastes or aversions. I will so trust that what is deep is holy, that I will do strongly before the sun and moon whatever only rejoices me, and the heart appoints. If you are noble, I will love you; if you are not, I will not hurt you and myself by hypocritical attentions. If you are true, but not in the same truth with me, cleave to your companions; I will seek my own.[18]

He proclaims the value of society but sees its limits, though "it is easy to see that a greater self-reliance must work a revolution in all the offices and relations of men; in their religion; in their education; in their pursuits; their modes of living; their association; in their property; in their speculative views."[19] Finally, though, for all his broad idealism, Emerson falls into the trap that ensnares many who extol self-reliance:

Insist on yourself; never imitate. Your own gift you can present every moment with the cumulative force of a whole life's cultivation; but of the adopted talent of another, you have only an extemporaneous, half possession. That which each can do best, none but his Maker can teach him. No man yet knows what it is, nor can, till that person has exhibited it. Where is the master who could have taught Shakspeare? Where is the master who could have instructed Franklin, or Washington, or Bacon, or Newton? Every great man is a unique.[20]

In fact, all of the "geniuses" he mentioned *were* instructed and made it their business to accept instruction and to take to heart its lessons. Their "master" was tradition and was the heritage of language and of the knowledge of generations. The "geniuses" may have been unique, but they all and always used what others had done before them.

Like his friend Henry David Thoreau, Emerson held something of a naive though beautiful and laudable view of what the individual could do in the world, a view that stemmed, in part perhaps, from that old wishful pastoral vision of the world as a garden—a different genesis from the worldview of the Borderers but with much similarity all the same and, over the years since, showing much influence over developing Borderer attitudes.

*****

Written in response to the British writer and philosopher Thomas Carlyle's 1829 essay "Signs of the Times," which Marx depicts as a "passionate attack upon the 'Age of Machinery,' "[21] Timothy Walker's *North American Review* article "Defense of Mechanical Philosophy" also presents an argument quite in keeping with the sentiments of Borderers. The people of the frontier, as I have indicated, never had much interest in the myth of the pastoral, seeing their environment only as something to be fought and conquered—and used—by any means necessary. This attitude continues today. In his depiction of what he sees as Carlyle's doom-and-gloom attitude, Walker foretells similar attitudes by contemporary conservatives against what they see as the handwringers over global warming and environmental destruction. Writing specifically about Carlyle's attitudes, he says that

> throughout the whole article ... he draws most cheerless conclusions from the course which human affairs are taking. If the writer do not, as he humanely assures us in the end, ultimately despair of the destinies of our ill-starred race, he does, nevertheless, perceive baleful influences hanging over us. Noxious ingredients are working in the caldron. He has detected the 'midnight hag' that threw them in, and her name is Mechanism. A more malevolent spirit, in his estimation, does not come from the hateful abodes. The fated inhabitants of this planet are now under her pernicious sway, and she is most industriously plotting against their weal.[22]

He goes on to state his counterposition, again not unlike that of contemporary "red staters":

> We cannot perceive that Mechanism, as such, has yet been the occasion of any injury to man. Some liberties, it is true, have been taken with Nature by this same presumptuous intermeddler. Where she denied us rivers, Mechanism has supplied them. Where she left our planet uncomfortably rough, Mechanism has applied the roller. Where her mountains have been found in the way, Mechanism has boldly levelled or cut through them.[23]

All that we have are tools and resources given to us by God; therefore, we have the God-given right—duty, in fact—to use those tools and resources for our own betterment:

> When we attempt to convey an idea of the infinite attributes of the Supreme Being, we point to the stupendous machinery of the universe. From the ineffable harmony and regularity, which pervade the whole vast system, we deduce the infinite power and intelligence of the Creating Mind. Now we can perceive no reason, why a similar course should not be pursued, if we would form correct concepts of the dignity and glory of man. Look at the changes he has effected on the earth; so great, that could the first men revisit their mortal abodes, they could scarcely recognize the planet they once inhabited.[24]

Anyone who has ever walked behind a plow understands the advantage of the tractor to a degree well beyond the understanding of the writer who simply appreciates the evolution from the quill to the typewriter to the computer.

The intellectuals of the East and of Britain saw a difference between the mechanical world and the natural world that few Borderers were quick to accept. As poor farmers, for the most part, they interacted with the natural world on a level no longer even possible for the city dwellers and the gentry of the 18th century, who had already experienced the split between the lives they now led and the land, a split that becomes the heart of the urban experience. What the urban people and the intellectual elite (and even those who became the new working class) would feel to be a further alienation from nature through machines was seen, in agricultural places, as simply an augmentation of processes that had gone on for generations. Mechanization allowed farmers to do more with land with a little less physical effort, but the change is one of degree, not substance. Where the city dweller might see a break with the past, the farmer may very well only see a continuum of advancement:

> We cannot go back to the origin of mankind and trace them down to the present time, without believing it to be a part of the providence of God, that his creatures should be perpetually advancing. The first men must have been profoundly ignorant, except so far as the Supreme Being communicated with them directly. But with them commenced a series of inventions and discoveries, which have been going on, up to the present moment. Every day has beheld some addition to the general stock of information. When the exigency of the times has required a new truth to be revealed, it has been revealed.[25]

Walker goes on the claim that genius "was not the result of accident, but the work of an overruling Providence."[26] Even the greatest possible individualist, in this view, would have to humble himself or herself before God—something many of even the staunch individualists of today's Borderers would agree is true (though the followers of Rand probably would not).

Having presented a case much in keeping with the mind-set of the frontier—probably more than with the views of New England, where the pastoral and other myths still had a great deal of influence—it is hardly surprising that Walker had left his native Massachusetts by the time his article appeared, settling in what was then the great city of the West, Cincinnati. He founded a law school there, and his grandson, Nicholas Longworth, would be the Speaker of the U.S. House of Representatives in the late 1920s.

Cincinnati, right on the Ohio River, where Mrs. Trollope had also proposed to settle, had become an important Borderer town by the time Walker got there. Its population, in 1800, was less than 1,000. In 1810, there were more than twice as many people in town, about 2,500. By 1820, Cincinnati was home to almost four times as many as that, approaching 10,000. By 1830, a year or so after Walker moved there, nearly 25,000 people lived in the city. In 1840, it had nearly doubled once more, having reached 46,000. This, of course, was the pattern of the West, and it would be repeated over and over again. The first people there were Borderers, old and new. They were followed by immigrants from the East and abroad, people like Walker who, no matter how much affinity they might feel for the westerners, brought in another, more powerful culture and grafted it on top of that established by the Scots-Irish and those who had first joined them.

*****

As we see with Emerson and Thoreau, the rural world of westward expansion was not the only place of growth of American visions of individualism. Even these two were not the only ones in the East developing a strong individualist tradition, often starting from the ideas and writings of Franklin. So, though the urban cultures did not arise from a Borderer base, the experience of the city can also be used to illuminate this American phenomenon, if for nothing but contrast or complement to Borderer vision—or for both. After all, the cultures of America have never existed in silos. Each one influences all of the others and vice versa. Just like African American culture influences the lives of white Americans, and vice versa, the rural-based culture of the Borderers has influenced the cities and has been influenced by them. This was just as much the case in days before mass media. Population movement in America has always been so strong that few groups have been able to live their lives in relative cultural isolation. This is why it is only in Appalachia, one of the poorest regions of the United States and, for a long time, one of the most uninviting to urban outsiders, that the older Borderer culture remains immediately and clearly distinct from the greater American whole.

The general bifurcations of America can be expressed in quite a number of ways: North/South, of course, and Black/White. In this book, I am using the Borderers against the other British folkways, calling them, together, the secular-liberal culture. Again, that is not the only way in which fundamental American differences can be characterized. This is particularly significant today, when demographic shifts are ensuring that, soon, the majority of the

American population will not have strong ancestral ties to the British Isles and Europe.

Another way to describe the American dualities is through its political parties. The debates that led to their development, the struggle between those wanting a strong centralized government and others seeking a much more diffuse system, have continued ever since bickering started among George Washington's advisers (particularly between Alexander Hamilton and Thomas Jefferson), and it too can be used to pin a basic philosophical differences to American contentions. One of the other common ways to see the divide is, as I have alluded, to place it as one between urban and rural; another sees an essentially immigrant sensibility (or an ethnic or even panracial one) against an older one, stemming from British colonial roots. There are more, including other obvious ones built around attitudes toward apparent race. The differences between these, however, are simply differences in starting points: Each one sheds useful light on the American experience just as each helps us better understand the others. They all lead to a similar place, often with the same people and groups on each side—even though they do all remain distinct.

✶✶✶✶✶

It is impossible to pin one's arguments about American culture successfully to a single approach alone, not if one does not wish to paint oneself into a corner, for the American experience, like the human experience, is varied and multidimensional. For that reason, I am going to turn my attention away from the specifically Borderer experience for a few pages to look at the opposite end of the spectrum: that of American cities, particularly the larger ones. Here, though the culture may be based on secular-liberal ideals, the impact of groups other than the remaining English folkways is even greater, if that is possible, than it has been on the Borderers. Sheer numbers make the case:

> In 1890, as in many cities on the Atlantic seaboard, the proportion of foreign stock in San Francisco was 78 percent, in Salt Lake City 65 percent, in St. Louis 67 percent, in Duluth 75 percent, in Chicago 78 percent, and in Milwaukee 86 percent. Nor was immigration merely a big-city phenomenon. Immigrants and their children at the end of the nineteenth century constituted a majority in the still heavily rural and small-town states of Minnesota, the Dakotas, Montana, Arizona, Wyoming, Utah, Nevada, and California.[27]

Though immigrants were important in many parts of America in the 19th century, the greatest impact of immigration was, not surprisingly, on the coasts or near the great inland waterways. It was not until well into the second half of the century, after all, that the railroads would be able to compete in numbers with the traffic on the rivers and coastal waterways. The states of the old Confederacy are noticeably absent from the list above, as are those adjoining. "Of the thirty-eight million to arrive between the end of the Napoleonic Wars and the onset of the Great Depression in 1929, half came before 1900. Some five million entered prior to the beginning of the Civil War in 1861, with the result that by 1860 Boston's population was 36 percent foreign-born, Brooklyn's 39 percent, and New York's 48 percent."[28] The impact of these numbers was phenomenal, of course, immigrant attitudes melding with established ones, creating a culture even more different than it was before from the Borderer culture and the southern culture, which were now irrevocably linked in eastern eyes through the losses of the Civil War and the devastation of Reconstruction.

To start to understand the differences in culture between "red state" and "blue state" America, one need look no further than the different visions of individualism and self-sufficiency exhibited within the two cultures, especially in their rural and urban incarnations. In the Borderer culture, as we have seen, individuality has a great deal to do with lack of restraint, with being left alone to make or create. In the secular-liberal culture, as we will see in the following discussion, individualism is more often linked to opportunity and to the taking advantage of it. The self-made person, in the former, succeeds through throwing off a yoke. In the latter, he or she finds ways to make themselves successful through working around, or even with, existing constraints. The former stresses freedom; the latter, ingenuity.

*****

In many Borderer families, there remain vestiges of what was once a great sense of shame even at the *idea* of being "on the county" (as public assistance was once known in rural communities). This would be not only a last resort but also an absolute moral and personal catastrophe. Public assistance meant subservience and a loss of independence. Though families with backgrounds in the secular-liberal culture may similarly see public assistance as something to be avoided, they may (and many do) also see it as opportunity, as a bit of breathing room allowing them to get back on their feet or to allow them time, if they happen to be new immigrants, to learn enough about America to negotiate it successfully. The safety net, for the former, may stop a fall;

for the latter, it can also spring one back. This simple description of differing attitudes toward public assistance, though perhaps seeming to be making a distinction without a practical difference, points out something of real conse-quence: When one group sees another seeming to embrace what the first believes is a negative, all sorts of conclusions can easily be drawn, many quite distinct from the truth. Images such as that of the "welfare queen" result and resentments grow as the rural Borderers see what they think is a gaming of the system by the urban poor who often do not appear to be native born or either culturally or racially similar to the Borderers (who feel they are paying for the services) themselves.

The received wisdom in much of nonurban America is that welfare has become an urban lifestyle, something that people are proud of. The Borderers do not understand this. Though there is not the same sense of shame associated with welfare in the cities, the desire there is to use welfare not merely for survival but as a means to other ends. It is not the defeat of the individual that drives one to it but rather the desire *not* to be defeated. Such differing cultural attitudes, however, are rarely explored and almost never explained in ways allowing either side to understand the other.

One of the underlying secular-liberal assumptions of immigration to America in the 19th century was that an individual comes to take advantage of what the United States has to offer, not to change it. Opportunity was there; it needed only to be grasped, not created. This is quite different from the Borderer necessity of building from the bottom up (after destroying what was already there, Native American cultures, for example), of *making* oppor-tunity instead of grasping it.

The most iconic of the American writers on urban success in the 19th century is surely Horatio Alger, whose books show boys rising from rags to, if not riches, the middle class. These are tales not of cultural change or of assimilation but of people in dire circumstances who, when given a chance, take it. Alger's most famous character is "Ragged Dick" Hunter, who later tells a boy who had helped him along in the first book of the series, " 'If I'm changed, it's because of what you said to me then, you and your father. But for those words I might still have been Ragged Dick.' "[29] There is never a sense that Richard Hunter has been able to do it all on his own, as in the wil-derness tradition of a Daniel Boone. Here, it is the goal not to get away from society but rather to use the benevolent aspects of society for one's own progress. After all, " 'Dick may have been lucky,' said Mr. Rockwell, 'but I generally find that luck comes oftenest to those who deserve it. If you will try to raise yourself I will help you.' "[30]

The goal of the Alger books is not simply to encourage boys (and they really were written for boys) to make the most of themselves but rather to make clear to them that they also have to help others. Rarely is there one boy alone in the stories. In most, one who is beginning to gain a little success reaches a hand back to others: "Nobody had ever taken any interest in him before. Life to him had been a struggle and a conflict with very little hope of better things."[31] This helping of others, to Alger, is the heart of what makes success in America possible, what makes individual effort meaningful. He expressed the importance of such help frequently: " 'He has been a rough customer, but then he has never had a chance. I believe in giving everybody a chance.' "[32] And " 'I was once a poor boy like you, and found friends. I'll be your friend.' "[33] And "He never forgets his humble beginnings, and tries to show his sense of God's goodness by extending a helping hand to the poor and needy boys whose trials and privations he understands well from his own experience."[34] And " 'We ought all to help each other,' said Mr. Bates. 'I believe in that doctrine, though I have not always lived up to it.' "[35] Then this:

> "I congratulate you on your advance in life. Such a rise shows remarkable energy on your part."
> "I was lucky," said Dick, modestly. "I found some good friends who helped me along."[36]

To Alger, it is not "God helps those who help themselves" but rather "helping others moves one toward God."

The type of success that an urban individual, in Alger's eye, can aim toward is quite different from that which a Borderer might imagine, for it is success within a framework of society and of commerce. Hunter, for example, does not necessarily aim to be the owner of a company: "By a series of upward steps, partly due to good fortune, but largely to his own determination to improve, and hopeful energy, Dick had now become a bookkeeper."[37] Being an employee is sufficient. However, the type of employee considered sufficient or desirable falls within a narrow scope that ignores actual economic reality. "That certain kinds of labor were intrinsically destructive to health and well-being was ignored for the most part by a literature clearly directed more to clerks than to coal miners."[38] Not everyone can aspire to office work. Weiss, in the quote above, is referring specifically to New Thought literature, but his words apply just as well to Alger. The consequences of the job on the employee were always assumed to be benign, assumed so by simply ignoring dangerous professions.

Of course, Alger was not against anyone working for himself or reaching the top. His characters, after all, often start out self-employed but at the bottom, working as bootblacks or paperboys. It is their energy in pursuing even so lowly a calling that leads them upward. He describes the attitude of one of his characters: "Now he was working for himself, and this seemed to put new spirit and courage into him. Then again he felt that he had shaken off the hateful thralldom."[39]

Success did not mean being at the pinnacle, though. What it did mean was having a job with a future, and an increasing income—and being able to put some of it aside for investment: "The feeling that he was his own master, and had a little hoard of money for present expenses, gave him courage."[40] It also meant understanding one's place in the realm of commerce—understanding that even the boss is not completely free. In this sense, Alger was well within the tradition of literature as a depiction of class structure and struggle for success within it, much as was James Fenimore Cooper, one of his personal favorites and to whom he once wrote a fan letter:

> "Permit me to take this opportunity to express to you, Sir," he wrote, "the great gratification with which I have perused many of your works—more especially the Leatherstocking Series." He concluded his letter with "the hope that your life may long be spared to add to the works with which you have already enriched American literature." Not surprisingly, Alger would often allude later in his juvenile fiction to Cooper stories he had enjoyed in his own adolescence.[41]

At one point, Alger, intentionally or not, does almost parody the Borderer attitude of freedom: " 'I wish I had a store of my own,' he thought, discontentedly. 'Then I could do as I pleased without having anybody to interfere with me.' "[42] This is from a character destined for failure, for no one is every really one's own boss in Alger's world. Even someone owning a business is constantly at the beck and call of customers. This character, from *Mark, the Match Boy*, does not understand the needs of the real individualism of the city. Alger writes of him, "But there was one thing he did not understand, that the greatest obstacle to his advancement was himself."[43] He explains, "According to his theory, the world owed him a living; but it seemed as if the world were disposed to repudiate the debt."[44] Alger's urban aesthetic of individualism, clearly, is one not of the solitary striver but of the man in constant negotiation with a world that is not always going to provide for him or work with him. This is quite distinct from the Borderer vision of a world that, though it may be harsh, is his or hers for the taking—if he or she can.

In the late 1960s, Richard Weiss wrote that he thought it curious that Alger, of all of writers of juvenile fiction during the decades after the Civil War, had "entered the American vocabulary, though his books are scarcely read any longer."[45] Furthermore, he found Alger to have not been "a representative of his time, but a nostalgic spokesman of a dying order. Of middle-class rural origins, he was always an alien to the industrially dominated society of his adulthood."[46] Like Jeffery Decker, who finds this depiction "inaccurate," I believe that, though they were not industrial workers, the ability of Alger's protagonists "to secure respectable white-collar work is characteristic of Progressive Era standards for middle-class success"[47] and even of the Gilded Age, that of Alger proper, that preceded it.

By the 1920s, though Alger was no longer read, his name had become a convenient description for almost any rags-to-riches story. So forgotten was he personally that Herbert Mayes, who went on to a successful career as a magazine editor at *Good Housekeeping* and *McCall's*, was able to write a fabricated biography of Alger that would long be accepted as the standard source for information on the writer. Only in the 1970s were the "facts" of the biography debunked. The irony, of course, is that Alger once again had helped another man's career—this time, though, not through his writing but through his name. Appropriately enough, Alger also had been, in truth, tutor to the sons of banker Joseph Seligman in New York City, one of whom, Edwin, would later become a renowned economist and one of the founders of the American Association of University Professors. Alger was not quite so intellectually meager as some would make him out to be.

The success and individualism myths hawked by Alger are much more muted and tame than are those of the West and of the Borderers and their descendants and much more cognizant of the relationship between individual success and the society as a whole. This, in a way, was part of what the secular-liberal easterners saw as their own much more sophisticated view of what it means to succeed, especially in terms of money, society, and even religion, setting themselves above the mass of Americans. Henry Adams, a confirmed follower of New England culture, expressed the prevailing attitude of disdain toward what was, by 1900, the mass of Americans:

> Indeed, the American people had no idea at all; they were wandering in a wilderness much more sandy than the Hebrews had ever trodden about Sinai; they had neither serpents nor golden calves to worship. They had lost the sense of worship; for the idea that they worshipped money seemed a delusion. Worship of money was an old-world trait; a healthy appetite akin to worship of the Gods, or to worship of power

in any concrete shape; but the American wasted money more recklessly than any one ever did before; he spent more to less purpose than any extravagant court aristocracy; he had no sense of relative values, and knew not what to do with his money when he got it, except use it to make more, or throw it away. Probably, since human society began, it had seen no such curious spectacle as the houses of the San Francisco millionaires on Nob Hill. Except for the railway system, the enormous wealth taken out of the ground since 1840, had disappeared. West of the Alleghenies, the whole country might have been swept clean, and could have been replaced in better form within one or two years. The American mind had less respect for money than the European or Asiatic mind, and bore its loss more easily; but it had been deflected by its pursuit till it could turn in no other direction. It shunned, distrusted, disliked, the dangerous attraction of ideals, and stood alone in history for its ignorance of the past.[48]

The cultural split, by the end of the century, just at the height of belief in a unitary American vision and a national "manifest destiny," was as great as it ever had been.

*****

Yet the split between the two cultures did not mean that the Borderers were interested only in money or in doing it all on their own. Like many on the other side of the divide, Borderers had taken advantage of the Lyceum movement that had been promoted by Emerson and grew out of the writings of Franklin and that provided libraries, lectures, and more that could be useful to the working man who had not had the benefit of a strong education in his youth. The tradition of self-improvement remained strong throughout the 19th century and into the 20th and in both cultures, with the New Thought and Chautauqua movements (among others) succeeding the Lyceum movement and attracting adherents from both sides of the divide.

Just as the visions of success promoted by these movements crossed cultural boundaries, none of the success movements, particularly those of the late 19th century, was completely independent of the others:

> The impact of New Thought was further enhanced because certain of its key ideas were disseminated by other groups, among them Christian Scientists, Spiritualists, Theosophists, and psychical researchers. Their common ground was an antipathy to "mere" materialism and a commitment to some kind of philosophical idealism. All affirmed

the primacy of spirit over matter which was fundamental to the new gospel of success.[49]

Another significant point about New Thought, particularly in relation to attitudes today, is that, echoing Walker, "New Thought found it important to say that 'man need not be the victim of his environment, but can be the master of it.' "[50] This is another part of what has led to contemporary splits in attitudes toward the causes of climate change or global warming. If man's actions have led, unconsciously, to a worldwide shift in temperature and weather patterns, then man never really was master of the environment but was simply fooling himself. The inheritors of New Thought optimism cannot accept this. After all, they devoutly believed that "men suffered from aspiring to too little rather than too much."[51] Accepting environmental limitations, then, is stultifying.

This view was rather overly optimistic—or worse. According to Weiss,

New Thought writers turned common sense insight into extravagant exaggeration. This was particularly true of the notion that states of mind can affect objective reality. Clearly, the results of most objective conditions are to some degree determined by our subjective response to them. But inspirationalists encouraged the belief that thought did not only condition circumstances, but controlled them entirely.[52]

The impact of this belief continues, showing up even in such popular culture icons as the various productions of *Peter Pan* starring Mary Martin in the 1950s, where Martin (as Peter) asks members of the audience to save the fairy Tinkerbell from the poison she has drunk by *believing* they can save her and showing their belief by clapping their hands. As Weiss says,

The commitment to individual power was too great to be surrendered to a social determinism. The problem of drawing the line between individual and social causation was certainly not exclusively American, but our particular history did have a unique emphasis. No other nation had experienced such an unsupervised development; no other country was so lacking in communal controls; no other people had known such freedom from institutional restraint. In other societies, existing institutional restrictions might be adapted to changing social needs; in America they had to be created from scratch. Historically, Americans had been compelled to discover individual solutions where social ones were lacking. Self-sufficiency, developed in response to need, in time became a cherished value and, even when inadequate, was too deeply ingrained to be scrapped overnight.[53]

The Chautauqua movement, which began at about the same time as New Thought, was a little less centered in theology (though it still had a strong religious aspect), making it more clearly the inheritor of the Lyceum movement. Something of adult summer camps, the Chautauquas were events allowing people to take advantage of groupings of lectures by many of the more prominent figures of the time. They were extremely popular into the 1920s and served as vehicles for introducing Americans of all types to the intellectual debates of the day. Like the Lyceum movement and New Thought, they emphasized the responsibility and possibility of the individual: "Men seeking success must regard their task as one of realizing an abundance which, though latent, was infinite."[54]

*****

Norman Vincent Peale, a 20th-century inheritor of the New Thought mantle, opens his phenomenally successful *The Power of Positive Thinking* with these lines:

> Believe in yourself! Have faith in your abilities! Without a humble but reasonable confidence in your own powers you cannot be successful or happy. But with sound self-confidence you can succeed. A sense of inferiority and inadequacy interferes with the attainment of your hopes, but self-confidence leads to self-realization and successful achievement.[55]

Peale, one of the most successful American preachers of his time, reflected for *new* generations the attitudes of New Thought and other success movements of a generation before his, movements that, once again, often crossed the divide between the Borderer culture and that of much of the rest of America outside of the educated urban elite. The old ideas did not die but were simply incorporated into new presentations.

*****

Two of the most influential American writers on the Lyceum movement, New Thought, the Chautauqua movement, and others emphasizing "success" were Franklin and Emerson. A third, influential on both New Thought and Chautauqua, was the psychologist and philosopher William James. None of these could be called an intellectual lightweight. Yet Horatio Alger, who has (perhaps undeservedly) no intellectual reputation at all, also had a great deal to do with the success of these latter two movements though generally unacknowledged. After all, though Alger's heroes "are patient and virtuous, much more akin to the ideal bourgeois of ante-bellum time,"[56] they are also in keeping with the restrained New Thought ethos. In general, this and the other movements promoted the idea that individual virtue was rewarded and was its own reward, for both individual and community (for Borderers, the "community" aspect was probably not accented quite as much as elsewhere). Excess was frowned upon, especially in the "bad habits" (like smoking and drinking), which were seen as causes for slipping into poverty (and not as some of poverty's results) but also for consumption beyond constraint and massive accumulation of wealth.

The idealism of these movements was a little excessive, though that did not diminish their impact, which can still be felt. Weiss writes, for example, that

> success writers would not admit any necessary antagonism between the boss and his workers. All were engaged in a common enterprise with *mutual* obligations. The employee owed his boss loyalty, hard work, and intelligence. The employer owed his worker a fair living wage, decent working conditions, and courteous consideration. Hard feelings and conflict were due to personal misunderstanding and suspicion.[57]

This idealism, also the idealism of Alger, has led both to the sense of betrayal that many Americans (and not just Borderers) feel in contemporary employment situations where there seem to be few obligations to the employees (aggravating nascent beliefs that one should never rely on anyone but oneself and thereby contradicting the Alger ideal) and, paradoxically, to the belief that the rich, if left alone, will use their money in ways that benefit everyone— Ronald Reagan's "trickle-down" economics. As employees, the Borderers want to be treated with respect. As potentially rich (their optimism often knows no bounds), they want the freedoms of the rich to remain unrestrained.

* * * * *

Though the books of Horatio Alger have not lasted as long as his name has, the type of story for juveniles that he crafted became a notable part of the American publishing industry over the first half of the 20th century. A number of other series directed at boys and with themes of moral struggle for success were eventually launched, some of them also becoming touchstones for their times. Among them was the Tom Swift series created by Edward Stratemeyer. Stratemeyer, who had a connection to some of Alger's unfinished manuscripts, published the first Tom Swift books in 1910, including *Tom Swift and His Motor-Cycle* and *Tom Swift and His Airship*. Among the boys who gobbled up the books was likely an eight-year-old in Minnesota, already probably dreaming of his own future. If he did in fact read the books, that boy, Charles Lindbergh, read the following words:

> "Now do be careful," cautioned Mr. Swift, the aged inventor, once more. "I'm afraid you two have set too hard a task for yourselves this time."
> "No we haven't, dad," answered his son. "You'll see us yet skimming along above the clouds."[58]

The "we," of course, was not a man and his plane, as it would become when Lindbergh would write his best seller *We* about his flight across the Atlantic, but the idea is there, an idea of adventure racing far beyond what an older generation could imagine. It was an idea of individualism as strong as any put forward by Emerson or lived by Boone—and it combined elements of the individualism of both sides of the cultural divide. Technology was what gave it its drive, and technology is what made the Tom Swift series, which focused on inventions, so very popular. The technological genius no longer needed to rely on society but could build machines to do for him (and, as yet, it was most always a "him") that which he did not wish to rely on other people for.

To Americans of the 1920s, Lindbergh seemed to be "a compelling Horatio Alger story as he became the most famous American of his time"[59] More appropriately, he was Tom Swift taken from the pages of that other, later series of boys' books (though a series deeply indebted to the Alger books) and made real. Tom Swift had a motorcycle; young Charles Lindbergh had a motorcycle. As Lindbergh would do on his trip across the Atlantic, Tom Swift "had to rely on himself. Tom was a resourceful lad, and he had often before been obliged to depend on his wits."[60]

Like Tom Swift, Lindbergh appeared to be able to do everything connection with his projects:

> During the first weeks of production, Don Hall [chief designer for the Ryan Company that built Lindbergh's plane] recalled, Lindbergh participated in every aspect of the plane's construction, "and he did not leave San Diego until he was absolutely sure that the smallest part, the weakest link in the mechanism of his ship was strong enough to withstand strain before which other planes had succumbed."[61]

This followed the time-honored tradition of "if you want it done right, do it yourself," a tradition that had become, by the boyhood and young manhood of Lindbergh, an American mythology in its own right. By the time of his famous flight, Lindbergh "had become entirely self-reliant in the air. He could fix his own plane and plan his own route and possessed remarkable hand-eye coordination."[62] *This*, to Americans on both sides of the cultural divide, was what American individualism was all about, though each side considered it in its own different light.

As it does in Lindbergh's best seller about his flight, technology becomes part of the individual from the 1920s on—but in general today it is stripped of the humans who created it and of its history (at least it is by many in the Borderer culture). As with language and ideas, generally the only people of importance concerning technologies are, ultimately, those who use them, not those who created them.

Both Lindbergh and the fictional Swift were involved in the creation of their crafts, but this has become more rare as the complexity of our machines necessitates increasing specialization. Once, the pride of many young American men was the car that they had restored and augmented, the work of their own hands reflected in all aspects and usages of the product. Today, there is very little possibility of becoming an ace backyard mechanic, of making a new part if need be or cobbling together pieces found in a junk-yard. Now, pride is found in using well the creations of others, leading to the encompassing of products as manufactured, so to speak, in one's own individualism. Customization, for the moment, has fallen away.

The new attitude of incorporating technology into individualism does have antecedents, however, even in Lindbergh's *We* (the "we" referring to himself and his aircraft), and it finds precedence in *Tom Swift and His Airship*:

> "We'll soon be flying through the clouds on your back," he remarked, speaking to the apparatus as if it could understand. "I guess we'll smash some records, too, if that engine works as well when it's installed as it does now."[63]

Technology, like family and friends, becomes part of the individual and not the group. It is excused from the web of interactions that make up society. In science fiction, its antecedents are sometimes removed from human beings completely, as it is in *Forbidden Planet* (Fred Wilcox, 1956), allowing it to be even more closely associated with the individual wielder of it, questions of creation becoming moot.

*****

More than 80 years after the fact and in a milieu of continual media-celebrity overload, it is hard for us to imagine how absolutely unexpected was

Lindbergh's flight over the Atlantic and landing at Le Bourget Field outside of Paris on May 21, 1927, and how unique the reactions of the public. The plucky solo flier, so young and looking so innocent, caught the imagination of Europe and America in a way no person ever had. Imagine: More than half the number of New York City's population of nearly 7,000,000 turned out to see Lindbergh after he had landed (from a ship, not his plane) at the Battery and made his way up to Central Park just a few weeks after the flight, little more than a month after the then-unknown flier had, without fanfare, brought his little *Spirit of St. Louis* to Curtiss Field on Long Island to try for the first successful nonstop flight from New York to Paris.

What made Lindbergh's feat so moving to so many? A great deal of it had to do with who he was—and with the fact that he seemed to be just one man attempting a feat against incredible odds. When he took off, others were preparing for the same trip, but in bigger, fancier aircraft with multiple engines and larger crews. Not to mention, they were doing so with access to money and publicity. Lindbergh did the flight alone, and it seemed as though he had done it *all* alone. And he had done it on the cheap (comparatively). He was just the sort of loner guaranteed to spark the American imagination (and the European, too, for that matter). His childhood, Americans saw once they started to learn the details, even carried resonances of Boone, America's great 18th-century loner.

Growing up, Lindbergh had learned to hunt early and had developed self-sufficiency on his parents' farm. Like Boone, Lindbergh had an indulgent mother who "understood his urge for the outdoors and for freedom from structure. She would pull him out of class every once in a while to take him for hikes in the woods."[64] Self-reliance was crucial to both men. Lindbergh's "father had warned him about 'depending too heavily on others.' The old Minnesota settlers had a saying: 'One boy's a boy. Two boys are half a boy. Three boys are no boy at all.' "[65] As soon as he could, Lindbergh developed another American type of self-sufficiency, learning to ride and maintain his motorcycle, again like Tom Swift, providing himself with individual mobility and a sense of freedom.

* * * * *

On the Borderer side, people believed that, if they were left alone, they could become Charles Lindberghs themselves. On the secular-liberal side, people believed that, if they just had access to the resources, they could become Charles Lindberghs themselves. For the Borderers, however, another aspect of individualism was also growing, and that was of the individual as free from restraint like the pilot soaring in the air. Up there, whatever one did was nobody's business but one's own. And that is the way, they thought, that it should be.

That this, too, was not simply a Borderer attitude but spread to other American cultures is evidenced in African American pianist and composer Porter Grainger's 1922 song "Ain't Nobody's Business," which includes verses much like this one:

> If I should take a notion
> To jump into the ocean
> Ain't nobody's business if I do.
> If I go to church on Sunday
> Then cabaret all day Monday
> Ain't nobody's business if I do.

Along with reliance on technology, the forced integration of human activities in closely packed urban environments has made this idea nothing much more than a pipe dream for almost anyone today—outside of the few privileged to operate in the remaining and rapidly closing "wide-open spaces"— even in the air. Yet it has persisted among Borderer descendants and has had a large impact on their view of the American political system.

At the same time, the "only in it for myself" attitude certainly did also arise in urban environments, especially among those of the poor who started to see the lack of success among those around them as the fault of the people themselves and not the fault of lack of possibilities or of anything or anyone else. Almost a parody of the Horatio Alger stories, this new paradigm of success came through a willingness to step on anyone and do anything at all—if it helped in getting ahead.

Perhaps one of the most famous of the examples of this paradigm is Sammy Glick, the title character in Budd Schulberg's 1941 novel *What Makes Sammy Run?* In many ways, Glick is the antithesis of Lindbergh. He is the person with ambition but no skill but who is willing to "steal" the skills of others to get his way. To Glick, it is the result that matters, not the way one gets there or even what one learns along the route.

At one point in the book, the narrator, Al Manheim, tries to school Sammy on the old secular-liberal idea of what it means to be a successful individual:

> "Sammy," I began wisely, "society isn't just a bunch of individuals living alongside of each other. As a member of society, man is

interdependent. Not independent, Sammy, *inter*-dependent. Life is too complex for there to be any truth in the old slogan of every man for himself. We share the benefits of social institutions, like take hospitals, the cops and garbage collection. Why, the art of conversation itself is a social invention. We can't live in this world like a lot of cannibals trying to swallow each other. Learn to give the other fellow a break and we'll *all* live longer."

I felt pretty pleased with myself after I said that because I was convinced that it was one of the most sensible things I had ever said. But I might as well have been talking to a stone wall. In fact that might have been better. At least it couldn't talk back.

Sammy's answer was, "If you want to save souls, try China."[66]

Sammy, the ultimate cynic, shows exactly the other side of the Lindbergh coin of self-reliance: " 'Talent can get you just so far,' " he [Glick] said. " 'Then you got to start using your head' "[67]—and must start using what other people have done. Even thievery does not matter—as long as one is not stupid enough to be caught.

For the cynic like Glick, one can even look to Thoreau for justification, even if a false one and a purposeful misunderstanding of Thoreau's purpose: "Law never made me a whit more just; and, by means of their respect for it, even the well-disposed are daily made the agents of injustice."[68] So why respect laws of any sort?

Though Thoreau's "Civil Disobedience" can be misconstrued as primarily antistate, its real purpose is to justify resistance to an unjust state. The difference comes in an understanding of "what men are prepared for,"[69] as in understanding just what the role of government should be. To Thoreau, an overreaching government is as bad as an overreaching man. The government must depend on the governed, but the governed must be dependable:

The authority of government, even such as I am willing to submit to—for I will cheerfully obey those who know and can do better than I, and in many things even those who neither know nor can do so well—is still an impure one: to be strictly just, it must have the sanction and consent of the governed. It can have no pure right over my person and property but what I concede to it. The progress from an absolute to a limited monarchy, from a limited monarchy to a democracy, is a progress toward a true respect for the individual. Even the Chinese philosopher was wise enough to regard the individual as the basis of the empire. Is a democracy, such as we know it, the last improvement possible in government? Is it not possible to take a step further towards recognizing and organizing the rights of man? There will never be a really free and enlightened State until the State comes to recognize the individual as a higher and independent power, from which all its own power and authority are derived, and treats him accordingly. I please myself with imagining a State at last which can afford to be just to all men, and to treat the individual with respect as a neighbor; which even would not think it inconsistent with its own repose if a few were to live aloof from it, not meddling with it, nor embraced by it, who fulfilled all the duties of neighbors and fellow men. A State which bore this kind of fruit, and suffered it to drop off as fast as it ripened, would prepare the way for a still more perfect and glorious State, which I have also imagined, but not yet anywhere seen.[70]

Instead of being shrunken to the point where it could be drowned in Grover Norquist's bathtub, the state becomes a respecter and, by implication, a supporter of the individual. The implication is that the state can wither away, but only when the individual makes full use of his or her "higher and independent" power. Those "few" who could live "aloof" from the state, "not meddling with it, nor embraced by it," can do so because they have learned to respect their neighbors and can live with them without conflict.

Thoreau's vision melds well with the ideals of individualism in America of both the Borderers and the secular-liberals. However, it has always surprised me that he has never been quite so popular with the Borderers as with the secular-liberals. The reason probably has to do not with his views on government but with those on nature. *Walden* can seem extremely naive, though still gorgeous and energizing, to those who grow up without the removal from the land that industrialization has forced on a growing percentage of people everywhere.

*****

At one point late in *What Makes Sammy Run?*, Manheim tries to explain his feelings about Glick to a woman:

I told her a little of how balled up I felt inside because there were times when I wanted to say what I had to say as honestly as possible, and times when I felt as ambitious as Sammy without being able to free myself from the sense of relationship with everybody else in the world, which made it difficult to do anything which I thought might cause them pain.[71]

Sammy has no such constraints. As Manheim explains,

I saw Sammy Glick on a battlefield where every soldier was his own cause, his own army and his own flag, and I realized that I had singled him out not because he had been born into the world any more selfish, ruthless and cruel than anybody else, even though he had become all three, but because in the midst of a war that was selfish, ruthless and cruel Sammy was proving himself the fittest, the fiercest and the fastest.[72]

This is the perversion of individualism that scared—and still scares—so many Americans of the secular-liberal tradition, people who see the individual as best residing within, or at least respecting the constraints of society. What was becoming more and more apparent over the course of America's cultural development, however, was that it was the Glicks, for the most part, who were getting ahead. More and more, as the 20th century progressed, Lindbergh was appearing to be the anomaly.

The Borderers are not Glicks, of course. Their individualism, though it can be scarily like the completely amoral selfishness of Schulberg's imagination, has a great deal more to it—and a great deal more restraint. Though they can talk a good Glick/Rand line, most Borderer followers of the cult of individualism temper their beliefs through strong allegiances to family and friends —and through their commitment to religion. The secular-liberals, who do not view either family or religion as central elements to public (as opposed to personal) action, often fall into the trap of seeing this as corruption and bias rather than as, the way Borderers see it, personal responsibility and faith, the very building blocks, to Borderer minds, of real and successful community.

The Borderer vision of individualism starts within each of them, with faith in the person and in God. It next moves, in a spreading circle, to family, to friends, and only then to others in the broad realm of human interaction. If each person acted responsibly, by these lights (and just as Thoreau argues), there would be little need for government—each individual having a tempering effect on those they interact with. The secular-liberal vision starts in a different place, with a structured base created and maintained by the group. Once responsibilities to it are met, the individual is free to—is encouraged to—act on his or her own to whatever ends seem appropriate, as long as those ends do not threaten or compromise the group structure. Here again we see Thoreau, but from another perspective. The secular-liberal sees a duty to resist the state when it becomes corrupt, while the Borderer seeks to avoid it in the first place, to move away from it, as has been done since first arrival in America, if not before.

In these ways and others, these two visions are fundamentally different, even if they do overlap a great deal of the time or end up looking the same—even if the word used to describe them is the same. In fact, it is that similarity that causes much of the problem between Borderers and those from the secular-liberal culture: Though the words are the same, the meanings are not, so the two cultures end up speaking at cross-purposes, neither one able, at the end of the day, to understand how the other half lives.

CHAPTER 6

The Townspeople, the Hero, and Alienation

Perhaps it seemed like the cult of individualism in America reached its height in the decades after World War II when the "loner" became the usual hero of popular media and when that loner, appropriately, was of a different sort than had been seen before. This hero became the icon of the Beats and then of the drug culture of the 1960s, exemplified by the solo motorcycle rider and by existential angst. It became the symbol of a cultural chasm that opened out of what had seemed a unity of wartime effort. In the popular mind, the new individual became both what was good for America and its actual best—as well as a lightning rod for what was its worst.

World War II saw not only the defeat of Germany and Japan but also the first signs of what would soon *seem* to be the final defeat of America's rural Borderer ethnicity as a distinct culture, the defeat of a vision of America rooted in small towns across the country from the mountains of Appalachia to California, a vision rising from much older Scots-Irish sensibilities. This vision did not actually die, of course, but it was pushed aside by a new "consensus" view of America, promoted not by Borderers but from within growing American print and electronic media and crafted by the Northeast and the upper Midwest—with strong aid from California and the Northwest.

To these cultural powers of the United States, there was much not worth mourning within the defeated vision. Its "wrongs" has been apparent for years—especially the essential wrongs of racism that had long warped the United States. For other Americans, the older vision was lamentably pushed aside by adulation for that new type of loner individualist—not a Daniel Boone trying to live alone but a person who could live alone even in a crowd.

Nonetheless, the once-idealized rural America of the self-sufficient Borderer remained a powerful and suggestive force, never dying but simply moving to the side in the face of the powerful new figure of individualism exemplified by superstars such as John Wayne (in his postwar incarnation), Marlon Brando, and James Dean. These were what Americans *should* be. The older individual, mired in family and friends, was now passé, its adulation naive—fit only for consumption by children watching television.

Looking back from a time of conservative resurgence, however, one can easily see that the Borderer ideal never should have been so ignored or treated with disdain. Doing so only widened splits already present in American society.

* * * * *

Ultimately, the attitudes of those who saw the Borderer culture as backward, instead of demolishing Borderer attitudes, contributed to the culture's revival and, eventually, to its political domination. Starting with the Reagan era, this revival has shifted the entire American political debate far to the right. Referring to people as "hillbillies" and "rednecks" because their beliefs do not conform to the dominant media pattern has proven to be insufficient for dismissing the Borderers from the political realm. Instead, it turned them into an opposition—and a powerful one even in their days in the "wilderness" of the Barry Goldwater disaster. Then it led them back to a power that conservatives had lacked in America since 1932, power that, though it seems to be waning in 2013, is still potent in American political discussion, still defining the parameters of the debate itself.

In its rise from its own ashes starting in the 1960s, the American conservative movement has made effective use of the older vision of American individualism as well as of the resentment of the defeated, much as Democratic politicians in the South had done almost a century earlier. Unfortunately, from that low point after Goldwater's 1964 defeat, the movement's successes have also exacerbated American divides (red state/blue state, conservative/liberal, rural/urban) even as they have renewed the strength of that older but battered vision of America.

The media, through fascination with the "star" at the expense of the cast, have been complicit in the attempted cultural theft of the older Borderer identity of individualism. The theft has even helped lead to many of the resentments that the conservative movement has harnessed so effectively. Early on, as far back as the 1920s, Hollywood took hold of a stereotype and a cultural divide that had been beneath East Coast radar, used it, and then, after the war, pushed it aside. By then, it had found a replacement for the older "naive" view of small-town America so no longer felt it needed to pander to it. Focused on the new individualist at the expense of the old, the movies turned the Judge Priest of Irvin Cobb's short stories into Judge Roy Bean (*The Life and Times of Judge Roy Bean*, directed by John Huston, 1972) and Will Rogers (who played *Judge Priest* in the 1934 John Ford film) into Larry "Lonesome" Rhodes of the Elia Kazan's 1957 film *A Face in the Crowd*. Hollywood turned the small farmer into a hillbilly bumpkin, helping to marginalize him, and turned the hero of the people into the hero of himself.

Yet Hollywood could not completely destroy the older vision of the individual so long embedded in the "hayseed" population. Its reality was too strong a presence, even when it was converted into parody, in too much of America. It is an element of all American lives, whether they love to hate it, hate to love it, or just plain love it. As Appalachian studies scholar J. W. Williamson writes,

> The hillbilly lives not only in hills but on the rough edge of the economy, wherever that happens to land him. Meanwhile, in the normative heart of the economy, where the middle class strives and where cartoon hillbillies and other comic rural characters have entertained us on a regular basis since at least the mid-1800s, we take secret pleasure in the trashing of hallowed beliefs and sacred virtues—not to mention hygiene. . . .
>
> As rural memory, the hillbilly is not so easily dismissed. Hillbillyland is coated in barnyard, and the residue sticks like mud. Its denizens perversely refuse to modernize, obliviously miss the need to be in squalor. Free of our squeamishness, the hillbilly thrives in squalor. He's the shadow of our doubt.[1]

The hillbilly is also the repository for all the negative attitudes in sophisticated quarters for that other, that Borderer America—and, at the same time, he has become the Borderer thumb in the eye to the coastal elites. He is the image of the defeated "worst" of America (the stereotypical Borderer) as well as the symbol of their rise from the ashes. The Confederate soldier in a soiled and torn uniform on unofficial license plates in the 1960s south over the words "Forget, Hell" was more than just a statement on a century-old war. It was a challenge, one that seemed forlorn at the time, to the secular-liberal culture that seemed on the verge of dominating every aspect of American life.

Williamson's point, that the hillbilly may be easy to dismiss but always remains with us, on the edges of our consciousness and our politics, is well taken, of course, but I do not think he goes quite far enough. As politics of the past decade (the decade after the publication of Williamson's book) have shown us, it is dangerous to dismiss the Borderer as hillbilly, and not simply because he figuratively (and literally) hangs around the edges. The hillbilly (as Williamson knows and also argues) is no simpleton, no bumpkin, though often is dismissed as such in popular culture. Instead, he is a vital force in America, the image even donned by the likes of David "Mudcat" Saunders, a liberal political activist from Virginia who sleeps under a Confederate battle flag. Saunders is proud of his heritage and culture yet is neither beholden to it nor a part of what has often been presented as its decaying monolith. Today, the hillbilly image is worn, by Saunders and many others, as much as a rebuke to the East Coast elites as that Rebel license plate of 50 years ago. They wear the image with pride and as a much more sophisticated statement than those it is aimed at often realize—which is part of the point.

Country musician Brad Paisley's 2013 song "Accidental Racist" (recorded with rapper LL Cool J) shows the confusion that the battle flag can also engender, especially among Southerners and Borderers. The song is confused itself, from both sides of the racial divide, but it is a genuine attempt to come to terms both with racism and with Southern (and often Borderer) pride. The white character apologizes for a tee shirt with the battle flag upon it, saying he didn't mean to offend, only to say that he is a fan of the 70s rock band Lynyrd Skynyrd. Then, oddly, the black character addresses him as "Mr. White Man," rapping in completely stereotypical terms about whites while wanting to be treated as an individual himself. Both characters want to be treated as individual human beings, but both complain in stereotypes about the other while presenting themselves as stereotypes:

> I'm just a white man
> (If you don't judge my do-rag)
> Coming to you from the southland
> (I won't judge your red flag)

The racial attitudes presented in the song aren't mean-spirited but are simply ignorant of the other—on both sides. The hillbilly and the gangsta are here, but with very little understanding of what these images mean.

The hillbilly image is also a rebuke to that other image, the one of that different kind of individualist that has grown since World War II, the individualist as someone standing against the community (for whatever reason). In many of these newer cases, the community is depicted as debased or, at best, wrongheaded—instead of in need of a savior. The people, the

Borderers, in this vision, are the enemy of all "right thinking" secular-liberal Americans.

In this sense, the hillbilly is the other side of the modern individualist coin, the tail to the head that is shown in contemporary media. Instead of the person who rises above the crowd, the hillbilly deliberately falls below it. Both individualist and hillbilly are proud, but the stereotype of the former is of a principled person, the latter appearing depraved.

As Rodger Cunningham writes in *Apples on the Flood*, Appalachians have long been stereotyped as having almost any characteristics beside, for example, Saunders's intelligence and skill:

> Mountaineers have been categorized by the dominant culture as "contemporary ancestors," as noble or ignoble savages. . . . In this disconfirmation, the dominator implicitly denies the dominated an inner self and an ability to think and act on one's own behalf. Such disconfirmation can take "benevolent," patronizing forms, which are perhaps most damaging.[2]

In part, today's hillbilly is a rebuke to these attitudes through the taking on the negative aspects as badges of pride. Though the elite have long claimed to want to "help" the poor of the Borderers, the words they use for them make one suspicious of their motives and, if a Borderer, makes one want to lash back at them somehow. Is it any wonder? Just think of the words today's liberals use to disparage their conservative, small-town opponents: knuckle-draggers, rednecks, know-nothings (harkening back to an older time), and, of course, hillbillies.

Even back in the 1930s, the view of many secular-liberal Americans toward Appalachia and Scots-Irish-based Borderer cultures in the rest of America's interior certainly *was* patronizing. But these Borderers, though relatively poor, were also a source of income for many in the secular-liberal world, not least for those in the growing media empires like the ones of Hollywood. This was not quite so much true for the big studios (though they made out well in the small towns, too), but it certainly provided the bread and butter for the Poverty Row studios whose output was often tailored for the small venues that could not afford the rental for "A" movies. The little towns did not draw enough to be attractive to the chains the big studios supplied and sometimes owned, but they did want movies. Poverty Row supplied their small mom-and-pop cinemas.

After the war, with the growth of suburbia and a further shift of cultural power to urban centers, it became even less profitable for studios to cater solely to the small-town theaters. Also, there were enough films made now so that the less successful and the fading movies could be shifted to venues of lower profitability without incurring loss elsewhere. In addition, television, though centered on the powerful urban stations, was beginning to make inroads into smaller markets. This, coupled with cultural movements from the other side exemplified by actions such as the witch hunts of the House Un-American Activities Committee (HUAC), allowed the Borderer/secular-liberal divide to widen, growing to the point of ignorance where positive depictions of small-town or rural life were now considered naive by those within the urban media powerhouses, where even parodies of hillbillies (like the Ma and Pa Kettle movies) were taken as lowbrow humor themselves. Rather than seen as they actually were, that is, as urban visions of the country, they were taken by the metropole as country views of itself. Or even as the truth.

Because they are necessarily urban based, what the media present of rural and small-town life is rarely close to actual Borderer life. Certainly it has little relation to the reality behind the image. When it comes to the Borderers, the media just do not know what they are seeing. Even when media figures themselves have Borderer backgrounds, they have had to become immersed within a milieu dominated by secular-liberal sensibilities and preconceptions. Having shed much of the culture of their youth, a necessary trade-off for success in the new environment, not even *they* can go back home and report on it with any real understanding. Instead, they fall back to presenting nothing more than stereotypical images, ones generally created by others within the secular-liberal tradition, anyway, people with no direct experience of the culture so often being parodied.

* * * * *

Henry Shapiro, in the preface to his book *Appalachia on Our Mind*, writes,

> We insist that ideas are not natural emanations from objective reality but are the creation of men, and stand between consciousness and reality; and that insofar as ideas become the surrogates for experience and representations of reality, they become also the subjects of discourse and the objects of action. It was not reality that concerned those who saw Appalachia's existence as a bothersome fact to be explained or altered, but reality defined in a particular way.[3]

So it has long been with the media. It is the defining, not the truth about the Borderers or small-town America in general, that has created the resentments that have in turn helped deepen much of the current American cultural and political divide. Unfortunately, the defining is done primarily on one side (or was, until the rise of conservative talk radio and Fox News): that side with the media power. And that is not, of course, the Borderer side—even today.

As Dwight Billings writes in his introduction to *Back Talk from Appalachia*, there is no singularity to Borderer culture anyway, making stereotyping and singularity even more distant from any actuality: "While the peoples and cultures in the Appalachian Mountains are decidedly plural, outside the region in the arts, the academy, and popular culture, many representations of them now, as for the past one hundred years, are often monolithic, pejorative, and unquestioned."[4] Billings, writing before 2000, goes on, a few pages later,

> Television networks recycle endless repeats of *The Beverly Hillbillies* and *Dukes of Hazzard* on cable. . . . Hollywood has not only brought a new version of *The Beverly Hillbillies* to the big screen but has contributed *Next of Kin* as well, the laughably violent story of eastern Kentuckians who arm themselves with antique firearms. . . . But this is nothing new for Hollywood. Appalachian scholar J. W. Williamson reports that in its early days the film industry made more than four hundred silent movies exploiting the nation's fascination with Appalachian feuds and moonshine making.[5]

This exploitation has never stopped; witness the 2012 television miniseries *Hatfields & McCoys* and John Hillcoat's movie *Lawless*, also of 2012.

* * * * *

To some degree, Williamson limits his discussion in *Hillbillyland*, his study of Appalachia in the movies, to the stereotypes themselves. Taking on lives of their own, these stereotypes have become an active force in shaping cultural oppositions in America, building on ethnic and cultural distinctions that are centuries old, arising even before arrival in North America. These have helped deepen the cultural divide between Borderer and secular-liberal, building resentments that the often clueless media establishment rarely notice even as they perpetuate them.

To understand this, we need only look so far as the western, a type of movie closely associated with small-town audiences (especially in its early day) and once made specifically for them, made with recognition of their specific cultural and entertainment traditions. As Peter Stanfield points out,

> As Westerns are allegorical forms especially open to reinvention, producers of Westerns understood that their films were presenting sets of

presupposed meanings, which their audience recognized as allegories on the state of the nation. ... Moreover, series Westerns display a marked use of nineteenth-century performance traditions drawn from theatrical melodramas, song forms, variety skits and blackface minstrelsy. These anachronisms help form a shared imagined heritage for the series Western's audience.[6]

Though, early on, westerns were strongly reflective of vaudeville and melodrama traditions, the genre changed after World War II (starting right before the war, actually, with John Ford's 1939 movie *Stagecoach* providing something of a bridge but with the big push coming later), becoming a powerful A-picture genre with a new focus. The career of John Wayne shows the arc. He began his career in westerns working for Republic Pictures, where, generally, he saved the town. *Stagecoach* moved his career up a level. During the war, his nonwestern pictures focused on battle, on leadership, and on groups of men. After the war, his roles were as loners, more and more, as men with little need for others and little desire to respond to their wants—even when he led them. Perhaps his greatest role, as Ethan Edwards in John Ford's 1956 film *The Searchers*, shows a man determined to sacrifice anything in order to reach his goal—even the lives and well-being of others he loves.

Though he never resonated with the baby-boomer generation, which looked to different kinds of film rebels, to actors like Marlon Brando and James Dean, Wayne certainly influenced younger actors, including those two, just as he would soon for other actors who played to the individualist tradition, stars like Paul Newman (when he was younger), Steve McQueen, Lee Marvin, and others. The difference between audience views of Wayne and those who followed appears to have been primarily political and cultural, Wayne coming down on the conservative side of things (the Borderer side) in the 1960s. In terms of screen image, there is probably very little difference, looking back from half a century on. The media establishment saw that the new individualist could be used across cultural and political boundaries.

That the western had changed—and Wayne with it—is a reflection of cultural change but also and more significantly of the change in media power in the culture at large, of the centralization of media and the increased control over it within the moneyed establishment of the East Coast and West Coast. In addition, it was a result of that weakening of the cultural and political strength of the small towns and of the rise of the suburbs. The audiences that had given Wayne his start were still there and still supported his movies. It was his roles in them that had greatly changed, making him marketable to a much wider audience.

Before World War II, American westerns presented what later came to be seen as a "naive" view of Borderer frontier culture and its conflicts. The "good" of the Scots-Irish-based and European immigrant and settler population was not just an underlying assumption but was a central and explicit thesis in these movies, most made by Poverty Row studios such as Republic Pictures and Monogram Pictures and distributed to rural and small-town theaters. After all, they were intended to be seen by the grandchildren of the very people portrayed. By the 1950s, this was no longer the case, the distance a generation greater. At the same time, the movie western had moved firmly into the "mainstream" controlled by secular-liberal sensibilities. Along with a changing social and political climate and better production values, actors, writers, and distribution, this led to a western quite different from what had been presented before. Though many of the westerns of the 1950s are among the best the genre has ever seen, something is lost whenever a change of this magnitude occurs. In this case, it was the people of the towns of the westerns who were lost.

Protection of the people once having been the rationale behind the action of the western, they now found themselves playing—at best—the role of oppressor in scenarios where attention is turned to other problems. In many instances they even found they had now disappeared completely from any foreground consideration. Questions concerning an alien (to the older rural and small-town audiences) sort of individualism and a new sort of personal morality (responding to the concerns of the growing urban/suburban audiences) unknown to them were now beginning to dominate the genre.

It is true, of course, that the negative side of rural and small-town Americans (scathingly parodied at least since the time of Mark Twain) had long been recognized in the western—witness the deliberate drawing on cliché in the expulsion of dance-hall girl Dallas and alcoholic Doc Boone from the town of Tonto, New Mexico, at the start of *Stagecoach*—but the essential "goodness" of the American people generally triumphed. It does so, too, in *Stagecoach*, where the passengers on the stage, pointedly including Dallas and Boone, prove to be the "real" salt-of-the-earth Americans—not the sour people in the town left behind. Yet, after World War II, the "good" population began to disappear from sight in the western. Even in *Stagecoach*, right before the war, a split was portrayed between the people of the West and the more "gentrified" officer class of the cavalry, representing the distant urban elite and the rational authority of the federal government. After the war, the split widened so far that the townspeople could no longer be seen over it.

Other divisions shown in *Stagecoach* point in the same direction. Each of the people in the stage represents something apart from the townspeople left behind in Tonto—and many of them prove to be, in one way or another, better for it. Dallas, the prostitute, presents a morality out of keeping with the prudes who drive her away—along with Doc Boone, an alcoholic doctor. Not only is he an open alcoholic, but Boone's very profession sets him apart from the people of the town. Joining them is a whiskey drummer, a traveling salesman—never to be trusted, though this one seems one of the meekest of the breed. There is also the wife of a cavalry officer, a gambler, a banker trying to escape town with embezzled funds, and, eventually, an outlaw. Except for the banker, these are all outsiders. And even the banker, an exploiter and a thief, is unacceptable to the culture of the western towns. But the passengers on the stage are also the people the film portrays most favorably, except, again, for the banker.

Why is this? What was happening to the tried-and-true formula of the western (those in which the townspeople need a hero/protector), to this genre that was now making its first forays into the top tiers of American cinema?

Why, also, two decades after *Stagecoach*, was a cultural split added to *The Magnificent Seven* (John Sturges, 1960), the Hollywood remake of *Shichinin no samurai* (Akira Kurosawa, 1954)? In the original, the townspeople are simply poor and oppressed; they share a cultural background with the samurai they hire to protect them as well as with the audience, the people who were expected to see the film. In the American remake, the townspeople are alien—to their protectors and to most of the film's intended American audience. Why? Why make it a *Mexican* town in need of protection by *Americans*?

Why was *Shane* (George Stevens, 1953) one of the last movies to follow the older pattern, such a throwback that it has seemed, to urban viewers since, incredibly naive? Why is the attitude toward the hero associated with older westerns vested most clearly, in *Shane*, in a child?

There are two answers to these questions. They are not contradictory but are complementary, though only one has been adequately explored. Speaking of *The Magnificent Seven* along with *The Alamo* (John Wayne, 1960), Stanley Corkin says,

> Both films ... see the role of western heroes as geographically wide-ranging and the frontier itself as a place lacking not civilization per se but the correct manner of civilization and the necessary forces to define that state correctly. However, in keeping with the sense of national

disquiet that preceded the presidential election of 1960 and upon which Kennedy built, both films are explicitly concerned with lands that are under the government of another nation.[7]

The "correct manner of civilization" is, of course, a secular-liberal conceit, a way of acknowledging the cultural divide without naming it. In this view, also, the topic of the films is not really America or its population at all but rather its place in the world, a reaffirmation of American strength and cohesion, projecting problems within to an external situation where they can be explored without too much self-examination or self-criticism. Or, as Richard Slotkin puts it, "The premise for *The Magnificent Seven* begins with the classic trope of American myth/ideology: the translation of class difference into racial difference, and the projection of an internal social conflict into a war beyond the borders."[8] Rather than presenting the struggles of a Borderer culture trying to put down roots and establish identity in the face of the same predatory bankers and politicians who had plagued their spiritual grandparents on the frontier of the 18th century, these westerns were now focused on external threats to what was, really, a mythical cohesive American culture (with attention subtly turned away from the people of Borderer culture), on showing the strength of that culture, and on distinct visions of the type of person best representing American ideals. In addition, they began to focus on the hero in a new way, making the hero not a savior, though still a self-contained individualist, but an antagonist to the surrounding culture.

Perhaps Slotkin does not go quite far enough when he writes of the translation of "class difference into racial difference." Certainly, the townspeople in *The Magnificent Seven* can be seen as stand-ins for African Americans beleaguered during the exploitative Jim Crow era with the bandits, of course, standing for American racist culture (though the bandits are of the same culture as the townspeople) and the seven as the equivalents of northern whites risking their livings by entering into a distant fray. But the differences involved are also cultural differences from inside white America, simplification of the problems into class or race masking a much more complex situation. In addition, the heroes are removed from cultural concerns anyway, for the most part, their conflicts becoming personal and internal.

The other answer is that small-town Borderer Americans had fallen completely out of favor by 1960, out of favor, at least, with the "New York and Hollywood elite" (whose negative attitude toward the rest of the country continues today, with some even calling the space between the coasts the "fly-over country"). Filmmakers could no longer see a way of making the white townsfolk seem worthy of protection without being accused of a naive and, eventually, racist viewpoint. For many, also, the McCarthy era of blacklists and low-level persecution, among other things (including the growing civil rights struggle), had soured them on the "everyday" American, though most continued to maintain their protective posture in terms of an idealized America and the rest of world.

Of course, acknowledgment in movies of the dangers of the intolerant and the mob certainly predate the McCarthy period, but in the earlier era this was leavened by at least a pretense of admiration for the pioneer spirit and strong religious belief that was imagined as the core of rural and small-town culture. In the postwar period, however, films extolling the life of small-town and rural America were increasingly seen as naive, as pap for television (and therefore unworthy of the theaters). *The Wizard of Oz* (Victor Fleming, 1939) and *It's a Wonderful Life* (Frank Capra, 1946) eventually became this in actuality through perpetual, annual holiday replays. With that increasing divisiveness associated with the civil rights movement and HUAC and McCarthyite investigations, American intellectuals and artists felt more and more alienated from what had once been considered the small-town "backbone" of America. In their eyes, the veneer of acceptance and toleration had been stripped away, revealing hate and venom beneath. Proving that a creative mind is one that can hold contradictory ideas simultaneously, many of them also saw America as the champion and exporter to the rest of the world of all that is right and good. But that was on the global stage, not for domestic consumption.

So it was that, in the eyes of many filmmakers, the only farmers worth protecting, by 1960, were poor Mexicans or other nonwhites, people who could learn from the American example but who did not carry the racist, small-minded baggage that had become so associated in the minds of the secular-liberal elite with the Borderer American. This was easier for the filmmaker, too, in that these non-American peoples could be shown as weaker, as less able, than it would have been possible to do with Anglo-Americans—with that massive Borderer audience around, people who just might have recognized a direct slap at them. So it is that *The Magnificent Seven* can be seen almost as racist in its depiction of the Mexicans and absolutely elitist in a way that *Shichinin no samurai*, even with its recognition of the samurai as a distinct class, is not.

The Magnificent Seven is no isolated example. The blockbuster western of the previous year, *Rio Bravo* (Howard Hawks, 1959), also excludes American townspeople. Though there are two mentions of crowds of people in town, the only characters (aside from gunslingers, cowboys, and Angie

Dickinson) given even the slightest prominence are the Mexican couple who own the hotel and, in a much briefer role, a Chinese undertaker. Hawks's elitism shows up in a number of other films but it is explicit here, where John Wayne's John T. Chance even turns down help from Pat Wheeler (Ward Bond) and his men on the grounds that they are amateurs. The only one he accepts is a young gunfighter called "Colorado" and played by Ricky Nelson. Chance and Dude (Dean Martin) talk about him:

CHANCE: It's nice to see a smart kid for a change.

DUDE: I wonder if he's as good as Wheeler said.

CHANCE: I'd say he was. I'd say he was so good he doesn't feel he has to prove it.

This is the real individualist, the person with such confidence that he does not need the approval of anyone else. Today, such an elitism smacks of the attitudes of the neoconservative acolytes of the late Leo Strauss, a group that "hawks" (and both Wayne and Bond, for that matter) would be quite comfortable with. Strangely, it is also similar to the attitude identified with the "New York liberal and media elite" that the true small-town conservatives have long felt they were bitterly opposing. This is John T. Chance as Walter Lippmann, as we will see, but with his intellectual opponent John Dewey nowhere to be found. Nothing in this cultural divide, as in attitudes toward individualism itself, is simple or clear-cut.

Americans, both so-called elite and common, conservative and liberal, had come together remarkably during World War II, but many now felt betrayed by the very people they had fought and worked with, shoulder to shoulder. It did not matter one's class or political persuasion: Many people now felt that others who had claimed to be their friends were now doing them wrong. This is another reason for the divide that has dominated the American political landscape ever since, with each side imagining the moral high ground for itself, injury done only by the other. One other result, of course, has been a further retreat into an insular individualism.

As we have seen, this is no simple divide easily defined. The coastal elites often see the political conflict today as one between themselves as individuals and a corresponding conservative elite, who they see as lying to and manipulating a gullible populace—a feeling that points obliquely to why they often write the populace out of the movies. Those people are victims, too—but the "elite" are unable to see who the real villains are and blame the people. As a result, when they do show rural and small-town populations, they end up pointing out their inability to negotiate a complex cultural divide and their *own* contradictory feelings toward the other half of America. It is no wonder the secular-liberal "elite" have such a hard time reaching out to "average Americans," the present-day Borderers.

Though the Hollywood blacklist is looked back on as an abhorrent aberration, the conservative critics of Hollywood, then and now, do have a point: The film industry tends liberal. There is nothing surprising about this: People involved in the arts generally are more willing to take certain types of risks (outside of monetary risks), and risk is an inherently anticonservative undertaking. Different callings attract different mind-sets, anyway. Academia, where exploration of the unknown is supposed to be part of professional activity, is generally of a rather liberal bent. Business, on the other hand, where risk needs to be weighed much more carefully (given its greater consequences in economic arenas), leans to the conservative, as does government, where stability is the ultimate watchword. Media tend toward elitist sensibility. And it is, ultimately, a basic elitism that led to the degradation of the place of the small farmers and townspeople in the movies.

*****

In *High Noon* (Fred Zinnemann, 1952), the first great film of the new model of western individualism, Marshall Will Kane (Gary Cooper) cannot find sufficient townspeople to support him, even for their own good. His actions, furthermore, prove not to be for the good of the people (though he tries to couch them in those terms) but for the good of his own moral code.

When Johnny Logan rides to Vienna's in response to her summons in *Johnny Guitar* (Nicholas Ray, 1954), he rides below the dynamiting of a pass for the railroad and above a stagecoach robbery. The incidents box him in, the new and the old, setting up a situation of riled-up townspeople he has no control over and a conflict between two groups caused by the events he witnesses. Made just two years after *High Noon*, *Johnny Guitar* shared its release year with *Riding Shotgun* (André De Toth, 1954), *another* western where the townspeople turn on the hero, even if he is Randolph Scott.

In the western, the trend toward explicit mistrust—and then exclusion—of white townspeople can be traced at least as far back as *The Ox-Bow Incident* (William Wellman, 1943), something of an anomaly for its time and rather a box office failure (*Stagecoach* does not focus nearly so much on the actual townspeople of either Tonto or Lordsburg, merely using them as framing, as an initial and final backdrop). However, the movie is actually more sophisticated and more nuanced than those later movies that denigrate the townspeople, the ones that followed once the war was over. A lynch mob forms, yes, and the lynching is carried out, but the exploration is one of how this happens, not a simple, blanket condemnation of the participants. Also, *The Ox-Bow Incident* does not show leaders who are somehow better or worse than the townspeople. If anything, they are exactly as culpable.

None of these films could have been made before the start of the war. In fact, a film of *The Ox-Bow Incident* had been proposed since 1940, with no success. Yet even before the war, of course, some Americans worried about the impact of mob mentality—witness Sinclair Lewis's 1935 novel *It Can't Happen Here*—but the problems of economic depression and then external threat put off most consideration of this problem in film until the war was safely won and the economy was once more booming.

On the other hand, there were also plenty of films made just before the war and during it that could never have been made later—except those by the few directors still willing to pour what had come to seem simply syrup, people like George Stevens, whose *Miracle on 34th Street* (1947) is as nostalgic as his later *Shane*. Before the war, movies like *The Wizard of Oz*, though they certainly accented the difference between black-and-white Kansas and Technicolor Oz, could still focus on the value of a rural existence, lifestyle, and populace: After all, "there's no place like home." *It's a Wonderful Life*, released just after the end of the war, is even more patently nostalgic for a small-town Borderer culture—one that is beset by bankers just as the early Borderers in America were and just as the townspeople were in prewar westerns. But that sort of film became increasingly rare. Given that films were becoming targeted more and more often toward suburban audiences, letting television become the prime medium for the rest of the country, it is not surprising that during the 1950s these movies of an older type became holiday television staples aimed at "old-fashioned" audiences.

*****

As the western changed once the war was over, so did its definition. Robert Warshaw, in a 1954 essay, even went so far as to argue that much of what had been significant to the western (though he did not phrase it that way), including the townspeople, was actually irrelevant—and always had been.[9] As John Lenihan describes his view, "Matters of plot, secondary characters, and perspective merely provide background for the exploits and character of the hero. An *Ox-Bow Incident* or *High Noon* fails as a Western because a social problem and message remove the hero from the center of attention."[10] The women of the town could never save the day, as they do in *Destry Rides Again* (George Marshall, 1939). But this was a definition of the western as the new sort of John Wayne film fitting the needs of a new time, not of the genre as it had been or of what had once been the expectations of its primary audience.

Though they come from points of view across the political spectrum, the postwar films did begin to address questions being raised through HUAC and Joe McCarthy, even if only obliquely at first, questions about the role of the populace—and almost all of them come to the conclusion that the people are unable to take care of themselves on their own (a conclusion in keeping with earlier westerns)—a repudiation of John Dewey's belief that the people, given education and information, can best handle their own affairs. Both left and right were tending toward an elitism that disregarded the populace, leading to situations such as that of *High Noon*, where the film can be read as a polemic for disparate political points of view, as long as they are elitist, not populist. The individual as carrier of a social ideal is what is important, not the people.

Trying to put this in the best light possible, Lee Clark Mitchell writes of *High Noon*,

> Yet less important than pedigreeing any single reading of plot is the need to recognize how closely [screenwriter Carl] Foreman's liberal polemic resembles the arguments of those he attacked. McCarthy viewed liberals as responsible for selling out the nation; opponents instead viewed him as the threat to fundamental freedoms. But pro- and anti-McCarthyites shared a conviction as deep as anything dividing them: that the true enemy was civic complacency. And this capacity to provoke a common assessment of America's current malaise explains much of the film's appeal. No matter one's political stripe, all agree that the citizens of Hadleyville have regressed to a state of infantile dependency, requiring a paternal figure to protect them.[11]

Significantly, the marshal is no longer one of their own in the town. More specifically, he has decided to abandon the people he had served and is about to begin the process of setting up as a shopkeeper elsewhere. This turns the pattern of the classic Poverty Row western on its head. In those, the hero is quite often someone who left home long ago but has returned—either to avenge a wrong to himself or a member of his family or to protect a community he felt he had abandoned. The hero would more likely be the Frank Miller character in *High Noon*, returning to town to see that "justice" is done. Here, of course, Miller is evil. Of note, Miller and his gang come close to the hillbilly stereotype, characters such as the one played by Lee Van Cleef presaging the "degenerate" rapists of *Deliverance* (John Boorman, 1972).

Where Mitchell is wrong is in his suggestion that the enemy is "civic complacency." Yes, both the old conservatives and old liberals *were* similar, certainly in their disdain for what they would see as the lower-class American (the Borderer, actually). It was this similarity, of course, that was at the heart of the problems, not complacency. As a result of it, traditional northeastern Republicans never were able to fully take part in the new conservative movement of the late 20th century or of the Tea Party of the early 21st, movements sponsored by a new type of elite conservative, ironically, people who had made money not on a traditional base but elsewhere and who never looked to older wealth for guidance.

The putative split between liberals and conservatives in the 1950s was not as deep as the cultural split beneath it. Joe McCarthy was defeated not just by his own extravagance and alcoholism but also by the fact that he never was a part of the Republican establishment, which was as much a part of the secular-liberal establishment as the Democratic Party. He was a Borderer outsider *used* by an establishment that sought a temporary advantage through him. McCarthy imagined himself an individualist, but he was, in the final analysis, only a tool.

Even *Shane*, which does provide a sympathetic picture of small farmers faced with the anger of a rich cattleman who sees them encroaching on his range, shows that it is the hired professional (again, that archetypal individualist of the western, especially of the newer sort), ultimately, who will decide the issue—unless another professional, one who has, in this case, turned sentimental, blocks him. Here, however, we see a more direct reflection of the attitudes of the prewar (and postwar television) western, where the hero often really *does* play the role of savior. And this is probably why many of us who grew up in the postwar period, nursed on television westerns, found *Shane*, when we discovered it (for the most part in the 1960s, when we had developed our own "sophisticated" visions of film), naive and annoying. Mitchell calls the film "a distillation of the Western itself, glorifying the larger social processes of American history in a glowingly nostalgic mode."[12] More accurately, it is a distillation of what *had been* the western itself, glorifying something that had become increasingly problematic, especially in the more intellectually oriented corners of American society. Behind its gunslinger elitism, it promotes a Jeffersonian ideal that was increasingly seen as naive and passé, especially in a dangerous world where Lippmann's "realist" vision dominated both sides of the 1950s cultural divide.

Reflecting what was becoming the elite consensus, both from conservative and liberal sides, in *Public Opinion*, Lippmann writes,

Every democrat feels in his bones that dangerous crises are incompatible
with democracy, because he knows that the inertia of masses is such
that to act quickly a very few must decide and the rest follow rather
blindly. . . .

The democrats had caught sight of a dazzling possibility, that every
human being should rise to his full stature, freed from man-made limitations. With what they knew of the art of government, they could, no
more than Aristotle before them, conceive a society of autonomous
individuals, expect an enclosed and simple one. They could, then, select
no other premise if they were to reach the conclusion that all the people
could spontaneously manage their public affairs.[13]

This was written soon after the end of World War I. Lippmann's attitude had
become the underpinning of beliefs on both left and right (the "right" of
northeastern Republicans, that is) by the end of World War II. In a way this
is the underpinning of the cult of individualism in its postwar incarnation.
The people, once viewed as so strong and able, were now seen as weak, as
needing guidance:

Whether a conservative bemoaned liberal deviance from the constitutional framework of limited government or a liberal faulted
Eisenhower with inaction and drift, political criticism, like the
intellectual-social criticism of rampant conformity and individual anxiety, connoted dissatisfaction with an America that had lost all sense of
direction and purpose. America, it was believed, could ill afford such
weaknesses at a time when the rest of the world either challenged or
depended upon U.S. leadership.[14]

Such an attitude moves concern from the people to the leaders, heroes, or
antiheroes, for it is there that (in this view) any possible action or progress
originates.

*****

Though the dangers of the mob had been obvious to American intellectuals,
artists, and elite long before World War II, few of these people had felt its ire
personally, and they generally viewed what they imagined as the "common
person" with affection, though affection tempered with condescension.
Even the intellectuals attracted to communism and the idealistic left of the
1930s had believed that theirs was a task of converting essentially good-
hearted people, convincing them to see the truth and what was good for
them. Not only did they not understand that they were looking at the

"people" from the far side of a divide difficult to cross but they believed that the real enemy lay elsewhere.

Though there had long been persecuted Americans (lynchings were once common, of course), they had not previously included the educated and artistic elite. Now, however, they did—figuratively, at least (sometimes literally), and with the complicity of a part of the elite (until the McCarthyites went too far). To make matters worse, the persecutors and persecuted had recently made common cause against Germans and Japanese (with few on either side raising a peep about the internment of the Nisei, an action at least as bad, if not worse, than anything McCarthy sparked). The betrayal felt by the American left in the changed postwar situation was intense—and it soon began to show up in the movies in, as I said, an industry that (like most relating to the arts) relies on creative impulses that tend to come from people of liberal bent. This sense of betrayal did not show up simply in westerns: The movie of *Inherit the Wind* (Stanley Kramer, 1960) may present as negative a portrayal of small-town Americans as can be found anywhere this side of out-and-out parody, providing an indication of just how great the divide between the two Americas was becoming. The individual was now one who could stand up to the mob instead of, as had been the case, the one who protected the people.

The confusion felt by the left was unintentionally summed up early on in a 1945 Gary Cooper western *Along Came Jones* (Stuart Heisler). Cooper's character, Melody Jones, is mistaken for an outlaw with the same initials. To keep the townspeople from discovering the real outlaw, who is hiding out at her place, the outlaw's girlfriend, played by Loretta Young, feeds the frenzy against Jones. The idea is that the common people are easily duped, setting up the destruction of perfectly innocent people, victims of another's machinations and of manipulation of the crowd.

★★★★★

Movies showing the ire of the town relate to those showing the anger of the alienated, a film tradition with earlier roots that begins in earnest after World War II and that continues today in numerous incarnations, its greatest reach from its beginnings being, perhaps, the zombie (and related) movies. Their roots can be traced back to many things, including vampire tales, the Jewish golem tradition, and even to Mary Shelley's *Frankenstein* (though the zombies, one could argue, descend from the townspeople, not the monster). The zombies were not always the dead. They could even be something like, say, motorcycle gang members, like the characters in *The Wild One*

(László Benedek, 1953). Though the gangs, in this instance, are not portrayed as unrelentingly evil, they do seem to be, in large part, made up of emotional zombies.

Brando, of course, confirmed his individualist image with this movie, where he and Lee Marvin play heads of rival gangs terrorizing a small and sleepy town. His individual, though, is of a new type, like nothing imagined for Daniel Boone or by Henry Thoreau—or even Charles Lindbergh.

At one point, Brando's character, Johnny Strabler, is asked by a young woman who has learned that his gang is called the Black Rebels Motorcycle Club, "What are you rebelling against, Johnny?" After a beat, he replies, "What have you got?" This becomes the essence of 1950s cool, with "rebel without a cause" becoming the essential phrase for the alienated hero as well as the title of Nicholas Ray's 1955 film starring James Dean, the other epitome of young screen cool of that period.

Essential to any understanding of Brando's character in *The Wild One* is the motorcycle itself. An icon of freedom since at least the days of Tom Swift, it characterizes freedom on the ground—within society but no longer responsible to its strictures. At the end of *The Wild One*, Strabler comes back into the town to see the girl he has fallen for, giving her his one smile of the film (his affirmation that he is not, after all, a zombie) before leaving. The townspeople let him go without interference this time.

Compare that with the end of *Easy Rider* (Dennis Hopper, 1969), where the two main motorcyclist characters are gratuitously shot by a couple of "rednecks" in a pickup truck, the shooters being the zombies, this time. At the time of *The Wild One*, Hollywood's own alienation from a great part of the American public had not progressed to the point it would reach as a result of the passions of the Vietnam War—and the different ending reflects the change.

Since the time of *The Wild One*, the motorcycle has become an increasingly important symbol of the individualist in American popular culture. When John Kerry, while running for president in 2004, posed a number of times on motorcycles, he was generally laughed at—though he is, in fact, a motorcyclist. His straight-laced image just could not meld with the popular imagining of the motorcycle as an outlaw machine. Yet, by that time, many baby boomers who had never ridden motorcycles in their youth were taking up the machines, donning leather jackets and wrapping bandannas over their scalps—proclaiming freedom and individuality and staving off the staid image of preretirement years. Paradoxically, most of these riders are from Borderer backgrounds and the political right, quite far removed in their own lives from the stances of the motorcycle "outlaws" who were alienated from what was, essentially, Borderer society in the 1950s and 1960s.

In *The Wild One*, reconciliation across cultural divides is still considered possible, as the last interchange between Johnny and Kathie shows. It is not easy or simple and may not be effective—but the chance is there. The same is not true in *Easy Rider*, less than a short generation later. Though the two main characters, Wyatt and Billy, are drug runners and drifters, they are the "good guys" of the movie—and the two "rednecks" who do them in are stereotypically evil in a way that many secular-liberals, certainly by the 1960s, saw much of Borderer culture. There is no possible reconciliation.

The final scene of the movie begins by showing the two motorcyclists on the road to the sound of Roger McGuinn singing the first verse of Bob Dylan's "It's Alright Ma (I'm Only Bleeding)," one of the great 1960s songs of alienation and defeat. The verse played includes the lines

> To understand you know too soon
> There is no sense in trying.

The counterculture movement of the 1960s from whence the film arises was extremely conflicted over the role of the individual, but it fully embraced an alienation from at least the Borderer half of America's broader culture.

Though wanting communal activity and life, the great heroes of the youth of the 1960s were figures who reject the former and are conflicted about the latter, like Brando and Dean and Jack Kerouac's Dean Moriarty in *On the Road*. Kerouac's character is based on Neal Cassady, who would later have intimate connection with 1960s counterculture just as he had with 1950s Beats—he became the driver of the bus named "Further" that Ken Kesey and his "Merry Pranksters" painted in bright colors and used for crossing the country in 1964. These were all people who had given up "trying" in favor of "being." To them, the ending of *Easy Rider*, strangely enough, becomes not one of defeat but of triumph, for the characters die true to themselves, taking an unbending existential pose to their graves.

* * * * *

The cultural and political split that one sees today between the predominantly rural Borderer America and the much more urban secular-liberal America (with the suburbs somewhere between), though as old as the oldest American city, was exacerbated by McCarthyism after World War II and abetted by an entertainment industry shaken by the related controversies that threatened to tear it apart. The industry was changed in ways still evident, residual resentment toward small-town attitudes continually showing up in film, reflecting a feeling that it was the "red state" Americans (and not another faction of the elite) who were the cause of McCarthyite and HUAC persecutions—and who continue to want to attack the intellectual and artistic communities of the country. The retreat from social causes led to a changed type of individualism, one based on a rejection of society and not a rising above it. Hero status was gained ironically and by disapprobation, not by adulation.

*****

Often remarked upon, the implications of the changes in the United States on the heels of World War II are rarely really examined in terms of the broader American perception of rural and small-town communities except in noting their gradual disappearance while examining the growing suburbs. A passing lament for *rural* decline is usually all one hears. Instead, even the cultural historians have concentrated on the new, the young, the urban, and the suburban that were now becoming the focus of American society. And why not? After all,

> this [postwar] economy favored young adults as never before. First, a rapidly expanding postwar labor market was absorbing a generation originating in the low fertility period of the late 1920s. This would create a tight labor market, which in its turn would push up wages. There was also a massive government subsidization for adult education in the immediate postwar years through the GI Bill, which resulted in a major increase in years of schooling for a large share of the population who would never have been able to afford the schooling. These two factors help to explain a major shift of young workers into higher status and better paying jobs.[15]

These factors also help explain the rise of a new vision of Borderer culture in general: Many of these newly educated, well-paid young people may have been from small towns, but they had turned their backs on their homes; they now populated the new suburban tract houses springing up near every urban center. They did not want to hear about what was, to them, the past. America, after all, was racing into the future—and they expected to go with it.

The dramatic nature of the changes at that time can be seen in the changing nature of employment, once dominated by rural activities:

> In 1910, half of the native white stock was still occupied in farming, com-
> pared with only about one-sixth of the foreign white stock.... The
> foreign white stock's labor supply was directed principally toward meeting
> the labor demands of industrialization in the larger towns and cities,
> particularly the requirements for manual labor.... The native white
> stock also dominated business and craft occupations in the smaller towns
> and villages.[16]

This predominance of farming had pretty much disappeared by World War II,
and the percentage of the working population involved in agriculture continued to slide even afterward, with not 12 percent of white Americans (and only
19 percent of black Americans) making their livings as farmers in 1950.[17]
Furthermore, while "in 1900, about two thirds of the native white stock lived
in rural areas, by 1950 close to two-thirds were in urban areas."[18] Clearly, the
action, in this "new" America, centered more than ever on the cities—and
even the "native white stock" (and, though to a lesser degree, the African
Americans) were finally getting their piece of it.

American culture was rapidly emerging into a new configuration. The suburbs were suddenly growing at an astonishing rate, and the cities were experi-
encing a serious population shift as the upwardly mobile opted for that ranch
house with its carport and deep backyard. On the other hand, the money, if
there had ever been much, that had left the small, rural towns during the
Depression did not return—at least not in comparison to the wealth now accru-
ing to the new "metropolitan areas." This change, in particular because the shift
in wealth was so clear, also affected how different parts of America were viewed.

The rural population now seemed even poorer, older, and more quaint
than it had in the period between the wars—books like James Agee and
Walker Evans's *Let Us Now Praise Famous Men* showing white poverty in
the depression notwithstanding. Though there had been depictions of "hillbillies" in film and elsewhere for more than half a century (or even further
back to Mark Twain's Pap Finn and before), the rise in popularity of Ma
and Pa Kettle, starting with *The Egg and I* (Chester Erskine, 1947), with its
pattern of story centering on the couple's interactions with the "new" world,
accented the desire of many of the children of Borderer families to put the
"mountains" behind them—to be part of the new sophisticated urbanite
population that knew, as did Robert Mitchum's character in *Thunder Road*
(Arthur Ripley, 1958), how to order in a fancy restaurant and even could tell
what a mobile sculpture is.

In a certain respect, the Kettle movies exacerbated a filmic debasement
of what has since been further reduced into the political catchphrase

"small-town values," values that had once actually been seriously examined (for better and worse), in Hollywood movies. More and more frequently, especially in film, Americans now found mainly caricatures of rural life (or of community) or discovered that rural and small-town Americans were serving simply as the backdrop for explorations of new visions of alienated individualism.

Given the cultural and economic situation of the time, it should not be surprising that the attention of much of America turned away from the problems of survival faced by small-town and rural American communities. Focus was now on new questions centering on urban life and myth, many of them focusing on individual identity and on national and generalized (as opposed to local and specific) responsibility. The Depression was over anyway, and the American spotlight had been forced away from home by war and its aftermath; the individual, having had to subsume personal desire in the national effort, now had the opportunity to let personal desires dominate. The federal government, once generally a distant specter, now played up close and personal in almost all American lives, providing both counterpoint and companion to personal desire. While people and the media emphasized the individual "me," everything, in fact, was becoming more centralized and unified—bringing new sets of problems and even responsibilities along with certain advantages. These competing yet coupled trends also found reflection in the arts, particularly in the popular arts.

Of course, even in the new urban-centric America, entertainment for rural communities continued. Radio, with its high population penetration and relatively cheap community-based broadcasting arm, was the mainstay in the countryside into the 1960s, even while television was sweeping up urban and suburban attention. The movies, however, were in a much more unsure position. Fearing the small screen, Hollywood was in the midst of an attempt to make sure its products would be differentiated from what could be shown on television, leading to expensive innovations such as the dynamic widescreen 1.85:1-ratio picture that soon became standard and the even wider Panavision/CinemaScope (up to 2.35:1) formats, along with elaborate productions with mis-en-scène detail impossible to discern through the muddy television picture of the time, changes that boosted the costs of moviemaking. Together, all of this added up to a perceived necessity of aiming for the broadest market possible with each picture. And that, after the war, meant focusing on the suburban market. Fewer and fewer movies were made specifically for small-town and rural markets.

One of the exceptions was *Thunder Road*, which ran for years in small the-aters in Appalachia, becoming something of the *Gone with the Wind* of the mountains.

The Poverty Row studios, which had relied more heavily on rural audi-ences for their successes, were not able (or were not farsighted enough) to capitalize on the changes in culture and population after the war. Their out-put dwindled, and by the 1950s they had pretty much disappeared from the scene (though a new type of B operation aimed at youth audiences would soon replace them). As a result, though there were still occasional paeans to rural life and community even from the major studios, such as *I'd Climb the Highest Mountain* (Henry King, 1951), these looked increasingly passé and even naive, given the new cultural focus on urban situations and on that new type of individualism personified by the Beats or by characters like Brando's Johnny Strabler in *The Wild One*. As we have seen, Johnny is the alienated individual, a new phenomenon, a person with no goals and, more important, no family ties, so fitting in neither older vision of individualism. The breaking of family bonds in this type of alienation can also be seen, of course, in the Stark family of *Rebel without a Cause*, presenting a challenge to the myths of both of the major American cultures.

*****

It was not only the young, the Beats, leftist artists, and intellectuals who felt alienated after the war. To be effective, "Tailgunner Joe" McCarthy spoke to another sense of growing alienation—a new sense of removal from what many people in American Borderer culture had once thought of as "theirs." The country, at least through the way it was portraying itself in the rapidly expanding electronic media, was moving in directions at odds with their hopes and dreams—away from what they thought American had been and could be. McCarthy's accidental genius was to stumble on a focus for the inchoate resentments that many of the more rural Americans were discover-ing within themselves.

While political strength, perhaps, rested to a slightly greater extent with the more conservative strain of America (now that the Depression was over), the media strength, for all of the blacklists and hearings, remained with the "liberal elite." The "common folk" were no longer simply appearing as basi-cally decent, hardworking, and willing but were now portrayed as cowardly—once the veneer is scraped off—and unwilling to stand up for what, deep down, even they know is right and proper. Or, as in *A Face in the Crowd*, they were just stupid, easily bamboozled.

Reflecting an urban sensibility, many of the films of the time, as I have said, even seemed to get rid of "the people" altogether. They had more akin with John Steinbeck's youthful view of the city than with rural life, where population paucity brings each individual into a position of importance: "During all this time, I never once knew or saw one New Yorker as a person. They were all minor characters in this intense personal drama."[19] This was a far cry from the worlds Steinbeck himself would create, where the individual is irrevocably connected with community—a vision that had begun to seem passé and a little naive during the postwar period, though it should never have been given the short shrift that it experienced. It does, however, reflect the aesthetic of, among others, film noir, an urban genre of extreme secular-liberal sensibilities.

In reference to James Mangold's 2007 remake of Delmer Daves's 1957 *3:10 to Yuma*, *New York Times* film critic A. O. Scott wrote, "The best of the old westerns were dense with psychosexual implication and political subtext. Often dismissed, then and now, as naive celebrations of dubious ideals, they were in many ways more sophisticated than their self-consciously critical (or 'revisionist') heirs."[20] This itself may seem to be something of a revisionist point of view, given the decades of seeing the westerns of the 1950s in particular as head and shoulders above any others before or since, but revisionism is not always simply an attempt to get out from under the prevailing wisdom. Sometimes, and this may be one such time, the revisionist may be right. The sweeping away of the older western as naive and simplistic was itself part of the cultural change America experienced on the heels of World War II. It replaced an older model that concentrated on individualism within social contexts with examination of individualism focused on the inner dynamics of the character, a much more clearly Freudian model. Not everyone had wanted the change, though, and sometimes even felt squeezed out by the "new" America. Certainly, the Borderers did not want it.

One of the odd things about the shift in focus in the western is that, even though it was now moving to reflect new urban sensibilities, it ultimately reverted to what seemed like a reflection of that older sense of individualism that the Borderer population had held for generations before falling into what can appear to have been an idea of individualism much more in keeping with the traditions of New England and urban America. The difference is, however, that the traditional Borderer view keeps family and friends as part of individualism's purview, as we have seen, while the responsibility for equality and fairness, so important to secular liberalism, anchored the concept in much of the rest of the country. The new alienated individual fit neither of the old patterns, but it was something that the artistic temperament of the coasts could encompass and make part of their own conceptions (for it really did not conflict with their own older views), while, to the Borderers, it was a direct threat to the responsibilities that they believe an individual must hold.

As we have seen, one of the most widely remembered of the postwar films portraying the new individualism and attempting to show the reasons for alienation is *High Noon*. Though the film presents a cast with experience in westerns going back to the 1930s and whose association with the genre would continue through the 1960s, *High Noon* was, in many ways, not just a new sort of western but also a statement of a new political vision of the role of the individual. The model of the lawman or other savior working for and with the community is turned on its head in more ways than our earlier discussion shows; here, the lawman acts through personal commitment and ideals, both greater and more individual than the specifics of the town or even its perceived needs. Here, the loner is indeed alone, but not as a rebel like Brando in *The Wild One* or even as rebels in other westerns, whose loneliness, as in *Shane*, can come from personal moral conflict and inability to deal with community. No, here it is the loneliness of the idealist, an egotistical faith (as some would see it) that places belief before people—an idea completely alien to Borderer culture but somewhat able to coexist with urban sensibilities. As a result, the townspeople (who do not understand that the marshal's ideals would ultimately save them—or do not want to) abandon him, perhaps reflecting the betrayal felt by some of those associated with the film—including Zinnemann, screenwriter Carl Foreman (who also wrote an early draft for *The Wild One*), and actor Lloyd Bridges—during that era of Hollywood witch hunts.

In the film, while responsibilities of the individual toward ideals (and not toward people) are emphasized, the position of the townspeople (and the wife) is correspondingly debased. This, I am sure, was not the intent of the filmmakers, whose point deals with the individual standing against the forces of evil—here represented not by the townspeople but by a killer and his gang. Similarly, in *A Face in the Crowd*, the point was to show how crass the manipulation of the public could be—the implied insult to that public for being so easily fooled (instead of scared, as in *High Noon*) may not have been consciously meant by director Elia Kazan or by writer Budd Schulberg (both of whom had faced HUAC and had "named names"), but it is there, nonetheless.

So focused were the filmmakers on their own points and on self-justification, perhaps, that they did not see that others might not also be zeroing in on the individual as idealist but might be considering the depiction of the community—or the individual as responsible first to parts of the community (family and friends) immediately. One film where this conflict is almost screamingly evident is, again, *Inherit the Wind*, where the population of the town, with its adherence to fundamentalism, is presented, though almost accidentally, as venal and small-minded.

Other films of the time that tried to get rid of community in order to concentrate on concerns of the individual and idealism and individualism include *The Searchers*. It fails to remove community completely, however, providing a counterpoint to Ethan Edward's (John Wayne) obsession through the desire of Martin Pawley (Jeffrey Hunter) to marry and return to society once he has fulfilled his commitment to the memory of the family that raised him. Both characters harken back to the returning savior of earlier westerns, but Edward's single-minded passion takes it into a new direction. A similar emphasis on the individual with a corresponding pushing of the community into the background became a hallmark of film noir where, as in *The Asphalt Jungle* (John Huston, 1950), the city often seems all but empty except for criminals and cops. "The dark, depopulated look for the film"[21] *Crossfire* (Edward Dmytryk, 1947), a movie whose director and producer (Adrian Scott) would find themselves among the "Hollywood 10" before HUAC, may have allowed for a close look at anti-Semitism, but it also reduced community to close to zero. Idealism wins out; personal relations wither.

Film noir, by the late 1940s, had begun to have an influence on westerns, helping push group responsibilities back in favor of study of an individual as an alienated loner but also as an idealist. *Pursued* (Raoul Walsh, 1947), for example, brushes aside questions of community for a Freudian examination of past on present.

＊＊＊＊＊

The loss of the importance of community in film must certainly have been in the back of Robert Mitchum's mind when he wrote the story for *Thunder Road*. The star of *Pursued* may have been remembering past pictures of his where the individual is everything—or might even have been thinking back to *The Night of the Hunter* (Charles Laughton, 1955), where he showed how an individual can twist a community's beliefs into terror. Whatever the reason, Mitchum now created what was becoming a rarer sort of loner, one with ties to his family that he, quite consciously, will not sever but that have been irreparably torn:

As the returned soldier Lucas Doolin, Mitchum somehow stands outside of the events in which he is participating. He is nostalgic for a past that he has lost and is not able to recover. Too much affected by the war, his connection with family and community has been severed beyond repair. At one point Lucas says, "I know what I want. I wanna stop the clock, turn it back to another time in this valley that I knew before." He knows that he can't stop that clock and he knows what his fate will inevitably be. Mitchum was a great actor, and there is a cool intelligence at work in *Thunder Road*, both behind and in front of the camera. It is this cool intelligence which lends structure to *Thunder Road* and, in the end, makes it work.[22]

Mitchum's personality and background certainly were critical factors to the creation of *Thunder Road*, as might be expected, given that he wrote the story, produced the film, had a hand (uncredited) in the directing, and co-wrote the songs. Son a of Scots-Irish South Carolinian, Mitchum clearly felt a kinship with the mountain people who surrounded him as he made the film from a base in Ashville, North Carolina. Even his method of working fit well with the culture he now saw around him:

The way they made those B Westerns [that were Mitchum's start in the movies], no frills, no pretense, just-get-it-done, strict egalitarianism—everybody swallowed the same dust, ate the same chow, used the same honey wagon—this would remain in Robert Mitchum's mind the ideal, the most comfortable and lease embarrassing way of making movies, an approach he would try to encourage no matter how far from those innocent and threadbare productions his career would take him.[23]

The first we see of the hollow at the heart of the movie is a view of a neat farm down a dirt road. The buildings may be old, but they appear well kept. The house may be hand built of rough wood, but the porch and its pillars are straight, and everything is in its place. The kitchen, when we see it, is large and tidy, and "Ma" is ironing. She is certainly in command in the house, even forcing grace before meals on her sons.

Everyone in the movie works, in some form or another. Even the teenage girl, Roxanna Ledbetter, does, minding the family store. When the Doolin brothers talk about the car that Lucas uses for running moonshine, they fuss about it, clearly capable and knowledgeable. The younger brother, though he has not reached his majority, is obviously already a master mechanic. All of this is in direct opposition to the stereotypes of Appalachian Borderers.

And it all shows a type of individualism that had generally been superseded in film by the 1950s.

High Noon and *Thunder Road* share a number of thematic elements. Each features a local populace, the law, a gang, a loner hero, and a love interest—actually two in each case, one representing passion and the past and the other idealism and the future. The difference between the usage of each feature, thematically, is that Mitchum's movie does not back away from consideration of any of these elements, while *High Noon* ultimately pushes aside all but the hero, his individualism and his idealism, reducing even his love interest from an independent actor to simply his lone support. In *High Noon*, as in secular-liberal culture in general, the individual is committed to ideals. In *Thunder Road*, as in Borderer culture, the individual is committed to family.

To make its point unmuddied, *High Noon* has to show the town's folk backing away from the marshal (significantly, he is not a sheriff with authority coming from the community but a marshal, with authority stemming from a distant central authority). Though this is a device necessary to the progression of both plot and theme, it does distort any image of the people, making them (as a whole) an object of scorn. The last scene shows them trickling back, now that the Marshal Kane has saved them. Kane, however, in what is probably an accidental bow to Borderer sensibilities, is embracing his wife. But they no longer need the others.

In *Thunder Road*, on the other hand, the local community is extremely involved in what goes on with Lucas Doolin, both for good and for bad. No one imagines that the pressures faced because of gangster Kogan are anything but the responsibility of the group. In fact, when Kogan approaches each moonshiner with an offer to include him in his new network, the answer he gets from each is the same, as Vernon Doolin tells his son, "They all said they'd let 'em know." Nobody is willing to act without consulting the others. When they do meet, it is while their wives and children are in church—that central symbol of Appalachian and early American community—and they meet with the blessing of the preacher. In contrast with that of *High Noon*, the last scene shows a caravan of cars bringing Lucas Doolin's body back home to his community while his younger brother holds hands with the young woman who represents the future of the family.

In *Thunder Road*, the law is represented by Treasury Agent Troy Barrett, played by Gene Barry, who would soon become television's Bat Masterson, a dapper, citified lawman in the Wild West. He does not hate the moonshiners, and they know it. They say to one another that the revenuers do not kill—a sign of a certain amount of respect or, at least, understanding on the part of the lawmen. However, it is the law, ultimately implacable and unyielding, that sets up Doolin's death.

The law, in the person of the marshal in *High Noon*, is just as implacable and unyielding. How much so is indicated by his very name, Will Kane (an indication, also, that the movie is not attempting realism as much as it desires to make a point). This is a story meant to show the importance of the "will" of the individual and the law, to be followed even if it means acquiring the "mark of Cain" that will condemn this upholder of law and order to wander from place to place, never finding community—or even family (it really makes no sense, in terms of the film's setup, that Kane's wife becomes an integral part of the climactic battle and reunites with him; this was probably necessitated by worries about alienating a large part of the American audience). The intent of creating such a cowardly populace was not simply to comment on any general timidity (though that can be an important point) but to allow room for Kane to deal with his own commitment to law and ideals. Even so, the movie provides a slap in the face to small-town pride, which (in much of America) contains the Borderer ideal that the community can and will stand up for itself—that it does not even need others (like a marshal from outside) to act for it.

In contrast, the law in *Thunder Road*, though just as dedicated, acts neither for the community nor in unsympathetic opposition to it. When Roxanna Ledbetter shows up at Barrett's house, she is treated with compassion by his wife Mary. The cultural differences illustrated by the suburban-style middle-class house and the much more rustic dwellings of the hollow are used simply to show distance, not lack of understanding. Still, as in *High Noon*, the law of *Thunder Road* is removed from the people and is forced on a reluctant populace. The difference is that, in the former movie, it is for the people's good, whether they understand that or not, a point of view maintained most strongly in the metropole. In the latter, the law is seen as, at best, a necessary evil or, at least, a force that can only be avoided, never defeated—much more of a Borderer conception.

In both movies, the gang of outlaws is headed by a man with a clear agenda. In *High Noon*, it is to take revenge on the marshal who had sent him to prison. In *Thunder Road*, it is to create an illegal whiskey syndicate covering manufacture, transportation, and distribution. The town in the western had been "cleaned up" by the marshal some years in the past, in the older tradition of the western, bringing in the rule of law and sending the miscreants to the state penitentiary. Now, his work may come undone, sending the town back to a brutal past. This, again, is part of the myth of the West as understood in the metropole. The gang attempting to take over the moonshine business, on the other hand, is centered in the city, reaching out to the hollow as just another instance of a metropole trying to control the periphery. Doolin, representing the rural community, is able to take care of the gang—perhaps the most famous moment in the movie comes when he coolly flicks a cigarette onto the lap of the driver of a gangster car trying to force him off the road—while Kane has to defeat the gang not just for himself but also for his ideals—and almost incidentally for the community, which has already proven unable to do it for itself.

Though both Doolin and Kane dissociate themselves from their communities, the purposes and meanings of their loner and individualist status are quite different. Doolin had been torn from his community by the military, another intrusion by the metropole. He learned too much of the greater world while away but was too tied to his family to leave it completely. The role of whiskey runner, then, proved perfect for him, allowing him to indulge himself in the city with his woman there while returning frequently to the home base he needed for spiritual survival. The situation, as it was before the Kogan gang showed up, suited him.

Kane, on the other hand, neither came from the community nor planned on remaining in it. The movie takes place on the day of his leaving—or attempted leaving—with a new bride and hopes of a new life. Clearly, he has no real connection to the community, nor has he a concern for its future. His concern for the town is simply a result of his personal code of duty. In many respects, Kane exemplifies the newly dominant form of the western hero, the individualist who does not need community—a type taken to a further extreme by John T. Chance in *Rio Bravo*, who actually refuses help—the ultimate alienated idealist, the professional. If so, Doolin plays a different role, one seen in many older westerns, of the man who returns, who works with the community even though he must, at times, act alone (doing so for his family and not for his own needs).

Both movies stick to stereotypes concerning the women. The "old" loves, women involved in entertainment (a saloon owner and a nightclub singer), are both dark. The two representing the future are fair. In *High Noon*, however, Amy Kane has little history with the town and is intent on taking her new husband from it. *Thunder Road*'s Roxanna Ledbetter is firmly embedded in the community of the hollow (her family owns the local store) but is never able to entice Lucas to stay back "home."

In *Thunder Road*, there is hesitation on the part of the people of the hollow when faced by "bad guy" Kogan, but they do not abandon Lucas Doolin as the townspeople of *High Noon* do Will Kane. To Kane, the simple life is an imagined future with his Quaker wife. To Doolin, the simple life of home and family is no longer possible: "But that's long gone, now. My head's full of so many other things. I've been across an ocean, met all the pretty people. I know how to read an expensive restaurant menu; I know what a mobile is." Still, unlike Kane, he is never completely pushed away by the community, nor does he abandon home. In fact, as the ending of the movie makes quite clear, his death wrenches the community.

Oddly, the fact that Kane lives and Doolin dies shows how much more sophisticated and nuanced was Mitchum's vision than that of the creators of *High Noon*; for all that, *High Noon* is considered the classic and *Thunder Road* merely a drive-in phenomenon. At the end of *High Noon*, the towns-people return to Kane in what is really a naive vision of a future where they recognize they were wrong, that he, acting alone, had saved them. But that does not satisfy: A community dependent on an individual has no future— nor does a relationship that has forced the wife to cast aside fundamental beliefs to try to save her strong-willed husband. Mitchum's movie, on the other hand, displays an understanding that the individual acting alone and by his own lights is as much a threat as a savior.

In *High Noon*, the actions of the individualist have brought unwanted attention on the community. In *Thunder Road*, two young men influenced by Doolin die—and he recognizes that they have served as his stand-ins; he understands that death has to stop before his own brother becomes a third, and it does stop, though through Doolin's own demise. By removing Kane so completely from the community of *High Noon*, such questions of influence and responsibility regarding the community are elided.

* * * * *

This is one of the major differences between the views of individualism in the Borderer and secular-liberal culture up at least through the 1960s: the respon-sibility of the individual. The tradition of personal responsibility to family and friends before ideals or laws remains strong in Borderer society, so much so that, to outsiders, it can make them look clannish and suspicious of outsiders. When another vision of individual responsibility intrudes, one like that of the secular-liberal one where responsibility is to personal ideals and not to others, a conflict is sure to follow. Neither side is in a position to understand the other, and the belief of each infringes on the other. Movies, which tend to simplify and accent cultural differences, present the results of culture clashes surrounding questions of what an individual should do but, unfortunately, primarily from one cultural viewpoint only, that of the secular-liberal. The same was true of much of the rest of popular media up until the rise of conservative talk radio in the 1980s.

One of the reasons for the success of the talk radio format is that it provides an outlet for frustrations that had built up for years against media that was seen as unresponsive—indeed, antagonistic—to Borderer sensibilities. Given the way they were treated in the movies and even on television, for the most part, it is no surprise that Borderers had begun to resent what Sarah Palin, in 2008, would call the "lamestream media."

What the movies in the decades after World War II show us is that there really was a culture clash going on between parts of the broader American society of European descent. Neither side understood the other, and neither even saw that the problem was culture, not class. As a result, they set the stage for a 21st-century cult of individualism quite different from what had come before.

CHAPTER 7

Keeping It All Apart

The cult of individualism, today, continues to have two parts, one associated with each of the major white American cultural groupings: the Borderers and the secular-liberals. Both, or the misunderstandings they generate, continue to be destructive to constructive discourse in the United States. Borderer individualism is retreating further behind the barriers of friends and families that were set up centuries ago, using the following twin justification for its actions (or inactions): First, the belief is that too many who do not work sponge off of those who do, necessitating creation of barriers against them. Second, the idea is that the individual, left alone, is always better able to do anything than the individual encumbered by societal dictates. Secular-liberal individualism, on the other hand, is premised on the metaphor of cream always rising to the top: The elite become elite because they know how to operate better, no matter the environment. They also see responsibility to ethical ideals as the highest commitment—not simply responsibility to law. Though these do not sound tremendously different, they are.

The differences between the visions of individualism do not manifest themselves simply in political divergences even though Borderer/secular-liberal distinctions are the basis for the American "red state/blue state" divide. Here again, there may be a high correlation between the two, but it is not one to one. As with the political diversity of the followers of Ayn Rand, many secular-liberals are also political conservatives—one of the reasons the right has been pulling itself apart since the 2012 election, for not even conservative secular-liberals can understand Borderer viewpoints, many of which are much more fundamental than expressed political affinities.

*****

In conservative Charles Murray's *Coming Apart: The State of White America, 1960–2010*, there is absolutely no mention of Appalachia, Borderers, or the Scots-Irish—or of any differentiation within the greater white culture of an America arising from older ethnic traditions. In fact, Murray goes so far as to assert that the "trends I describe exist independently of ethnic heritage."[1] Such a claim can be made only by ignoring *completely* the cultures and ethnicities of the U.S. population prior to 1960—which Murray does by taking the date of the John Kennedy assassination (November 21, 1963) as his real starting point. Such a claim, also, can be made only by focusing on the Enlightenment idea of the individual as a tabula rasa, as self-creation and self-responsibility, and by ignoring the influence of and responsibility for family—for family is the lynchpin of culture and the home of ethnic heritage and neither culture nor ethnicity can be considered without the other. Given the reality of human social organization, Murray's concentration on the self is as poor a focus as the opposite extreme, that of looking only at environment and history as the shaping factor in human success.

It also contradicts the much more nuanced (though incomplete) vision of American ethnicity presented by Nathan Glazer, another conservative (or neoconservative), who pretty much refuses to separate ethnicity and class, finding them caught up in different ways and percentages in different individuals. Glazer writes that "since the different identities are bound together in statistical clusters and are carried by a single human being, it is very hard to separate out the various identities people carry and to relate the varying interests that activate an individual to specific identities."[2] Glazer's own work illustrates the dangers he describes: A child of immigrants and one who grew up in New York City, Glazer does not question the monolith of "Anglo-conformity"[3] of the British-descended Americans, the idea of which, though incorrect, has been the received wisdom since at least the end of World War II.

What Glazer and Murray do agree on is that one's cultural orientation (ethnic, class, and more) has become something of a personal choice (à la "symbolic ethnicity"). This is one of the basic assumptions behind the secular-liberal cult of individualism and its promotion of the importance of a self-selecting societal elite. As on the census, ethnicity "is a matter of personal choice—no one will check on it and, presumably, no consequences will follow from giving an incorrect answer."[4] In this view, each person is free to create his or her own myth of personal background—even ethnicity, class, and culture becoming elements of individuality. This is quite different from the Borderer emphasis on family ties and an individualism framed by personal relationships.

Creating his own myth in his book, instead of tapping into older ones, Murray posits the formation of new and distinct upper and lower classes in America over the past half century. As he says, he takes his "new upper class" as a subset of what Robert Reich, David Brooks, Richard Florida, and Richard Herrnstein (in conjunction with Murray himself) have described as today's managerial and professional (or creative) class: "I am not referring to all of them, but to a small subset: the people who run the nation's economic, political, and cultural institutions. In practice, this means a fuzzy set in which individuals may or may not be in the upper class, depending on how broadly you want to set the operational definition."[5]

Like each of the four writers he refers to, Murray misses that the "new upper class" is not based solely on the accomplishments of individual members but has evolved from specific American ethnicities while excluding certain others. Arguing instead that the new class is based either on creativity or on economic success—or on both—he conveniently forgets that individuals trying to join it have to do more than prove creative or economic value. In most cases, they also have to come from more. To join this "new upper class," most people not there by birth would have to shed certain specific cultural and/or ethnic markers that illustrate the divide between their culture and, generally, the secular-liberal culture and adopt certain others. Murray can get away with this because, as he says, he is working with "fuzzy sets" and because, as we have seen in previous chapters, cultural and ethnic divides are *always* fuzzy.

The closest Murray comes to acknowledging that there actually were cultural and ethnic divides that created elites in the past is to nod his head in recognition to the old power of the Northeast. He says, however, that the members of that ruling elite, before 1960, "had little in common except their success,"[6] making his point through a distinction between David Rockefeller and the Jews involved in the creation of media empires. He also argues that Edward R. Murrow, Walter Cronkite, and Charles Collingwood belong in this elite in the same way a Rockefeller did, ignoring the fact that those media personalities were all employees, not the real elite at all but its paid public face.

By setting his discussion solely in terms of success, Murray misses the vital question of why *these* people were successful while others, many just as intelligent and able, were not. This, of course, is a question often elided by followers of the cult of individualism. The successful rarely want to acknowledge the role of luck or of their starting point. Murray further limits his "narrow elite" to the movers and shakers: lawmakers, media professionals, and corporate executives. His "broad elite" consists of those in managerial and professional positions. He also ties his elite into the concept of the "self-made man," one of the very myths so much at the heart of American cults of individualism. He argues that even the "elite" of Eisenhower's and Kennedy's governments were not elite at all (in the sense of being of an old northeastern upper class) but self-made—exactly as in his vision of the elite today. The difference, he argues, is a common cultural taste or preference—though he never actually tries hard to convince his readers that the earlier elite did not have the same commonality. Of course, it did. And, not surprisingly, it was this common culture of the elite that provided the easiest and clearest demarcation of the divide between the Borderers and the rest of white America, though Murray and the writers he cites never seem to have seen it.

One of those writers, Richard Florida, discusses the Great Depression and the experience of his father, the son of Italian immigrants in Newark, New Jersey, noting that his

> father's experiences were broadly shared throughout the country. Although times were perhaps worst in the declining rural areas of the Dust Bowl, every region suffered, and the residents of small towns and big cities alike breathed in the same uncertainty and distress. The Great Depression was a national crisis—and in many ways a nationalizing event.[7]

The truth is that (and this is what Murray, like the other followers of the cult of individualism today, ignores as well), the experience of Florida's father in New Jersey and that of the part of the country culturally descended from the Borderers was *quite* different—as different as lives and experiences in Italy and, say, Scotland at any similar point in time.

What Florida—like Murray and many others—is doing is making a case for individual initiative as the deciding factor in success, doing so in part by ignoring completely the cultural and ethnic forces both aiding and impeding any particular individual. The desire to do this is as strong as ever in America today, the growing cult of individualism cutting down any emphasis on culture and ethnicity—and even poverty—to the extent that it is even affecting education. Teachers are finding themselves blamed for the failure of students, even when outside factors of culture and ethnicity (and of poverty, of course) have clearly contributed directly to that failure.

As a grandchild of immigrants and growing up within sight of New York City, Florida likely had very little contact with the descendants of the Borderers during his childhood. Lacking that cross-cultural knowledge, he is willing to extrapolate from his father's experience to that of all Americans. His personal experience has given him no reason not to. This is something that too many in the secular-liberal American culture have been doing for generations, essentially ignoring the very real differences between themselves and the children of the Borderers, making the entire Borderer culture something of a ghost culture.

But it remains a ghost that has never really died.

Almost half of America has been living with that ghost for more than two centuries. They have been told constantly that their own experiences were no different than those of any other white Americans, effectively negating their unique cultural heritage. Life may have been a little harder in the Dust Bowl than in Newark, but that is all.

But it is not all. The heritage of the Borderer is quite distinct from that of the secular-liberal or even the Italian immigrant, and heritage has a huge impact on how people view their own possibilities. Perhaps, for example, it is appropriate to speak of "white privilege" when dealing with what once had been the dominant portion of the white population of America, that of the higher classes of the Northeast and the West Coast, but it is almost laughable when talking about much of the other half. Borderer lives have often been of rural hardship and deprivation—witness the James Agee and Walker Evans book *Let Us Now Praise Famous Men* showing Depression-era life for white tenant farmers in the South. Even when this reality is recognized, all that most people think about is remedying the poverty—that, they imagine, will make the groups equal. Just as Italian American, Jews, and others have risen from poverty into prominence in the greater culture, the children of Borderers should be able to do so, too, and by following the same path. This attitude, though, ignores the realities of cultural difference and leaves many Borderer descendants mired in poverty— just as it does for many African Americans.

It is not so simple as those who think that alleviating poverty or improving education can increase cultural equality might have one believe. The ghosts that Italian Americans and Jews and, of course, African Americans carry with them, religion and certain cultural stereotyping among them, have been recognized by the greater culture and are even explored by that culture in its arts and media. Even when there is discrimination against them, it is generally clarified and recognized and called abhorrent. Generally, people know it for what it is, even if they cannot always stop it. But discrimination against the Borderer culture is not considered discrimination at all—for the Borderer culture is not even considered a culture. At most, it is considered simply lower class, carrying no baggage aside from accent (like the myth of the 1956 Alan Lerner and Frederick Loewe musical *My Fair Lady* and even George Bernard Shaw's play *Pygmalion*, on which it is based), making it possible to "rise above" simply through work and desire. It is attitudes like this that make perfect fodder for those, like Murray and Florida, who argue that it is not culture or ethnicity at all that matters in contemporary America but rather creativity and ability. And it makes for the perfect opportunity to tell "hillbilly" jokes without the slightest twinge of unease.

Yet this idea that anyone can rise, that all one needs is within oneself, is as much a fiction today as it ever was. In a 2009 study for the Brookings Institution, Julia Isaacs compared family incomes from the 1960s with the family incomes of their children in the 1990s and 2000s. Her conclusions, which confirm what those with real experience of American cultural divides already knew, include this:

> Contrary to American beliefs about equality of opportunity, a child's economic position is heavily influenced by that of his or her parents.
>
> - Forty-two percent of children born to parents in the bottom fifth of the income distribution remain in the bottom, while 39 percent born to parents in the top fifth remain at the top.
> - Children of middle-income parents have a near-equal likelihood of ending up in any other quintile, presenting equal promise and peril for those born to middle-class parents.
> - The "rags to riches" story is much more common in Hollywood than on Main Street. Only 6 percent of children born to parents with family income at the very bottom move to the very top.[8]

One impediment for most people from the Borderer culture who do try to find success within the broader American society is that they have to hide their own heritage as they merge their lives with those of extant elites. Today, those from other "outsider" cultures do not have to do this quite as much. Imagine the conflict in *The Jazz Singer* (Alan Crosland, 1927): Jack Robin (aka Jakie Rabinowitz) has rejected the culture and music of his cantor father. We in the audience respect both cultures and understand the dilemma that Robin ultimately faces. Next, remember *Ray* (Taylor Hackford, 2004), whose Ray Charles offends a future wife by taking "church music" and making it pop. Here again, we in the audience are able to respect both cultures and can understand her negative reaction to what he is doing. Now, imagine a movie about a country boy who wants to play, say, classical piano. Likely, the only way we can envision this movie is as a comedy. Why? Because the home culture of the boy has no respect in most of the rest of America; no one takes it seriously. In fact, it is rarely seen as a culture at all. For this reason, successful Borderers abandon their cultural heritage with an alacrity seen much more rarely, today, in people arriving at American success from other cultures.

Fortunately for Borderer strivers, most people mistake style for substance. If one can learn the dialect of the rich and its touchstones for individual judgment, one can "pass" into their society. This common and ages-old error of accepting the mask as the reality is one that Murray makes in his discussion of the television series *thirtysomething*. Murray claims that the culture presented in the show "had no precedent, with its characters who were educated at elite schools, who discussed intellectually esoteric subjects, and whose sex lives were emotionally complicated. . . . The characters all possessed a sensibility that shuddered equally at Fords and Cadillacs, ranch homes in the suburbs and ponderous mansions, Budweiser and Chivas Regal."[9] Yet what Murray mistakes for "sensibility" is nothing more than another set of markers of a cultural divide, one that he apparently does not even know exists. The simpler divide implied by his pairing is one of reliance on money and advertising against an undefined "real" and developed "taste." The choices, in his mind, have nothing to do with the evolving cultural conventions of a long-established upper class within the old dominant secular-liberal culture, conventions far removed from brand names or styles of homes. However, though Murray may style them as "sensibilities," in fact, these are simply the new markers for delineating between this contemporary version of the upper class and American hoi polloi, be they Borderer or otherwise.

This is not new, and the "refined" tastes are "better" only in that the things Murray lists above are items the "in" group has decided against. In reality, their Saabs and brownstones and Laphroaig only cost even more money and are the subject of less advertising. They may indeed be better made, but they impart no inherent superiority of taste or culture. Shuddering at others is only the same snobbishness that has been the hallmark of class-conscious literature for generations. How people who hold such sensitivities today are different in substance from the people of Edith Wharton's 1920 novel (set in the 1870s) *Age of Innocence* or from the movie *The Philadelphia Story* (George Cukor, 1940) is never explained by Murray.

*****

The cultural markers of ethnic groupings within white America can be seen in American literature at least since the time of James Fenimore Cooper and his Leatherstocking tales almost two centuries ago, reflecting unspoken rules set even further in the American past and in its English heritage. It is possible to argue that Cooper was simply mimicking for America the class structures shown in the English novels of the time, but there is really a great deal more to what he was attempting. Like the Borderer in general, Natty Bumppo serves as a buffer between the expanding metropole and the "savage" Native Americans, characters not found in most English novels of the time. Within the rest of the white communities in the Leatherstocking books, however, easily recognized cultural markers of class distinction abound—and many of them are exactly of the same sort Murray claims are new today.

In many respects, Murray and Florida are reacting to what had been a strong tendency in cultural commentary to name environment as the primary shaper of behavior, creating a binary of individual and environment that adherents of the cult of individualism can be comfortable with. But it is never quite so simple. As conservative intellectual Thomas Sowell writes,

> Group cultural patterns may indeed be products of environments—but often of environments that existed on the other side of an ocean, in the lives of ancestors long forgotten, yet transmitted over the generations as distilled values, preferences, skills, and habits. The outward veneer of a new society—its language, dress, and customs—may mask these underlying differences in cultural values, which are nevertheless revealed when the hard choices of life have to be made, and sacrifices endured, to achieve competing goals.[10]

In other words, as Ralph Waldo Emerson claims in "Self-Reliance," "Society is a wave. The wave moves onward, but the water of which it is composed does not."[11] Sowell's point, clearly, was not even radical for 1994, when his book was published, so it strikes me as a little strange that, today, so many commenters on American culture, especially conservative ones, refuse to acknowledge the influence of ancestors. My only explanation for it is that they have been blinded by the secular-liberal cult of individualism, being its adherents themselves even while claiming affinity with the more generally conservative Borderer-based American culture.

Murray sees his new upper class as increasingly segregated from the rest of America, as if segregation even among whites had not existed prior to 1960—it certainly had, the coasts and urban areas walling out "poor" whites. The rural areas, except in the pristine resort and retirement communities, were left for the descendants of the Borderers. In addition, as most anyone from any cultural background knows, the isolation of the very rich from everyone except others of their economic status and the people who serve them has a very long tradition in America as elsewhere in the world. Walled estates and patrolled neighborhoods have been standard for eons. Yet, as if this were something new or different, Murray writes that

> Many of the members of the new upper class *are* balkanized. Further-more, their ignorance about other Americans is more problematic than the ignorance of other Americans about them. It is not a problem if truck drivers cannot empathize with the priorities of Yale professors. It is a problem if Yale professors, or producers of network news programs, or CEOs of great corporations, or presidential advisers cannot empa-thize with the priorities of truck drivers.[12]

Actually, it is a problem both ways. When the truck driver does not at least understand the priorities of Yale professors, a dialogue between the two can never be established. Murray has unwittingly bought into one of the reasons for the resentments of "red state" conservatives toward the "East Coast elite," that the elite need knowledge while the rest do not. Paradoxically, this is the problem such liberals as John Dewey were trying to address through creation of a system of education based on the concept of the citizen as informed decision maker and that conservatives such as Walter Lippmann resisted, believing the population best served by an informed elite crafting choices for the population as a whole.

That the divide between the professor and the teamster has been in existence since the early years of English colonization of America should be apparent to anyone who has made even the briefest study of the history of American culture. So wide has the divide appeared and so great the arrogance exhibited that it was always an easy base for comedy. Jean Hagan's comic line as Lina Lamont in *Singin' in the Rain* (Stanley Donen and Gene Kelly, 1952) skewers attitudes putting down the "little people" such as the one exhibited by Murray: "If we bring a little joy into your humdrum lives, we feel as though our hard work ain't been in vain for nothing." The surface joke, of course, is that Lamont, "lower class" in origin but removed from it by success, is no longer part of either group and understands neither—she certainly has not man-aged to take on the markers of the upper class. The deeper, unspoken joke is on the elite she apes. Depression-era films such as *My Man Godfrey* (George La Cava, 1936), *The Amazing Adventure* (Alfred Zeisler, 1936), and *Sullivan's Travels* (Preston Sturges, 1941)—just to name three—were built around the

wide gulf between the rich and the poor in America, of course, but also on the
lack of understanding and the cultural markers separating the two, the richer
secular-liberal culture and the generally poorer Borderer.

Murray at least *tries* to base his vision of the "new lower class" in history,
but it is a history that takes as truth the myth of "industriousness, honesty,
marriage, and religiosity"[13] as the basic aspects of American culture. This
has not really been the case at all, not even particularly in terms of the centrality of the myth. Still, Murray does manage to tap into certain other long-
term myths, claiming that early "Americans may not have been genteel, but,
as a people, they met the requirements of virtue."[14] This sort of self-
congratulatory vision of history is common to the myths within *any* culture
or ethnic group, part of the necessary intracommunication that, as Michael
Hechter claims, holds the group together. Common to all, it is no more true
for any one group than for any other.

Murray concludes that

> the trends of the last half century do not represent just the passing of an
> outmoded way of life that I have identified with "the American
> Project." Rather, the trends signify damage to the heart of the
> American community and the ways in which the great majority of
> Americans pursue satisfying lives. The trends of the last half century
> matter a lot. Many of the best and most exceptional qualities of
> American culture cannot survive unless they are reversed.[15]

But there never has been a monolithic American culture or community, not
even a monolithic American *white* culture—and we are not in a period of
decline from some past cultural height. Yes, there has been a constant and
growing divide between the Borderer culture and the other great American
culture that, until recently, had always been the dominant one (in terms of
media and intellectual activity). But what has happened over the past 50 years
is not a decline or even the development of new upper and lower classes; it is
simply the emergence of a Borderer culture strong enough to challenge the
long-dominant East Coast culture.

The central myth of this newly powerful Borderer culture focuses on its
unique Borderer vision of individualism, on the idea that one *makes* for oneself
and one's family. By the time of the 2012 Republican National Convention
with its catch phrase of "We Built It," the myth had become the basis for a successful cult that could now explicitly show its political muscle. Often called the
"Tea Party," this new cult of individualism is much more than a simple political
movement. It is a reflection of a cultural belief that "outside" forces have con-
spired to dampen individual initiative, that if people could only be left alone,

they could work miracles for themselves. Its attitudes are those behind the mania for guns that grew so strong over the first decade of the 21st century, stronger than it had ever been in American history. Guns, it is imagined, can keep at bay those who would keep one down. And there is a belief, a cultural conspiracy theory, if you will, that there *are* such enemies.

*****

Selfishness, as a devolution from individualism, to be clear, as it developed as a political symbol in American culture, is not the defining marker of "red state" or Borderer—or even Scots-Irish or Appalachian—culture. Yet it certainly has become a way of reacting to the assumptions underlying that other American culture, the one descended from the other three of David Hackett Fischer's four folkways and that has its own distinct cult of individualism. Selfishness is also a way of reacting to the aggressive domination of the northeastern culture that, though it is not always on top in the political realm, has long defined the terms of cultural discussion and stereotype. This is true today, thanks to media concentration, for even those parts of America far from its areas of physical prominence.

In his book on Appalachian culture and on interventions into it by the more powerful East Coast American culture, *All That Is Native and Fine*, David Whisnant discusses the importance of understanding culture and cultural interactions as a part of history, something that Murray, again, ignores. Whisnant claims that "to understand culture in the mountains—or indeed in any culturally enclaved area within a larger, formally pluralistic but essentially assimilationist social system—one must inevitably talk about the politics of culture."[16] This is also true for a culture that seems to have been assimilated, as today's Borderers, the non-Appalachian descendants of Scots-Irish culture, appear to have been. Only when we understand this can we finally see that the assimilation is never whole, never complete—that parts of the old culture always remain—and that these have a continuing impact.

Using economics, intelligence, and creativity as the new dividers of class, ignoring the fact that the older markers have never completely disappeared, Murray argues for a new "melting pot" for those who can rise above their origins. But no melting pot works completely. For many Borderers, it simply produced an *appearance* of assimilation that could be worn like a coat to be shed in the warmth of home. Rather than symbolic ethnicity, this might be called "symbolic assimilation."

In the Borderer case, because of the "cultural enclave" of the mountains that retains, more than elsewhere, the old base culture, we have the ability to see a bit more clearly just what "assimilation" from Borderer culture has really meant in America and why there are now two Americas that look the same but that are seeming less and less able to communicate with each other. We can also begin to understand the differences in vision of individualism and some of the resentments toward the "East Coast elite" (and toward the minorities that the elite seems, to the "red staters," to have embraced, minorities that, since the 2012 election, Democrats *have* embraced as part of a "new majority" reflecting demographic shifts leaving Borderers in a shrinking minority) that continue to dominate parts of American politics. One becomes "gradually aware that the manipulation of culture (at least, of culture construed in certain ways) inevitably reflects value and ideological differences as well as the inequalities inhering in class. Thus one must sooner or later consider the *politics* of culture, which show some signs of being reasonably predictable, even in widely separated circumstances."[17] And predictive they are, especially today, when those politics have become literal, have become a major component of American electoral competitions. Whisnant claims that "culture must inevitably be construed in political terms, *especially* in an encounter between two cultural systems that are socially or economically unequal."[18] Many "red staters," today, feel that they are living in exactly such a situation. Their response, all too often, is to retreat into a pugilistic stance of protective individualism, where one imagines that one has gained what little one has on one's own and that everyone else is trying to get it, especially those even lower on the scale.

Furthermore, Borderers feel that insult has been added to injury through the agency of what Whisnant calls "intervenors." He is speaking specifically of those who went from the "advanced" coastal and northern regions into the mountains both to help make lives better and to preserve the quaint culture. Their descendants, in the eyes of many Borderer-descended Americans, are the government programs that try to force certain types of social change through control over school curricula and college admissions ("equal opportunity"), over housing, medical care, and other aspects of life tantamount to "social engineering." Such programs leave many feeling frustrated and helpless for the "intervenor, by virtue of his or her status, power, and established credibility, is frequently able to define what the culture *is*, to normalize and legitimize that definition in the larger society, and even to feed it back into the culture itself."[19] To make matters worse, the " 'culture' that is perceived by the intervenor (even before the act of intervention) is rarely congruent with the culture that is actually there. It is a *selection*, an *arrangement*, an *accommodation* to preconceptions—whether of mountaineers, of Indians, or Georgia blacks, or Scotch Highlanders."[20] Naturally, the people so manipulated are going to start to feel, at some point, a little angry. Today, that anger is often exhibited in a strong "red state" anti–federal government stance and in the growth of a renewed cult of Borderer individualism.

The reasons for the stark and rancorous cultural splits of today are not buried in early American history. Many of them come from the experiences of the parents and grandparents of today's Borderers. After all, migration out of Appalachian and the intermingling of Borderer and secular-liberal cultures did not stop with the conquest of the continent. Huge numbers of Borderer Americans, especially of the generation that fought World War II, left the mountains, never to live there again. By the 1960s,

> Uptown, a Chicago neighborhood [had become] home to thousands of economically displaced Appalachians, mostly white, who had turned the area into a bastion of southern culture. Their families had moved North in search of work after mining and agriculture work started to disappear. But only a few found steady jobs. The rest scraped by on day labor, hustling and domestic work. By one estimate more than 40 percent of the neighborhood was on some form of welfare. It was their families the *Sunday Tribune* had deemed "a plague of locusts" descending on the city.[21]

Though the authors of this passage do not appear to understand the distinction between southern and Appalachian cultures, managing to conflate the two, they also point out something quite real about the migration out of Appalachia for approximately the 20 years after the end of World War II. Though the American economy, in general, was booming, it was not an easy time for Appalachian migrants, and most felt ignored by the federal government in particular, though they certainly did take advantage of what are now called "entitlements." Few of their children and grandchildren, however, are in that same state of distress: These are people whose economic condition has improved dramatically over the past 50 years—and they feel, for the most part, that they improved their lives on their own. This is another cause, of course, of today's cult of individualism.

That feeling is proving to be a major problem for the politics of the 21st century, in part because the period of economic progress for the migrants out of Appalachia corresponds with the period of civil rights advancements for African Americans. The Borderers looked at the blacks and wondered if they would also get some of this new "equal treatment" they were seeing come into play. They felt they did not. The children of Appalachia have watched the powerful of American government look favorably, or so it seemed to them, on African Americans while leaving poor whites to their own devices. That this is not the case is beside the point. That point, of course, is that belief itself. It is the myth behind it—a myth built upon perceptions of affirmative action and on tales of government preference in hiring and handouts for nonwhite Americans. It has led to real alienation from the federal government, and it has strengthened the cult of individualism.

Told they have had the advantage of being white, the descendants of the Borderers often react with indignation: Their own ancestors had been the unwanted, the pushed away. That their situation had been quite different from that of black slaves was irrelevant, in their eyes. What mattered is "today." Slavery, after all, is well over a century in the past. At the same time, they believe, with some justification, that it was those outcast ancestors of theirs who had built the United States (quite a few African Americans believe the same about their ancestors), making the past matter. Whatever the reality, to understand the Borderers, one certainly needs to understand their place in the history of the United States. Yet it is a place that, in its presentation within the broader culture, is almost always ignored, making understanding it next to impossible without a real and personal connection to Appalachian culture and the broader Borderer culture that is its cousin.

In Ken Kesey's novel *Sometimes a Great Notion*, an outside labor organizer tries to understand what has happened to a strike in a Northwest logging community, talking to a woman who has married in to the Stamper clan, the family central to the novel. She says to him, "You could never understand it all. You just want a reason, two or three reasons. When there are reasons going back two or three hundred years."[22] Those reasons writ large, reasons tied deep into Borderer culture, have not been, generally, part of the standard story of the nation—though they are disturbingly close by in that story, even when unheard. Had they been part of the standard history of the United States, it is likely we would not have the resentments and deep political divide we see today—and we might not even have a cult of individualism acting as a wrecking ball on our political process.

*   *   *   *   *

Many of us from Borderer backgrounds have lived our lives with a ghost of something just outside of reach, outside of consciousness. Many people attempting to assimilate into another culture have similar feelings, of course, but most Borderers have never recognized that they were (and are) outsiders in quite the same way. If they could recognize it, they might find that there are two ways that people respond to this ghostly doubleness. A friend of mine, raised a nonobservant Jew, embraced his religion in his 30s, learning

Hebrew and keeping a kosher household to try to make his life whole. Another friend, a Chinese American, repressed the Cantonese dialect he had spoken up to age five so completely that, when he, too, wanted to reconnect, he found it almost impossible to regain the language. He now visits China regularly, though, having regained a portion of his heritage. The second way is to deny completely what one's parents have given them—sometimes leading to tragic consequences. Like F. Scott Fitzgerald's Jay Gatsby, those who go down this path can let the lack of resolution of their cultural duality destroy them. Some of those in the second group manage to go over to the other side almost completely and often without disaster. But even they can never give up completely the culture that made them. No one can. Though they may be divorced from their root culture, that ghost of it, that doubleness, remains.

Seeing the cultural divide only in terms of class, Murray has a test in his book, one that scores "access" to the "rest" of America (the test is aimed at the members of the "new upper class"). It includes questions like "Have you ever lived ... in an American neighborhood in which the majority of your ... neighbors probably did not have college degrees?"[23] and asks if you have ever known an evangelical Christian or can identify Branson or Jimmie Johnson or have hitchhiked or ridden Greyhound—his idea of markers of the "new lower class." The higher your score, the more you know of the "new lower class." My score of 52 out of 100 puts me at the lower end of Murray's group of "lifelong resident[s] of a working-class neighborhood with average television and moviegoing habits"[24] and a little bit higher in his grouping of the first-generation middle class. I am toward the upper range of his upper-middle-class grouping and fall completely outside of his second-generation upper-middle-class grouping. All of this is ridiculous, for, like most Americans, I am a polyglot of backgrounds and experiences—most of which, however, do fall into a different sort of classification, one based on ethnicity and not on choice, education, or economic status—a Borderer classification that crosses all of Murray's boundaries.

One of the problems in trying to understand the influence of Borderer culture on the United States is that annoying fact that the Borderers look exactly like the rest of white America, a fact that has led to the common assumption of a monolithic American culture or, if division is recognized, one simply North/South. But the situation is a great deal more complicated. Rodger Cunningham, in "The Valley So Low: Kristeva, Freud, Mori, and Appalachian Uncanniness," a paper he presented at the 2012 Appalachian Studies Conference, shed some light on the sense of double exposure, of two almost identical but also extremely different cultures, that most

Appalachians recognize and that even the others feel, though (like Murray) they probably cannot explain it. Looking at it from the other side, from an Appalachian perspective, Cunningham writes about the reactions it engenders in secular-liberals:

> Appalachians simply cannot be around such people without waking in them an obscure discomfort, bewilderment, and anger. Examples from one's own experience will not fail to occur to many Appalachians. This reaction is not necessarily mediated by false assumptions but is simply a reaction to difference as such. Stereotyping is the result, not the cause, of the reaction, and the reaction itself is the real mystery to its objects. Stereotyping is a secondary reaction that only then assumes independent agency. What is happening here? I propose that this horror is paradoxically aroused by such small differences precisely because they *are* relatively small.[25]

Trying to convince anyone *not* from an Appalachian background that there is a difference and a reality behind it is, well, almost impossible—*even though* Borderers can almost always see that the others *feel* it. The visible distinctions between us, as Cunningham says, are too small.

Cunningham borrows from Masahiro Mori the concept of the "uncanny valley": The more like us something becomes, but still not *being* us (or one of us), the creepier we begin to feel in its presence. In terms of the relations between Appalachians and the rest of white America,

> for centuries Appalachians and their ancestors have occupied a space between binaries: tame/wild, civilized/savage, Anglo-Saxon/Celtic, settler/immigrant, North/South, "WASP"/"ethnic." We talk about "othering," but the problem here is precisely that Americans perceive Appalachians as *not other enough*. Mountain people's characteristics destabilize Americans' categories; the uncanny feeling is that of a taken-for-granted ground of thought suddenly tipping and sliding beneath the dominant culture's feet.

Thus, we have the strong reactions—both positive and negative—toward Appalachians by other whites. And, on the other side, the development of resentments toward the more powerful has helped lead to today's versions of the cult of individualism.

*****

Americans from the outside either want to embrace the "things" of Appalachian culture in particular, or they try to push that Borderer culture away completely. I remember secular-liberal friends enamored with the *Foxfire* books of Appalachian lore, with "old timey" music, and with weaving and other things they associated with the "simple" life "connected to the land." At the same time, they drank in without a problem typical disparaging depictions of Appalachians such as those found in the movie *Deliverance* (John Boorman, 1972). Obtuse attitudes toward Appalachians have been around, as we have seen (in chapter 3) since at least the 18th century. Ignorance has grown with immigration from abroad into urban areas that has provided the new Americans with little or no contact with the descendants of the Borderers—except, paradoxically, in primarily midwestern industrial centers where recent immigrants mingled with those displaced Appalachians who, after World War II, had followed routes north, such as Ohio's fabled "hillbilly highway," in search of factory jobs.

As recently as the late 1950s, writing in *Harper's Magazine*, Albert Votaw expressed urban frustration with those postwar Appalachian migrants arriving in Chicago, even buying into the conceit of Appalachians as "contemporary ancestors," primitives (like all of "our" ancestors supposedly were) in need of "our" help in coming forward into the modern age. To Votaw's frustration, however, this no longer seemed possible:

> These farmers, miners, and mechanics from the mountains and meadows of the mid-South—with their fecund wives and numerous children—are, in a sense, the prototype of what the "superior" American should be, white Protestants of early American, Anglo-Saxon stock; but on the streets of Chicago they seem to be the American dream gone berserk. This may be the reason why their neighbors often find them more obnoxious than the Negroes or the early foreign immigrants whose obvious differences from the American stereotype made them easy to despise. Clannish, proud, disorderly, untamed to urban ways, these country cousins confound all notions of racial, religious, and cultural purity.[26]

Is it any wonder then, that even a child of well-to-do Appalachians should experience a certain amount of mutual mistrust when entering the wider culture? Even as he tries to understand the other side of the double, Votaw reverts to stereotypes (if he had ever left them):

> If the Southerners are a nuisance to the city, the city is equally hard on them. The mountain folk, as one of their friends puts it, have been dodging revenue agents for hundreds of years, and there is no reason why their attitude should change overnight. Authority means trouble: police,

courts, jail; repossession of goods bought on time; snoopy social workers; the truant officer; the need to admit publicly—when asked to sign
for their youngsters' library cards—that they don't know how to read
or write.[27]

Though plenty of moonshine made it down the storied road from Wilkes
County, North Carolina (the home of my grandfather and of NASCAR pioneer and moonshine runner Junior Johnson) to Charlotte over the first half
of the 20th century, few people were actually involved in the trade. Most were
as honest and accepting of authority as people anywhere. Votaw's was an
attempt to exaggerate difference, perhaps out of fear that there *was* no difference, essentially, or perhaps simply out of inability to understand the
unknown that also seemed so familiar.

Making it even more difficult to understand the impact of Borderer culture
and Borderer reaction to the rest of America is the fact that almost all studies
of and commentaries upon the United States as a whole begin within and about
the other three of Fischer's four "folkways," leaving the Borderers almost completely out of the story—or as an unfortunate dead end, one best ignored—like
the family madwoman kept in the attic. For the most part, the cultural history of
"white" America details the evolution from Quaker and Puritan folkways into
the northern-states culture of the time of the Civil War and the Cavalier culture
into that of the antebellum South. The Borderers are nowhere to be seen—
except, of course, as cautionary tales of how people can devolve.

Obviously, that is never been the whole story. America has been built by
the Borderers as much as by any other of the American cultures, be they
"folkways," African American, or "ethnic." The desire for success has been
important to each. Many from each have succeeded and have worked within
the broader society, their stories probably more common than the situation
Votaw described. Borderers in particular believe quite strongly that they
made their successes themselves, that no one hand had helped them—and
that they had done it in the face of unfair external support for others. This is
not really true, of course, but the belief has left Borderers feeling angry when
they think that they see others, particularly African Americans, getting what
they imagined was a "free ride" where they had had to work. That anger, of
course, became part of the base for the Borderer cult of individualism today.

*****

These Borderers are not necessarily racist—not, at least, in the way Americans
from outside the region traditionally see racism or in the way of much of the
Deep South. Would they invite a black man or woman to sit at their table?

Not often. But they have nothing against the idea of a black person achieving as much as they have, themselves. "Separate but equal," to them, is not a means of ensuring that the races remain separate but unequal. Many Borderers do not care how well blacks do—as long as they do it elsewhere. After all, others felt the same way about their own ancestors—and the early Borderers took the hint and left, taking that Great Wagon Road away from the Quakers and the English. What they imagine is that African Americans are getting better treatment than they have ever had themselves. That Borderers do not know the history or the sufferings of slaves, the slaves' children and grandchildren, is another story.

The accusations of racism against Borderers today cause a great deal of resentment and confusion, as we saw with Brad Paisley's "Accidental Racist" in the last chapter—and become another factor in the development of the cult of individualism. "Just leave me alone" might be a better description of Appalachian attitudes, attitudes that can also be traced back to the reactions noted by that Anglican "missionary" Charles Woodmason, who tried to bring "proper" religion, dress, and comportment to the backwoods before the Revolution. The Scots-Irish Borderers did not like him very much and made that quite clear, often treating him with derision or anger. He was not "one of us" to the Borderers and would not become "one of us." After all, he was trying to change the Borderers into Anglicans, even to control them through the pulpit, rather than joining in with them as so many unattached young male migrants from Europe and the East had done for years.

Not surprisingly, the emphasis on self-sufficiency, along with the importance that the Borderers place on kinship, leads to an attitude toward the outsider that non-Borderers find hard to understand. It allows the Borderers "to embrace members of other ethnic groups rather than demean them. An individualistic society based on loyal service reaches to the person rather than to his or her ethnicity, although it certainly is capable of opposing an enemy on racial or national grounds if threatened."[28] This is the way the Borderer culture grew out of all proportion to the increase in the Scots-Irish population. It is also why the racism of Appalachia is quite different from the racism of the Deep South. It is based not on a tradition of servitude and oppression but on perceived threat from outsiders, both from African Americans themselves and from the East Coast elite that seems, in many Borderer eyes, to be championing blacks over the Borderer descendants.

Few, even beyond the old dominant but narrow-visioned secular-liberal culture of America, have ever understood the deep chasm between the inheritors of the other three "folkways" and the Borderers. Without a clear racial distinction, it has always been just too easy just to lump all American "whites" together. Even 1960s black activist Stokely Carmichael fell into this trap, telling the college students of the Students for a Democratic Society to take care of "their own" poor—as if most Harvard and Swarthmore students had any identity with Appalachian poor other than skin color (some did, of course, but very few). The Student Nonviolent Coordinating Committee had tried to support programs for organizing poor whites but "had trouble convincing white volunteers to live in white communities where the pace of change was far slower"[29]—where, to put it bluntly, the outside volunteers were not welcome but were seen as aliens and not as racial fellows. Here again, the intruders were attempting to bring change from the outside on the assumption that their economic superiority allows them to "know better" than the poor. Resentment at this was part of the reason that, also in the 1960s, Volunteers in Service to America (VISTA) was not well accepted in the mountains. Simply coming from a more "successful" milieu does not bestow ability to "help" others. This is a hard lesson to learn—as Teach for America, with its Ivy League volunteers working in inner-city schools, is starting to discover—and as Peace Corps Volunteers (including both me and Murray) have been finding out for generations now.

* * * * *

As Michael Hechter observes, the assumption of the sociologists and other students of culture, themselves mostly from the metropole (though he uses the word "core"), is that those who come into substantive contact with the dominant culture will be transformed by that culture, losing their own values and cultural orientation. That does not happen completely, as almost anyone who has moved from Appalachia to Chicago, Detroit, or anywhere else in the United States knows. That "doubleness," that ghost, is always present. What galls many Borderers even more than the expectation that they should *want* to join the majority is the belief they encounter that "the maintenance of peripheral cultural forms and customs is an irrational reaction by groups which seek to preserve a backward life-style insulated from the rapid change of contemporary industrial society."[30]

"Backward." That, as almost anyone from a minority or a less "developed" culture knows (or should know), is nonsense and is simply a reflection of the myths and biases of the culture of the metropole. It makes many of the outsiders to the metropole want to reject the powerful culture—though they rarely feel they have the ability to do so, unless an avenue appears, one that can provide them support like the cult of individualism can.

Hechter poses a question that has bedeviled those working in development for decades—or even centuries in the case of Appalachia: "Why is traditional culture so enduring in the periphery despite this substantial interaction with the core?"[31] Certainly, in the case of Appalachians, it is not simply a case of isolation. Yes, the hills and hollows can sometimes be hard to reach, but what about the millions of Appalachians who have left the mountains or their distant cousins in the broader Borderer culture, children of great-great aunts and uncles who led the western expansion? Why have they remained different from the East Coast–oriented dominant media and intellectual American culture, different enough (and strong enough) to create a political rift in the 21st century that is proving almost impossible to bridge?

On a cultural level, things such as the Creation Museum of Petersburg, Kentucky, serve as a thumb in the eye of the culture that has dominated American discourse at least since the time of Franklin Roosevelt. Beyond any belief in creationism, it is a reaction to the snooty and insulting depiction of "backward" Americans by the "enlightened" urbanites of the coasts, such as that shown in Jerome Lawrence and Robert Edwin Lee's 1955 play *Inherit the Wind* and Stanley Kramer's 1960 movie from it. Hechter points out that analysts from the "core" generally blame lack of economic development in a minority region or culture on the oppressive nature of the minority culture itself. The oppression, however, really comes from the outside and comes with and through the little understanding of the needs of the minority culture, which, after all, has generally been dismissed by the greater culture as having little value—except as a source for "primitive" arts, crafts, and music.

Alice Walker's 1973 short story "Everyday Use" deals with this problem in terms of an African American family whose daughter has in fact been assimilated into the larger culture, a daughter who comes back in search for artifacts of her "legacy" that can enhance her status in the metropole, providing a symbolic ethnicity. One passage of the story, narrated by the mother, highlights the difference in attitude between the assimilated daughter and her mother and another daughter who has stayed home:

"The truth is," I said, "I promised to give them quilts to Maggie, for when she marries John Thomas."

She gasped like a bee had stung her.

"Maggie can't appreciate these quilts!" she said. "She'd probably be backward enough to put them to everyday use."

"I reckon she would," I said. "God knows I been saving 'em for long enough with nobody using 'em. I hope she will!"[32]

The "things" of the minority culture are superseded in use by the "things" of the majority, generally (in the contemporary world) manufactured items of identical appearance—making the handmade "things" of the minority culture valuable not as usable items but simply as decoration and signs of ethnicity. In fact, the minority culture itself often comes to seem no more than that.

Most people from peripheral cultures are not so completely assimilated as the daughter in Walker's story appears to be. Even when they move from the periphery into the metropole (either literally or metaphorically), they take something of their home culture with them—as the daughter wants to do with the quilts. Unfortunately, the less immediate the appearance (at least) of assimilation, the greater the reaction, generally negative, of the larger culture—as seen in Votaw's depiction of Appalachians in Chicago. He judged them by standards completely unfair to them, holding them to cultural norms unfamiliar to them and imposing stereotypes upon them. Until they learned to at least look like they were conforming to the "standards" of the broader culture, they would continue to be looked down upon.

The descendants of the Borderers know this—and, though it annoys them tremendously, they also have a sense of humor about it. Witness the popularity of "hillbilly" knick-knacks among them, a popularity especially significant since they know that the "hillbilly" both amuses and frightens much of the rest of America. J. W. Williamson writes (with "us" being the broader culture),

> My assumption is that the hillbilly mirrors us, and like most mirrors he can flatter, frighten, and humiliate. As a rough-and-ready frontiersman, he can be made to compliment American men. He can also terrify. Put him in the same woods, but make him repulsively savage, a monster of nature, and he now mirrors an undeniable possibility in American manhood. In other words, we want to be him and we want to flee him.[33]

The hillbilly, who cares about no one and not even about the impression he makes, is also an exemplar, for better and worse, of individualism. What Williamson describes is a result of the long-term inability to recognize that there are two major white Americas (not to mention dozens of smaller ones)—even to suppress the idea—and it has led to creation of the comical/ horrible hillbilly, the embodiment of something "we" know is there but do not really want to admit as real, for, as Williamson also says, our "secret dread is that the dark, drunken hillbilly is no Other, but us."[34] This is true of the descendants of the Borderers, who, in light of the prevailing bias against Appalachian culture, often want to push away even a parodic representation of their past. It is also true of the rest of white America, who see that the Borderers are not so different, really, from themselves—though they know at the same time that they are very, very different.

The appearance of conformity crossing the two cultures combined with a knowledge of difference has compounded the problems in America between the "red state" and "blue state" cultures. Cunningham writes that

> the late Urban Appalachian activist Ernie Mynatt used to suggest, tongue in cheek, that Appalachians in Northern cities might acquire more respect if they painted themselves blue, thereby making themselves *marked* enough, *other* enough, to be safely so, not uncannily so. And this playful trope has been paralleled by Appalachian scholars in more sublimated attempts—straight-faced, research-based, and therefore less true—to paint their subjects as "other enough" by exaggerating, for example, the Celtic element of Appalachians' culture, the folk nature of their society, and/or the third-world status of their economy. This only has the paradoxical effect of strengthening stereotypes that are the secondary result of the original uncanniness.[35]

The irony of scholars trying to emphasize difference through externals in the face of widespread consideration of white American culture as a monolith should not be forgotten. In the popular mind, unless one speaks like an Appalachian, partakes in Appalachian crafts or music, or lives in poverty in the hills, one is not a part of Appalachian culture. The Borderer culture, to this mind-set, does not exist. The externals rule, and the resentment at being marginalized that many of the Borderers feel in contemporary America grows, as does, of course, the reactionary cult of individualism.

★★★★★

Hechter posits three propositions relating to the political integration of cultures on the periphery into the larger or dominant society:

1. The greater the economic inequalities between collectivities, the greater the probability that the less advantaged collectivity will be status solidary, and hence, will resist political integration.

2. The greater the frequency of intra-collectivity communication, the greater the status solidarity of the peripheral collectivity.

3. The greater the intergroup differences of culture, particularly in so far as identifiability is concerned, the greater the probability that the culturally distinct peripheral collectivity will be status solidary.[36]

In terms of the integration of Borderer culture into the mainstream of America, proposition 3 is extremely problematic, for the Borderer culture, so widely diffused and identifiable as different only in debatable fashion (through religion and politics, primarily—for the underlying attitudes stemming from the culture are much more difficult to quantify), has little obvious distinction—except, of course, the created or artificially enhanced distinctions that Cunningham alludes to, and those do not count. Yet there is a great deal of "status solidity," often identified simply as opposition to the "East Coast liberal elite," and this should not be discounted.

One of the reasons for the widening gap between the two major American cultures today is summed up in proposition 2. Until the advent of Fox News and then the Internet, there was no great conduit for intracollective communication among the Borderers, for most of American media was under the control of the dominant culture (or what once was the dominant culture: the two seeming to have achieved a certain amount of temporary parity recently). Over the period since World War II, the once economically "disadvantaged" Borderer descendants have definitely achieved a degree of economic parity within the greater culture, but the perception remains that others are getting more for less effort. This perception that achieves the same result, in this regard, that real economic disparity brings about, as in Hechter's proposition 1. After all, it is not often the reality that matters but the myths we develop, myths that we buy into as a group. One of the most common ones, for Borderer descendants, is that someone else is taking advantage of their hard work, getting rich (or lazy) at their expense. Anger at this, of course, is part of the impetus behind the cult of individualism.

*****

To reconcile the problems in what he was observing within the history of internal colonialism in the British Isles and the expectations that various social change theories would seem to set up, Hechter follows the pattern of dividing "culture" from "ethnicity," warning against the tendency to conflate the two terms:

> Let culture refer to a set of observable behaviors which occur independent of a group's relationship to the means and production and exchange. Thus variables describing religious affiliation or linguistic behavior may be considered to be cultural variables. On the other hand, let ethnicity refer to the sentiments which bind individuals into solidary groups on some cultural basis. Ethnicity therefore alludes to the

quality of relations existing between individuals sharing certain cultural behaviors.[37]

The problem with this, in terms of Borderer descendants in American culture, is that the obvious cultural variables or markers, as I have said, have often disappeared—or have become much less easily identified. Religion and political affiliation, for example, cross ethnic lines or themselves become the "homes" for ethnic conflict, as the Episcopal church is finding, as even the Republican Party is discovering. Yet a unique sense of the individual, unique to the children of the Borderers (metaphorical and literal), is the basis of the shared Borderer-like behavior that indeed seems to confirm Hechter's observation.

Hechter goes on to distinguish between the "functionalist theory" of ethnic change and the "reactive theory." He describes the former as claiming that "ethnic identification is ... a primordial sentiment, emanating in relatively undifferentiated social settings"[38] and one that is diluted by evolving economic similarities that eventually supersede them. He cites Max Weber as a proponent of this view, seeing a shifting affinity, as economic systems modernize, from "status groups" to class. Murray would also count as a proponent of the functionalist theory. This model has not been confirmed by events, as we have seen, turning Hechter's interest toward the "reactive theory," one that postulates that ethnic change stems from the prominence of markers of cultural distinction. Without them, the minority ethnicity tends to fade into the majority. Hechter writes, "Among many such minorities [in developed societies], ethnicity must be maintained in the face of considerable pressure for assimilation which arises from dominant cultural groups."[39] This has been the case, though often unstated and unnoted, for the Scots-Irish/Borderer (and Appalachian) culture in America almost since the time of the first arrivals from Ulster 300 years ago. Tellingly, for contemporary America, Hechter goes on to say that "ethnic solidarity might have a good deal in common with the phenomenon of political mobilization."[40] That is, as other markers fade, people seek out new ones to distinguish their own culture from the intrusive and more powerful one.

*****

The cult of individualism, though it may have new power on the right in contemporary politics, is certainly no new phenomenon, as we have seen. And it is not the purview of the Borderer alone or of political conservatives. In an essay published in *Harper's Magazine* in 1975, Peter Marin tells of listening to a woman who has just participated in an Erhard Seminar Training ("est") weekend. She told him she had learned

> (1) that the individual will is all-powerful and totally determines one's fate; (2) that she felt neither guilt nor shame about anyone's fate and that those who were poor and hungry must have wished it on themselves; ... (7) that whatever one thought to be true was true beyond all argument; ... (9) that my use of logic to criticize her beliefs was unfair, because reason was "irrational," though she could not tell me why.[41]

This could be used as a template for the arguments of Tea Party adherents today and even for the architects of Mitt Romney's political campaign. Romney strategist Ashley O'Connor even said that "fact checkers come to this with their own sets of thoughts and beliefs, and we're not going to let our campaign be dictated by fact checkers."[42] One of the main points of what really has grown into a cult of individualism is that what anyone else claims is irrelevant—if it conflicts what one believes or is trying to do.

Marin's article was rather prescient, probably in ways that, paradoxically, he had never intended. He writes that "selfishness and moral blindness now assert themselves in the larger culture as enlightenment and psychic health."[43] For a time, the American cultures seemed to have retreated from that. At least, it was not an overt part of popular culture in the 1980s and 1990s in the way it had been in the 1970s. But the attitudes were still there; they simply were shifting away from organized cultlike movements such as "est," becoming less codified but, also as the new century dawned, much more tied into politics. As Marin claimed, "The world view emerging among us centered solely on the self and with individual survival as its sole good."[44] This attitude certainly owes something to Ayn Rand, but its causes are deeper and stronger than anything and individual writer could create, and its reflection can be seen in presidential politics since World War II.

*****

The hold on the South of the Democrats, seen as the only opposition to emancipation-favoring Republicans since the Civil War, began to weaken in 1948, with four states going to that fervent follower of the cult of individualism Strom Thurmond on a states' rights ticket. Though Thomas Dewey, an old-fashioned establishment candidate, held onto much of the Northeast, the Midwest and the West were enough to give the election to Harry Truman, who did have a certain appeal to Borderer sentiments—the "Give 'em hell, Harry," yelled to him during the campaign, reflects nothing so much as Borderer pugnacity and individualism. Still, the Republican Party remained anathema in the South, so much so that even Dwight Eisenhower could not parlay his enormous popularity resulting from World War II into Electoral College victory in the South. Even though the Democratic candidate, Adlai Stevenson, was an avowed liberal and champion of secular-liberal values, the only states he carried in the 1952 or 1956 election were either in the old Confederacy or contiguous to it.

John Kennedy was able to turn his strength in the Northeast and the anti-Republican sentiments of the South into what would prove to be the last instance of the old Democratic coalition that included the "solid South" and, since Roosevelt's time, African Americans. Lyndon Johnson's civil rights legislation led to a regional shift in allegiance. Still, Johnson won in a massive landslide, taking all of the Electoral College votes except those of a rump confederacy and opponent Barry Goldwater's home state of Arizona. Johnson, like Truman, presented a strong Borderer image, keeping many Borderers within his party's tent. By the time of Richard Nixon's election four years later, the South was split between George Wallace and Nixon—but a conscious "southern strategy" made sure that would never happen to the Republicans again, not for another generation, at least. The immediate result was Nixon's great landslide victory of 1972 and the beginning of a Borderer romance with a Republican party that began, more and more, to cater to Borderer individualist instincts on questions of the role of the federal government, gun control, and more.

In 1976, Jimmy Carter, a favorite son of the South and an "outsider" in terms of Washington, D.C., was able to temporarily stem the tide of the "southern strategy," but he could not hold his coalition, losing disastrously to individualist Ronald Reagan, a Borderer champion who deliberately followed Nixon's plan and who put it to good use again four years later in his own landslide reelection victory against the very secular-liberal and much more communitarian Walter Mondale. His vice president, George H. W. Bush, was able to follow on his heels but lost to another southern favorite son, Bill Clinton, in 1992. Even so, Bush took a great deal of the South, the Midwest, and the West. Clinton's reelection showed a similar Electoral College pattern against Kansan Robert Dole.

What was remarkable about the two Clinton elections was not his own support but the alliance between southern states and western states (though not the West Coast), a coalition driven by Borderer sensibilities. This alliance propelled George W. Bush to victory in 2000 and again in 2004, reestablishing a somewhat erased 19th-century pattern of industrial North and New

England against the rest of the country. The same pattern held, but with not the same success, in 2008 and 2012.

The Borderer cult of individualism that has grown steadily over this period is currently extolled by free market advocates, libertarians, Tea Party advocates, and more, all of whom see the world through a simplistic lens ground by the cult of individualism. As Marin writes, "The end result of this retreat from the complexities of the world is a kind of soft fascism: the denial, in the name of higher truth, of the claims of others upon the self."[45] What we are now witnessing in American society and government may be further fallout on the heels of that result, the lack of willingness to work together for just about anything amid an "an endless litany of self-concern, self-satisfaction, self-improvement, self-assertion, self-gratification, self-actualization, and self-esteem."[46]

It has never been possible to live the ideals of individualism, Daniel Boone and Ayn Rand notwithstanding. In her journal, Rand wrote, "The secret of life: you must be nothing but will. Know what you want and do it. . . . All will and all control."[47] That may be nice to imagine, but, in reality, it falls apart when faced with the complexities of human existence. Not even Rand, in fact, could operate complete alone, completely originally:

> Rand was not shy about drawing from the work of other authors. Copying was one of the few honored traditions in Hollywood; no sooner had one studio released a popular movie than the others would rush a similar story into production. Similarly, Rand was inspired to write a play set in a courtroom after seeing *The Trial of Mary Dugan*. When her play *Night of January 16th* was first produced the *Los Angeles Times* noted uneasily, "It so closely resembles 'The Trial of Mary Dugan' in its broader aspects as to incorporate veritably the same plot."[48]

We are all dependent on the work of others. The ideas behind the cults of individualism, no matter their own cultural base, can never be more than illusion.

Afterword

In late September 2012, my wife and I spent almost a week in Mount Airy, North Carolina, for what is known as "Mayberry Days." The festival, in Andy Griffith's hometown and near where my mother grew up, celebrates not only his popular television show of the 1960s but also the culture portrayed in it. There were guitar and banjo pickers and fiddlers in some of the stores, on the streets, on the small stage in the old Earle Theater, in the Andy Griffith Playhouse, and in the town's small open-air amphitheater. People crowded the small cafés and diners for sandwiches in wax paper and for chat about characters who lived in the fictional Mayberry. Mount Airy's Main Street, which looks pretty much as it must have in 1960, would probably be as desolate as that of most small towns were it not for the festival that has grown up in the wake of the show's popularity.

While there, I spent time talking to local historian Thomas Perry, who had set up a table in front of a novelty store to sell his most recent book, *Beyond Mayberry: A Memoir of Andy Griffith and Mount Airy North Carolina*. He and I discussed Griffith and Appalachian culture, and I told him that, when I was a kid, I had distrusted *The Andy Griffith Show*, never watching it. I was used to television depictions of Appalachia that really made fun of the region, and I had suspected that *The Andy Griffith Show*, on some level, was doing the same thing. Perry nodded and told me that a professor of his at Virginia Tech had felt the same way, saying that Griffith's put-downs were like a knife so sharp that the victim never felt it.

That reminded me, though I did not mention it, of Griffith's Lonesome Rhodes character in his first big film role for Elia Kazan's 1957 movie

A Face in the Crowd written by Budd Schulberg. Close to the end of the movie, Rhodes says, "To those morons out there? Shucks, I sell them chicken fertilizer as caviar. I can make them eat dog food and think it's steak. Sure, I've got them like this. You know what the public's like? A cage full of guinea pigs." And that, I realized, is exactly what many in the secular-liberal culture think of the Borderers. They are morons who will buy anything. The secular-liberals know no more about them and wish to learn less.

The Rhodes character is an amazing individualist—but he is also a stereotype of the Borderer individualist preying on the stereotype Borderer. *A Face in the Crowd*, though it is a fine movie, is a secular-liberal film reflecting stereotypes secular-liberals concocted, even though it has a Borderer star. It was an attempt to explain a culture by and for people who had absolutely no understanding of it—who did not even know that it was a culture distinct from their own.

The filmmakers were faced with the same frustrations that many of the secular-liberal culture face today, over half a century later. To them, the Borderers often seem too stupid to believe, gullible, open to flimflam from the most obvious con artists—and the question is "Why?" Why was Senator Joe McCarthy so successful? Why is Senator Ted Cruz so, today? What is going on with America? Because they had no real experience with the "other half" of America, the secular-liberal culture created their own answers, *A Face in the Crowd* being one, but only one out of many.

The suspicion I had that *The Andy Griffith Show* was simply another putdown of Borderer culture was founded in the reality of popular media from as far back as the founding of the United States. It was a suspicion of a type shared by many Borderers for generations and with good reason. In this case, however, I think I was wrong.

In one of his last film roles, in *Waitress* (Adrienne Shelly, 2007), Griffith plays a wealthy old man who, knowing he is about to die, writes a large check to one of the employees of his pie shop. This I never would have been expected of him, early on in the movie. Having watched a lot more of *The Andy Griffith Show* over the last few years, I realized that I was wrong in my evaluation of Griffith's earlier work, too. He was not playing Sheriff Taylor for a secular-liberal audience or to explain or demonize the Borderers. He was playing to the Borderers themselves, presenting a gift to the culture he had grown up in. In a nonjudgmental way, he was poking fun at Borderers—but for themselves, not for snickering outsiders.

Judging from the visitors in Mount Airy, Griffith certainly did connect with a generation of Borderers. Most of the people on the streets were in their 60s or older. They knew the shows well and had come from Pennsylvania,

Ohio, Indiana, Tennessee, Virginia, Kentucky, and other states with large Borderer populations. We did not meet a single person from New York or New England.

The focus of talk was the characters, not so much the plots of individual episodes. Even minor characters were talked of with affection, their personality quirks chuckled over anew. The week seemed more of a celebration of the individuality of these slightly peculiar but extremely familiar (to any Borderer) personality types. It almost felt like the creators of the show—including Griffith—had decided to create an answer to negative media portrayals of Borderers by showing that, yes, they have weaknesses but that those weaknesses are different in each case. And, yes, they have strengths, strengths as different as each individual.

What they had done, I realized, was to create their own gentle study of Borderer individualism, but individualism quite different from that of the "cult" I write about in this book. What they present was and is the real individualism of Appalachia and, indeed, of Borderer culture anywhere, the individualism *behind* the cult. Though when they reflect stereotypes, the characters of *The Andy Griffith Show* rise above them. Even Barney Fife, the archetypal fool, has real human dignity that comes through just when he is looking his worst.

If there is ever going to be a reconciliation between the two dominant white American cultures, it is going to have to be through recognition by both sides that what they see of the other is not the entire story. There may be—there are—cults of individualism in America that are strong enough to destroy the country, but there is also a great deal more, even in the realm of individualism. Seeing this may allow each of us to emerge from our own cultlike beliefs long enough to reach out, one to another.

I hope that can happen.

Notes

INTRODUCTION

1. Richard Rorty, *Contingency, Irony, and Solidarity* (Cambridge: Cambridge University Press, 1989), 86.

2. Leo Marx, *The Machine in the Garden* (New York: Oxford University Press, 1964), 45.

3. Amiri Baraka, *Blues People* (New York: Harper, 1999), 4.

4. Baraka, *Blues People*, 7.

5. Baraka, *Blues People*, 8.

6. Michael Hechter, *Internal Colonialism: The Celtic Fringe in British National Development, 1536–1966* (New Brunswick, NJ: Transaction, 1999), xiv.

7. Jason Mosser, *The Participatory Journalism of Michael Herr, Norman Mailer, Hunter S. Thompson, and Joan Didion: Creating New Reporting Styles* (Lewiston, NY: Edwin Mellen Press, 2012), 51–52.

8. David Hackett Fischer, *Albion's Seed: Four British Folkways in America* (Oxford: Oxford University Press, 1989), 813–16.

9. Charles Lindbergh, "Des Moines Speech," September 11, 1941, http://www.charleslindbergh.com/americanfirst/speech.asp.

10. Budd Schulberg, *What Makes Sammy Run?* (New York: Random House Modern Library, 1952), 285.

11. Michael Ignatieff, *Blood and Belonging: Journeys into the New Nationalism* (New York: Farrar, Straus and Giroux, 1995), 6.

CHAPTER 1

1. Rodger Cunningham, *Apples on the Flood* (Knoxville: University of Tennessee Press, 1987), 158.

2. Leo Marx, *The Machine in the Garden* (Oxford: Oxford University Press, 1964), 143.

3. Peter Marin, *Freedom and Its Discontents* (South Royalton, VT: Steerforth Press), 1995, 43.

4. Michael Rogin, *Fathers and Children* (New York: Vintage Books, 1975), 13.

5. E. J. Dionne, *Our Divided Political Heart: The Battle for the American Ideal in an Age of Discontent* (New York: Bloomsbury, 2012), 56.

6. Nicholas Confessore, "Tramps Like Them: Charles Murray Examines the White Working Class in 'Coming Apart,'" *New York Times*, February 12, 2012, BR9, http://www.nytimes.com/2012/02/12/books/review/charles-murray-examines-the-white-working-class-in-coming-apart.html?pagewanted=all.

7. Jane Smiley, "Jane's Bingo! Award for Most Informative Book of 2006," *Huffington Post*, December 29, 2006, http://www.huffingtonpost.com/jane-smiley/janes-bingo-award-for-mos_b_37415.html?.

8. Smiley, "Jane's Bingo."

9. Smiley, "Jane's Bingo!"

10. Cunningham, *Apples on the Flood*, xxiv.

11. Cunningham, *Apples on the Flood*, 91.

12. Max Weber, *The Essential Weber: A Reader* (New York: Routledge, 2004), 150.

13. Richard Hofstadter, *Anti-Intellectualism in American Life* (New York: Knopf, 1969), 168.

14. Hofstadter, *Anti-Intellectualism in American Life*, 174–75.

15. Richard Alba, *Ethnic Identity: The Transformation of White America* (New Haven, CT: Yale University Press, 1990), 293.

16. Michael Tesler and David Sears, "President Obama and the Growing Polarization of Partisan Attachments by Racial Attitudes and Race," paper presented at the annual meeting of the American Political Science Association, Washington DC, September 2010, 7, http://mst.michaeltesler.com/uploads/sample_2.pdf.

17. Matthew Frye Jacobson, *Roots Too: White Ethnic Revival in Post–Civil Rights America* (Cambridge, MA: Harvard University Press, 2006), 20.

18. Nathan Glazer and Daniel Moynihan, *Beyond the Melting Pot: The Negroes, Puerto Ricans, Jews, Italians, and Irish of New York City*, 2nd ed. (Cambridge, MA: MIT Press, 1970), 314.

19. Mitt Romney, quoted in David Corn, "SECRET VIDEO: Romney Tells Millionaire Donors What He REALLY Thinks of Obama Voters,"

Mother Jones Magazine, September 17, 2012, http://www.motherjones .com/politics/2012/09/secret-video-romney-private-fundraiser.

20. Eric Hoffer, *The True Believer* (New York: Harper & Brothers, 1951), 47.

21. Marin, *Freedom and Its Discontents*, 36.

22. Tesler and Sears, "President Obama and the Growing Polarization of Partisan Attachments by Racial Attitudes and Race," 5.

23. Tesler and Sears, "President Obama and the Growing Polarization of Partisan Attachments by Racial Attitudes and Race," 15.

24. Friedrich Hayek, *The Constitution of Liberty* (Chicago: University of Chicago Press, 1960), 85.

25. Richard Weiss, *The American Myth of Success* (New York: Basic Books, 1969), 91.

26. Alba, *Ethnic Identity*, 342.

27. Margaret Mead, *And Keep Your Powder Dry: An Anthropologist Looks at America* (New York: Berghahn Books, 2000), 18.

28. Mead, *And Keep Your Powder Dry*, 18.

29. Mead, *And Keep Your Powder Dry*, 18.

CHAPTER 2

1. Stephen Asma, *Against Fairness* (Chicago: University of Chicago Press, 2013), ebook, Chapter 2: To Thy Own Tribe Be True: Biological Favoritism, section "Facts and Values."

2. Alexis de Tocqueville, *Democracy in America* (Chicago: University of Chicago Press, 2007), 482–83.

3. Suzanne Mettler, *The Submerged State: How Invisible Government Policies Undermine American Democracy* (Chicago: University of Chicago Press, 2011), 16.

4. Mettler, *The Submerged State*, 9.

5. Asma, *Against Fairness*, Chapter 1: Even Jesus Had a Favorite.

6. Ayn Rand, "Introduction," in *The Virtue of Selfishness* (New York: Signet, 1964), 5.

7. Nathaniel Branden, "Counterfeit Individualism," in Rand, *The Virtue of Selfishness* (New York: Signet, 1964), 128.

8. Branden, "Counterfeit Individualism," 129–30.

9. Peter Marin, "The New Narcissism," *Harper's Monthly*, October 1975, 48.

10. Steven Lukes, *Individualism* (Oxford: Basil Blackwell, 1973), 7.

11. Lukes, *Individualism*, 58.

12. Lukes, *Individualism*, 66.

13. Lukes, *Individualism*, 71.

14. Lukes, *Individualism*, 73.

15. Lukes, *Individualism*, 28.

16. Lukes, *Individualism*, 29.

17. Stephanie Walls, *The Impact of Individualism on Political and Community Participation* (Cincinnati: University of Cincinnati, 2008), dissertation, 16.

18. Walls, *The Impact of Individualism on Political and Community Participation*, 21.

19. Walls, *The Impact of Individualism on Political and Community Participation*, 144.

20. John Dewey, *Individualism Old and New* (Amherst, NY: Prometheus Books, 1999), 27.

21. Dewey, *Individualism Old and New*, 35.

22. Dewey, *Individualism Old and New*, 81.

23. Robert Morgan, *Boone: A Biography* (Chapel Hill, NC: Algonquin Books of Chapel Hill, 2007), 84.

24. Mitt Romney, "Full Transcript of the Mitt Romney Secret Video," *Mother Jones*, September 19, 2012, http://www.motherjones.com/politics/2012/09/full-transcript-mitt-romney-secret-video.

25. Mitt Romney, "Remarks in Irwin, PA, July 17, 2012," http://www.youtube.com/watch?v=NvYCeXAcdG4.

26. Barack Obama, "Remarks in Roanoke, VA, July 13, 2012," http://www.whitehouse.gov/the-press-office/2012/07/13/remarks-president-campaign-event-roanoke-virginia.

27. "BrooklynBadBoy," "Don't Explain, DOUBLE DOWN!," *Daily Kos*, July 19, 2012, http://www.dailykos.com/story/2012/07/19/1111638/-Don-t-explain-DOUBLE-DOWN.

28. Asma, *Against Fairness*, Chapter 2: To Thy Own Tribe Be True: Biological Favoritism, section "Moral Gravity."

29. Asma, *Against Fairness*, Chapter 2: To Thy Own Tribe Be True: Biological Favoritism, section "Rational or Emotional Motives."

30. Asma, *Against Fairness*, Chapter 2: To Thy Own Tribe Be True: Biological Favoritism, section "Rational or Emotional Motives."

31. Horace Kallen, "Democracy versus the Melting-Pot," in *Culture and Democracy in the United States* (New Brunswick, NJ: Transaction Books, 1997), 27.

32. Joel Klein et al., "How to Fix Our Schools: A Manifesto by Joel Klein, Michelle Rhee, and Other Education Leaders," *Washington Post*, October 10, 2010, http://www.washingtonpost.com/wp-dyn/content/article/2010/10/07/AR2010100705078.html.

33. Betty Hart and Todd R. Risley, *Meaningful Differences in the Everyday Experience of Young American Children* (Baltimore: P. H. Brookes, 1995), 15.

34. Hector Saint John de Crèvecoeur, *Letters from an American Farmer* (New York: Fox, Duffield, 1904), 55–56.

35. Leo Marx, *The Machine in the Garden* (Oxford: Oxford University Press, 1964), 108.

36. Randolph Bourne, "Trans-National America," *Atlantic Monthly* 116 (July 1916): 88.

37. Ayn Rand, *The Fountainhead* (New York: Signet, 1993), 24–25.

38. Rand, *The Fountainhead*, 694.

39. Mary Antin, *The Promised Land* (Boston: Houghton Mifflin, 1912), 7.

40. Antin, *They Who Knock at Our Gates* (Boston: Houghton Mifflin, 1917), 76–77.

41. Bourne, "Trans-National America," 89.

42. John Cawelti, *Apostles of the Self-Made Man* (Chicago: University of Chicago Press, 1965), 44.

43. Frederick Jackson Turner, "The Significance of the Frontier in American History," paper presented at the meeting of the American Historical Association, Chicago, July 12, 1893, first appearing in the Proceedings of the State Historical Society of Wisconsin, December 14, 1893 (*Report of the American Historical Association* for 1893, 199–227), http://xroads.virginia.edu/~hyper/turner/chapter1.html.

44. Christopher Lasch, *The Culture of Narcissism* (New York: Norton, 1979), 8.

45. Horace Kallen, "Meaning of Americanism," in *Culture and Democracy in the United States* (New Brunswick, NJ: Transaction Books, 1997), 18.

46. Bourne, "Trans-National America," 87.

47. Herbert Gans, "Symbolic Ethnicity: The Future of Ethnic Groups and Cultures in America," in *Making Sense of America: Sociological Analyses and Essays* (Lanham, MD: Rowman & Littlefield, 1999), 170.

48. Dan Carter, *From George Wallace to Newt Gingrich: Race in the Conservative Counterrevolution, 1963–1994* (Baton Rouge: Louisiana State University Press, 1996), 13.

49. Matthew Frye Jacobson, *Roots Too: White Ethnic Revival in Post–Civil Rights America* (Cambridge, MA: Harvard University Press, 2006), 178.

50. Jacobson, *Roots Too*, 22.

51. Jacobson, *Roots Too*, 7.

52. Jacobson, *Roots Too*, 7–8.

53. Jacobson, *Roots Too*, 9.

54. Bourne, "Trans-National America," 87.

55. Jacobson, *Roots Too*, 30.

56. Jacobson, *Roots Too*, 87.

57. Jacobson, *Roots Too*, 75.

58. Herbert Gans, "Symbolic Ethnicity," 177.

59. Bourne, "Trans-National America," 88–89.

60. Robert Merton, "Insiders and Outsiders: A Chapter in the Sociology of Knowledge," *American Journal of Sociology* 79, no. 1 (July 1972): 12–13.

61. Merton, "Insiders and Outsiders," 13–14.

62. Merton, "Insiders and Outsiders," 40.

63. Gans, "Symbolic Ethnicity," 170.

64. Jacobson, *Roots Too*, 32.

65. Asma, *Against Fairness*, Chapter 3: In Praise of Exceptions, section "Building the Grid of Impartiality."

66. Asma, *Against Fairness*, Chapter 3: In Praise of Exceptions, section "Building the Grid of Impartiality."

67. E. J. Dionne, *Our Divided Political Heart: The Battle for the American Ideal in an Age of Discontent* (New York: Bloomsbury, 2012), 4.

68. Dionne, *Our Divided Political Heart*, 214.

69. Jennifer Burns, *Goddess of the Market: Ayn Rand and the American Right* (Oxford: Oxford University Press, 2009), 284.

70. Burns, *Goddess of the Market*, 285.

71. Lasch, *The Culture of Narcissism*, 5.

72. Jacobson, *Roots Too*, 2.

73. Richard D. Alba, *Ethnic Identity: The Transformation of White America* (New Haven, CT: Yale University Press, 1990), xiv.

74. Jacobson, *Roots Too*, 181.

75. Peter Marin, *Freedom and Its Discontents* (South Royalton, VT: Steerforth Press, 1995), 42.

76. Lasch, *The Culture of Narcissism*, 9–10.

77. Marin, *Freedom and Its Discontents*, 47.

CHAPTER 3

1. Frederick Stone, "First Congress of the Scotch-Irish in America," *Pennsylvania Magazine of History and Biography* 14, no. 1 (April 1890): 69–70, http://www.jstor.org/stable/20083358.

2. Herbert Klein, *A Population History of the United States* (Cambridge: Cambridge University Press, 2004), 92.

3. Klein, *A Population History of the United States*, 91.

4. Joe Bageant, "Eat, Drink, Fight, Fuck: How the Scots-Irish Screwed Up America," *EnergyGrid Magazine*, January 2005, http://www.energy grid.com/society/2005/01jb-irishscots.html.

5. Bageant, "Eat, Drink, Fight, Fuck."

6. Colin Woodard, *American Nations* (New York: Viking, 2011).

7. Woodard, *American Nations*, Kindle version, Chapter 9.

8. James Leyburn, *The Scotch Irish: A Social History* (Chapel Hill: University of North Carolina Press, 1962), 88.

9. Leyburn, *The Scotch Irish*, 1.

10. Leyburn, *The Scotch Irish*, 11.

11. Leyburn, *The Scotch Irish*, 89.

12. Jim Webb, *Born Fighting: How the Scots-Irish Shaped America* (New York: Broadway Books, 2004), 73–74.

13. Nell Irwin Painter, *The History of White People* (New York: Norton, 2010), 133.

14. Leyburn, *The Scotch Irish*, 65.

15. Colm T. O'Dushlaine, Derek Morris, Valentina Moskvina, George Kirov, International Schizophrenia Consortium, Michael Gill, Aiden Corvin, James F. Wilson, and Gianpiero L. Cavalleri, "Population Structure and Genome-Wide Patterns of Variation in Ireland and Britain," *European Journal of Human Genetics* 18 (2010): 1248–54, http://www.nature.com/ejhg/journal/v18/n11/full/ejhg201087a.html.

16. Leyburn, *The Scotch Irish*, 66.

17. Leyburn, *The Scotch Irish*, 67.

18. Woodard, *American Nations*.

19. Judith Ridner, *A Town In-Between: Carlisle, Pennsylvania, and the Early Mid-Atlantic Interior* (Philadelphia: University of Pennsylvania Press, 2010), 8.

20. Ridner, *A Town In-Between*, 9.

21. Ridner, *A Town In-Between*, 23.

22. Ridner, *A Town In-Between*, 26.

23. David Hackett Fischer, *Albion's Seed: Four British Folkways in America* (New York: Oxford University Press, 1989), 6.

24. Fischer, *Albion's Seed*, 606.

25. Klein, *A Population History of the United States*, 60.

26. Henry Gemery, "The White Population of the Colonial United States, 1607–1790," in *A Population History of North America*, ed. Michael Haines and Richard Steckel (Cambridge: Cambridge University Press, 2000), 151.

27. David Galenson, *White Servitude in Colonial America: An Economic Analysis* (Cambridge: Cambridge University Press, 1981), 23.

28. Gemery, "The White Population of the Colonial United States, 1607–1790," 173.

29. Galenson, *White Servitude in Colonial America*, 178.

30. Klein, *A Population History of the United States*, 88.

31. Fischer, *Albion's Seed*, 611.

32. Rodger Cunningham, *Apples on the Flood* (Knoxville: University of Tennessee Press, 1987), 73.

33. Fischer, *Albion's Seed*, 615.

34. Fischer, *Albion's Seed*, 617.

35. Fischer, *Albion's Seed*, 621.

36. Fischer, *Albion's Seed*, 624.

37. Fischer, *Albion's Seed*, 626–29.

38. Fischer, *Albion's Seed*, 630.

39. Fischer, *Albion's Seed*, 612.

40. Fischer, *Albion's Seed*, 613.

41. Klein, *A Population History of the United States*, 93.

42. Klein, *A Population History of the United States*, 94.

43. Stephanie Walls, "The Impact of Individualism on Political and Community Participation," PhD diss., University of Cincinnati, 2008, 4.

44. Cunningham, *Apples on the Flood*, xvi.

45. John Major, *Historia Majoris Britanniae tam Angliae q. Scotiae …* (Paris, 1521), trans. in P. Hume Brown, ed., *Scotland before 1700 from Contemporary Documents* (Edinburgh, 1893), 44, quoted in Fischer, *Albion's Seed*, 656.

46. Walter Ong, *Orality and Literacy* (London: Routledge, 2002).

47. Webb, *Born Fighting*, 25.

48. Webb, *Born Fighting*, 37.

49. Webb, *Born Fighting*, 35.

50. Thomas Sowell, *Race and Culture: A World View* (New York: Basic Books, 1994), 3.

51. Webb, *Born Fighting*, 63.

52. Michael Hechter, *Internal Colonialism: The Celtic Fringe in British National Development, 1536–1966* (Berkeley: University of California Press, 1975), 18.

53. Cunningham, *Apples on the Flood*, xxi–xxii.

54. Wayne Franklin, *Discoverers, Explorers, Settlers: The Diligent Writers of Early America* (Chicago: University of Chicago Press, 1979).

55. Cunningham, *Apples on the Flood*, xxiii.

56. Cunningham, *Apples on the Flood*, xxiv

57. Cunningham, *Apples on the Flood*, 43.

58. Cunningham, *Apples on the Flood*, 43.

59. Octave Mannoni, *Prospero and Caliban: The Psychology of Colonization* (Ann Arbor: University of Michigan Press, 1990), 97.

60. Cunningham, *Apples on the Flood*, 21.

61. Cunningham, *Apples on the Flood*, xxviii.

62. Cunningham, *Apples on the Flood*, 72.

63. Fischer, *Albion's Seed*, 633.

64. Cunningham, *Apples on the Flood*, 78–79.

65. Fischer, *Albion's Seed*, 633.

66. Cunningham, *Apples on the Flood*, 93.

67. Frederick Jackson Turner, "The Significance of the Frontier in American History," paper presented at the meeting of the American Historical Association, Chicago, July 12, 1893, first appearing in the Proceedings of the

State Historical Society of Wisconsin, December 14, 1893 (*Report of the American Historical Association* for 1893, 199–227), http://xroads.virginia .edu/~hyper/turner/chapter1.html.

68. Horace Meyer Kallen, *Culture and Democracy in the United States* (New Brunswick, NJ: Transaction, 1997), 6.

CHAPTER 4

1. Robert Morgan, *Boone: A Biography* (Chapel Hill, NC: Algonquin Books of Chapel Hill, 2007), 11.

2. Marjoleine Kars, *Breaking Loose Together* (Chapel Hill: University of North Carolina Press, 2002), 16.

3. Colin Woodard, *American Nations* (New York: Viking, 2011), Kindle version, Chapter 9.

4. Henry Nash Smith, *Virgin Land* (Cambridge, MA: Harvard University Press, 1950), 215.

5. Michael Rogin, *Fathers and Children* (New York: Vintage Books, 1975), 3–4.

6. Charles Woodmason, *The Carolina Backcountry on the Eve of the Revolution* (Chapel Hill: University of North Carolina Press, 1953), 14.

7. Woodmason, *The Carolina Backcountry on the Eve of the Revolution*, 39.

8. John Mack Faragher, *Daniel Boone: The Life and Legend of an American Pioneer* (New York: Holt, 1992), xvi.

9. Morgan, *Boone*, 79.

10. Woodmason, *The Carolina Backcountry on the Eve of the Revolution*, 61.

11. Woodard, *American Nations*, Kindle version, Chapter 9.

12. Kars, *Breaking Loose Together*, 21.

13. Kars, *Breaking Loose Together*, 24.

14. Kars, *Breaking Loose Together*, 52.

15. Kars, *Breaking Loose Together*, 69.

16. Kars, *Breaking Loose Together*, 55.

17. Kars, *Breaking Loose Together*, 56.

18. Woodmason, *The Carolina Backcountry on the Eve of the Revolution*, 286–87.

19. Frederick Jackson Turner, "The Significance of the Frontier in American History," paper presented at the meeting of the American Historical Association, Chicago, July 12, 1893, first appearing in the Proceedings of the State Historical Society of Wisconsin, December 14, 1893 (*Report of the American Historical Association* for 1893, 199–227), http://xroads.virginia .edu/~hyper/turner/chapter1.html.

20. Thomas Slaughter, *The Whiskey Rebellion: Frontier Epilogue to the American Revolution* (New York: Oxford University Press, 1986), 29.

21. Slaughter, *The Whiskey Rebellion*, 78.

22. Slaughter, *The Whiskey Rebellion*, 13.

23. Slaughter, *The Whiskey Rebellion*, 35.

24. Rogin, *Fathers and Children*, 12.

25. Slaughter, *The Whiskey Rebellion*, 31.

26. Ron Chernow, *Alexander Hamilton* (New York: Penguin, 2004), 469–70.

27. Slaughter, *The Whiskey Rebellion*, 57.

28. Chernow, *Alexander Hamilton*, 470.

29. Slaughter, *The Whiskey Rebellion*, 59.

30. Richard Hofstadter, *Anti-Intellectualism in American Life* (New York: Knopf, 1962), 146.

31. Chernow, *Alexander Hamilton*, 487.

32. Smith, *Virgin Land*, 216.

33. Slaughter, *The Whiskey Rebellion*, 62.

34. Slaughter, *The Whiskey Rebellion*, 66.

35. Hofstadter, *Anti-Intellectualism in American Life*, 163.

36. Slaughter, *The Whiskey Rebellion*, 72.

37. Slaughter, *The Whiskey Rebellion*, 72.

38. Slaughter, *The Whiskey Rebellion*, 105.

39. Slaughter, *The Whiskey Rebellion*, 109–10.

40. Slaughter, *The Whiskey Rebellion*, 110.

41. Slaughter, *The Whiskey Rebellion*, 110–11.

42. Slaughter, *The Whiskey Rebellion*, 117.

43. Slaughter, *The Whiskey Rebellion*, 118.

44. Slaughter, *The Whiskey Rebellion*, 142.

45. Morgan, *Boone*, 54.

46. Woodmason, *The Carolina Backcountry on the Eve of the Revolution*, 33.

47. Morgan, *Boone*, 55.

48. Rogin, *Fathers and Children*, 19.

49. Morgan, *Boone*, 47.

50. Smith, *Virgin Land*, 59.

51. James Fenimore Cooper, *The Pioneers* (New York: Penguin, 1988), 109–10.

52. Cooper, *The Pioneers*, 21–22.

53. James Fenimore Cooper, *The Pioneers*, 356–57.

54. Christopher Lasch, *The Culture of Narcissism* (New York: Norton, 1979), 10.

55. Smith, *Virgin Land*, 223.

56. Smith, *Virgin Land*, 215.

57. Charles Haight Farnham, *A Life of Francis Parkman* (Boston: Little, Brown, 1901), 267.

58. Hofstadter, *Anti-Intellectualism in American Life*, 157.

59. Hofstadter, *Anti-Intellectualism in American Life*, 151.

60. Hofstadter, *Anti-Intellectualism in American Life*, 151.

61. Hofstadter, *Anti-Intellectualism in American Life*, 155–56.

62. Hofstadter, *Anti-Intellectualism in American Life*, 171.

63. Rogin, *Fathers and Children*, 15.

64. Rogin, *Fathers and Children*, 251.

65. Rogin, *Fathers and Children*, 253–54.

66. Rogin, *Fathers and Children*, 256.

67. W. E. B. Du Bois, *John Brown* (Philadelphia: G. W. Jacobs, 1909), 48.

68. Du Bois, *John Brown*, 31.

69. Du Bois, *John Brown*, 23.

70. Du Bois, *John Brown*, 50.

71. Du Bois, *John Brown*, 56.

72. Richard Weiss, *The American Myth of Success* (New York: Basic Books, 1969), 29.

CHAPTER 5

1. Leo Marx, *The Machine in the Garden* (Oxford: Oxford University Press, 1964), 73.

2. Marx, *The Machine in the Garden*, 82.

3. Marx, *The Machine in the Garden*, 98.

4. Henry Nash Smith, *Virgin Land* (Cambridge, MA: Harvard University Press, 1950), 224.

5. Smith, *Virgin Land*, 229.

6. Smith, *Virgin Land*, 237.

7. Andrew Carnegie, *Triumphant Democracy* (New York: Scribners, 1886), 23.

8. John G. Cawelti, *Apostles of the Self-Made Man* (Chicago: University of Chicago Press, 1965), 14.

9. Richard Weiss, *The American Myth of Success* (New York: Basic Books, 1969), 4

10. Cawelti, *Apostles of the Self-Made Man*, 15.

11. Cawelti, *Apostles of the Self-Made Man*, 23–24.

12. Cawelti, *Apostles of the Self-Made Man*, 3.

13. Frances Milton Trollope, *Domestic Manners of the Americans* (New York: Dodd, Mead, 1901), 281.

14. Trollope, *Domestic Manners of the Americans*, 160–61.

15. Ralph Waldo Emerson, "The American Scholar," in *Nature and Other Essays* (New York: Dover, 2009), 157.

16. Emerson, "The American Scholar," 159.

17. Emerson, "The American Scholar," 165.

18. Ralph Waldo Emerson, "Self-Reliance," in *Self-Reliance and Other Essays* (New York: Dover, 1993), 31.

19. Emerson, "Self-Reliance," 32–33.

20. Emerson, "Self-Reliance," 35.

21. Marx, *The Machine in the Garden*, 181.

22. Timothy Walker, "The Defense of Mechanical Philosophy," *North American Review* 33, no. 72 (July 1831): 122.

23. Walker, "The Defense of Mechanical Philosophy," 123.

24. Walker, "The Defense of Mechanical Philosophy," 126.

25. Walker, "The Defense of Mechanical Philosophy," 135.

26. Walker, "The Defense of Mechanical Philosophy," 136.

27. Arthur Mann, "From Immigration to Acculturation," in *Making America: The Society and Culture of the United States*, ed. Luther Luedtke (Chapel Hill: University of North Carolina Press, 1992), 69.

28. Mann, "From Immigration to Acculturation," 69.

29. Horatio Alger, *Fame and Fortune or the Progress of Richard Hunter* (Boston: Loring, 1868), Kindle edition, Chapter XXI.

30. Alger, *Fame and Fortune or the Progress of Richard Hunter*, Chapter XXII.

31. Alger, *Fame and Fortune or the Progress of Richard Hunter*, Chapter XXII.

32. Alger, *Fame and Fortune or the Progress of Richard Hunter*, Chapter XXIII.

33. Horatio Alger, *Mark, the Match Boy (or Richard Hunter's Ward)* (Boston: Loring, 1869), Kindle edition, Chapter 13.

34. Alger, *Fame and Fortune or the Progress of Richard Hunter*, Chapter XXIII.

35. Alger, *Mark, the Match Boy (or Richard Hunter's Ward)*, Chapter 4.

36. Alger, *Mark, the Match Boy (or Richard Hunter's Ward)*, Chapter 3.

37. Alger, *Mark, the Match Boy (or Richard Hunter's Ward)*, Chapter 1.

38. Weiss, *The American Myth of Success*, 169.

39. Alger, *Mark, the Match Boy (or Richard Hunter's Ward)*, Chapter 10.

40. Alger, *Mark, the Match Boy (or Richard Hunter's Ward)*, Chapter 12.

41. Gary Scharnhorst, with Jack Bales, *The Lost Life of Horatio Alger, Jr.* (Bloomington: Indiana University Press, 1985), 19.

42. Alger, *Mark, the Match Boy (or Richard Hunter's Ward)*, Chapter 16.

43. Alger, *Mark, the Match Boy (or Richard Hunter's Ward)*, Chapter 17.

44. Horatio Alger, *Rufus and Rose Or, the Fortunes of Rough and Ready* (Boston: Loring, 1870), Kindle edition, Chapter IV.

45. Weiss, *The American Myth of Success*, 48.

46. Weiss, *The American Myth of Success*, 49.

47. Jeffrey Louis Decker, *Made in America* (Minneapolis: University of Minnesota Press, 1997), 1.

48. Henry Adams, *The Education of Henry Adams* (Boston: Houghton Mifflin, 1918), 328.

49. Weiss, *The American Myth of Success*, 134.

50. Weiss, *The American Myth of Success*, 159.

51. Weiss, *The American Myth of Success*, 165.

52. Weiss, *The American Myth of Success*, 175.

53. Weiss, *The American Myth of Success*, 181.

54. Weiss, *The American Myth of Success*, 171.

55. Norman Vincent Peale, *The Power of Positive Thinking* (New York: Fawcett Crest, 1952), 13.

56. Weiss, *The American Myth of Success*, 59.

57. Weiss, *The American Myth of Success*, 117.

58. Victor Appleton, *Tom Swift and His Airship* (New York: Grosset & Dunlap, 1910).

59. Thomas Kessner, *The Flight of the Century: Charles Lindbergh and the Rise of American Aviation* (New York: Oxford University Press, 2010), xix.

60. Victor Appleton, *Tom Swift and His Motor-Cycle; or, Fun and Adventures on the Road* (New York: Grosset & Dunlap, 1910), 180.

61. Kessner, *The Flight of the Century*, 73

62. Kessner, *The Flight of the Century*, 118.

63. Appleton, *Tom Swift and His Airship*.

64. Kessner, *The Flight of the Century*, 7.

65. Kessner, *The Flight of the Century*, 58.

66. Budd Schulberg, *What Makes Sammy Run?* (New York: Random House Modern Library, 1952), 9–10.

67. Schulberg, *What Makes Sammy Run?*, 151.

68. Henry David Thoreau, "Civil Disobedience," http://www.gutenberg.org/files/71/71-h/71-h.htm.

69. Thoreau, "Civil Disobedience."

70. Thoreau, "Civil Disobedience."

71. Schulberg, *What Makes Sammy Run?*, 167.

72. Schulberg, *What Makes Sammy Run?*, 249.

CHAPTER 6

1. J. W. Williamson, *Hillbillyland: What the Movies Did to the Mountains and What the Mountains Did to the Movies* (Chapel Hill: University of North Carolina Press, 1995), ix.

2. Rodger Cunningham, *Apples on the Flood: Minority Discourse and Appalachia* (Knoxville: University of Tennessee Press, 1987), 117–18.

3. Henry D. Shapiro, *Appalachia on Our Mind: The Southern Mountains and Mountaineers in the American Consciousness, 1870–1920* (Chapel Hill: University of North Carolina Press, 1978), xviii.

4. Dwight Billings, "Introduction," in *Back Talk from Appalachia: Confronting Stereotypes*, ed. Dwight Billings, Gurney Norman, and Katherine Ledford (Lexington: University Press of Kentucky, 1999), 3.

5. Billings, "Introduction," 5.

6. Peter Stanfield, *Hollywood, Westerns and the 1930s: The Lost Trail* (Exeter: University of Exeter Press, 2001), 194–95.

7. Stanley Corkin, *Cowboys as Cold Warriors: The Western and U.S. History* (Philadelphia: Temple University Press, 2004), 180.

8. Richard Slotkin, *Gunfighter Nation: The Myth of the Frontier in Twentieth-Century America* (Norman: University of Oklahoma Press, 1992), 475.

9. Robert Warshaw, "Movie Chronicle: The Westerner" (1954), reprinted in *The Immediate Experience* (Garden City, NY: Doubleday, 1962), 135–54.

10. John Lenihan, *Showdown: Confronting Modern America in the Western Film* (Urbana: University of Illinois Press, 1980), 22.

11. Lee Clark Mitchell, *Westerns: Making the Man in Fiction and Film* (Chicago: University of Chicago Press, 1996), 192.

12. Mitchell, *Westerns*, 193.

13. Walter Lippmann, *Public Opinion* (New York: Harcourt, Brace, 1922), 272.

14. Lenihan, *Showdown*, 116–17.

15. Herbert Klein, *A Population History of the United States* (Cambridge: Cambridge University Press, 2004), 175–76.

16. Richard Easterlin, "American Population in the Twentieth Century," in *A Population History of North America*, ed. Michael Haines and Richard Steckel (Cambridge: Cambridge University Press, 2000), 634.

17. Easterlin, "American Population in the Twentieth Century," 644.

18. Easterlin, "American Population in the Twentieth Century," 643.

19. John Steinbeck, "The Making of a New Yorker," reprinted in Alexander Klein, ed., *Empire City: A Treasury of New York* (Manchester, NH: Ayers, 1955), 471.

20. A. O. Scott, "Review of *3:10 to Yuma*," *New York Times*, September 7, 2007, http://movies.nytimes.com/2007/09/07/movies/07yuma.html?8dpc.

21. Lee Server, *Robert Mitchum: "Baby, I Don't Care"* (New York: St. Martin's, 2001), 165.

22. Simon McLean, "Thunder Road," *Senses of Cinema*, http://www.sensesofcinema.com/contents/cteq/02/20/thunder.html#5, accessed September 5, 2007.

23. Server, *Robert Mitchum*, 79.

CHAPTER 7

1. Charles Murray, *Coming Apart: The State of White America, 1960–2010* (New York: Crown Forum, 2012), 13.

2. Nathan Glazer, *Affirmative Discrimination: Ethnic Inequality and Public Policy* (New York: Basic Books, 1975), 177.

3. Glazer, *Affirmative Discrimination*, 181.

4. Glazer, *Affirmative Discrimination*, 172.

5. Murray, *Coming Apart*, 17.

6. Murray, *Coming Apart*, 21.

7. Richard Florida, "How the Crash Will Reshape America," *The Atlantic*, March 2009, http://www.theatlantic.com/magazine/archive/2009/03/how-the-crash-will-reshape-america/307293.

8. Julia Isaacs, "Economic Mobility of Families across Generations," Brookings Institution, November 2007, http://www.brookings.edu/research/papers/2007/11/generations-isaacs.

9. Murray, *Coming Apart*, 24.

10. Thomas Sowell, *Race and Culture: A World View* (New York: Basic Books, 1994), x.

11. Ralph Waldo Emerson, "Self Reliance," in *Self-Reliance and Other Essays* (New York: Dover, 1993), 31.

12. Murray, *Coming Apart*, 101.

13. Murray, *Coming Apart*, 127.

14. Murray, *Coming Apart*, 129.

15. Murray, *Coming Apart*, 235.

16. David Whisnant, *All That Is Native and Fine: The Politics of Culture in an American Region* (Chapel Hill: University of North Carolina Press, 1983), 7.

17. Whisnant, *All That Is Native and Fine*, 8.

18. Whisnant, *All That Is Native and Fine*, 259.

19. Whisnant, *All That Is Native and Fine*, 260.

20. Whisnant, *All That Is Native and Fine*, 260.

21. Amy Sonnie and James Tracy, *Hillbilly Nationalists, Urban Race Rebels, and Black Power: Community Organizing in Radical Times* (Brooklyn, NY: Melville House, 2011), 1.

22. Ken Kesey, *Sometimes a Great Notion* (New York: Viking Press, 1964), 12.

23. Murray, *Coming Apart*, 103.

24. Murray, *Coming Apart*, 114.

25. Rodger Cunningham, "The Valley So Low: Kristeva, Freud, Mori, and Appalachian Uncanniness," paper presented at the 2012 Appalachian Studies Conference, Indiana, PA, March 23–25, 2012.

26. Albert Votaw, "The Hillbillies Invade Chicago," *Harper's Magazine* 216, no. 1293 (February 1958): 64.

27. Votaw, "The Hillbillies Invade Chicago," 66.

28. Jim Webb, *Born Fighting: How the Scots-Irish Shaped America* (New York: Broadway Books, 2004), 38.

29. Sonnie and Tracy, *Hillbilly Nationalists, Urban Race Rebels, and Black Power*, 28.

30. Michael Hechter, *Internal Colonialism: The Celtic Fringe in British National Development, 1536–1966* (Berkeley: University of California Press, 1975), 23.

31. Hechter, *Internal Colonialism*, 29.

32. Alice Walker, "Everyday Use," in *In Love and Trouble: Stories of Black Women* (New York: Harcourt Brace Jovanovich, 1973), http://xroads.virginia.edu/~ug97/quilt/walker.html.

33. J. W. Williamson, *Hillbillyland: What the Movies Did to the Mountains and What the Mountains Did to the Movies* (Chapel Hill: University of North Carolina Press, 1995), 2.

34. Williamson, *Hillbillyland*, 6.

35. Cunningham, "The Valley So Low."

36. Hechter, *Internal Colonialism*, 43.

37. Hechter, *Internal Colonialism*, 312.

38. Hechter, *Internal Colonialism*, 313.

39. Hechter, *Internal Colonialism*, 314.

40. Hechter, *Internal Colonialism*, 314.

41. Peter Marin, *Freedom and Its Discontents* (South Royalton, VT: Steerforth Press, 1995), 33.

42. Ashley O'Connor, quoted in Greg Sargent, "Fact Checking for Thee, but Not for Me," *Washington Post*, August 28, 2012, http://www.washingtonpost.com/blogs/plum-line/post/fact-checking-for-thee-but-not-for-me/2012/08/28/cccd6036-f11d-11e1-892d-bc92fee603a7_blog.html.

43. Marin, *Freedom and Its Discontents*, 31.

44. Marin, *Freedom and Its Discontents*, 32.

45. Marin, *Freedom and Its Discontents*, 37.

46. Marin, *Freedom and Its Discontents*, 35.

47. Ayn Rand, David Harriman, and Leonard Peikoff, eds., *Journals of Ayn Rand* (New York: Dutton, 1999), 28.

48. Jennifer Burns, *Goddess of the Market: Ayn Rand and the American Right* (Oxford: Oxford University Press, 2009), 28.

Bibliography

Adams, Henry, Leon Wieseltier, Ernest Samuels, and Jayne Samuels. *The Education of Henry Adams*. New York: Library of America, 2010.

Agee, James, and Walker Evans. *Let Us Now Praise Famous Men: Three Tenant Families*. Boston: Houghton Mifflin, 1960.

Alba, Richard D. *Ethnic Identity: The Transformation of White America*. New Haven, CT: Yale University Press, 1990.

Alger, Horatio. *Fame and Fortune or the Progress of Richard Hunter*. Boston: Loring, 1868.

Alger, Horatio. *Mark, the Match Boy (or Richard Hunter's Ward)*. Boston: Loring, 1869.

Alger, Horatio. *Rufus and Rose Or, the Fortunes of Rough and Ready*. Boston: Loring, 1870.

Alger, Horatio, and Alan Trachtenberg. *Ragged Dick, or, Street Life in New York with the Boot-Blacks*. New York: Penguin Books, 1990.

Antin, Mary. *The Promised land: By Mary Antin*. Boston: Houghton Mifflin, 1912.

Antin, Mary. *They Who Knock at Our Gates: A Complete Gospel of Immigration*. Boston: Houghton Mifflin, 1917.

Appleton, Victor. *Tom Swift and His Airship*. New York: Grosset & Dunlap, 1910.

Appleton, Victor. *Tom Swift and His Motor-Cycle; or, Fun and Adventures on the Road*. New York: Grosset & Dunlap, 1910.

Asma, Stephen T. *Against Fairness*. Chicago: University of Chicago Press, 2013.

Baraka, Amiri (LeRoi Jones). *Blues People*. New York: Harper, 1999.

Billings, Dwight B., Gurney Norman, and Katherine Ledford. *Back Talk from Appalachia: Confronting Stereotypes*. Lexington: University Press of Kentucky, 2001.

Boone, Daniel, and Francis L. Hawks. *Daniel Boone, His Own Story*. Bedford, MA: Applewood Books, 1995.

Bourne, Randolph. "Trans-National America." *Atlantic Monthly* 116 (July 1916): 86–97.

Burns, Jennifer. *Goddess of the Market: Ayn Rand and the American Right*. Oxford: Oxford University Press, 2009.

Carnegie, Andrew. *Triumphant Democracy; or, Fifty Years' March of the Republic*. New York: C. Scribner's Sons, 1886.

Carter, Dan T. *From George Wallace to Newt Gingrich: Race in the Conservative Counterrevolution, 1963–1994*. Baton Rouge: Louisiana State University Press, 1996.

Cawelti, John G. *Apostles of the Self-Made Man*. Chicago: University of Chicago Press, 1965.

Chernow, Ron. *Alexander Hamilton*. New York: Penguin Press, 2004.

Cooper, James Fenimore. *The Pioneers*. Cambridge, MA: Belknap Press of Harvard University Press, 2011.

Corkin, Stanley. *Cowboys as Cold Warriors: The Western and U.S. History*. Philadelphia: Temple University Press, 2004.

Crèvecoeur, J. Hector St. John de, Ludwig Lewisohn, and William Peterfield Trent. *Letters from an American Farmer; describing certain provincial situations, manners, and customs, not generally known; and conveying some idea of the late and present interior circumstances of the British colonies in North America. Written for the information of a friend in England, by J. Hector St. John*. New York: Fox, Duffield & Co., 1904.

Cunningham, Rodger. *Apples on the Flood: Minority Discourse and Appalachia*. Knoxville: University of Tennessee Press, 1991.

Decker, Jeffrey Louis. *Made in America: Self-Styled Success from Horatio Alger to Oprah Winfrey*. Minneapolis: University of Minnesota Press, 1997.

Dewey, John. *Individualism Old and New*. Amherst, NY: Prometheus Books, 1999.

Dewey, John. *The Public and Its Problems*. New York: Henry Holt and Company, 1927.

Dionne, E. J. *Our Divided Political Heart: The Battle for the American Idea in an Age of Discontent*. New York: Bloomsbury, 2012.

Du Bois, W. E. B. *John Brown*. Philadelphia: G. W. Jacobs & Company, 1909.

Eliasoph, Nina. *Avoiding Politics: How Americans Produce Apathy in Everyday Life*. Cambridge: Cambridge University Press, 1998.

Emerson, Ralph Waldo. *Nature and Other Essays*. New York: Dover, 2009.

Emerson, Ralph Waldo. "Self-Reliance." In *Self Reliance and Other Essays.* New York: Dover, 1993.

Faragher, John Mack. *Daniel Boone: The Life and Legend of an American Pioneer.* New York: Holt, 1992.

Farnham, Charles Haight. *A life of Francis Parkman.* Boston: Little, Brown, 1901.

Filson, John. *The Adventures of Colonel Daniel Boon: 1786.* New York: Garland, 1978.

Fischer, David Hackett. *Albion's Seed: Four British Folkways in America.* New York: Oxford University Press, 1991.

Fitzgerald, F. Scott, and Matthew J. Bruccoli. *The Great Gatsby.* New York: Scribner, 1996.

Franklin, Benjamin, and Leonard Woods Labaree. *The Autobiography of Benjamin Franklin.* New Haven, CT: Yale University Press, 1964.

Franklin, Wayne. *James Fenimore Cooper: The Early Years.* New Haven, CT: Yale University Press, 2007.

Galenson, David W. *White Servitude in Colonial America: An Economic Analysis.* Cambridge: Cambridge University Press, 1981.

Gans, Herbert J. *Making Sense of America: Sociological Analyses and Essays.* Lanham, MD: Rowman & Littlefield, 1999.

Glazer, Nathan. *Affirmative Discrimination: Ethnic Inequlaiy and Public Policy.* New York: Basic Books, 1975.

Glazer, Nathan, and Daniel Moynihan. *Beyond the Melting Pot: The Negroes, Puerto Ricans, Jews, Italians, and Irish of New York City.* 2nd ed. Cambridge: MIT Press, 1970.

Habermas, Jürgen. *The Structural Transformation of the Public Sphere: An Inquiry into a Category of Bourgeois Society.* Cambridge, MA: MIT Press, 1989.

Haines, Michael R., and Richard H. Steckel. *A Population History of North America.* Cambridge: Cambridge University Press, 2000.

Hart, Betty, and Todd R. Risley. *Meaningful Differences in the Everyday Experience of Young American Children.* Baltimore: P. H. Brookes, 1995.

Hayek, Friedrich A. von. *The Constitution of Liberty.* Chicago: University of Chicago Press, 1960.

Hayek, Friedrich A. von. *The Road to Serfdom.* Chicago: University of Chicago Press, 1944.

Hechter, Michael. *Internal Colonialism: The Celtic Fringe in British National Development.* New Brunswick, NJ: Transaction Publishers, 1999.

Higham, John. *Strangers in the Land: Patterns of American Nativism, 1860–1925.* New York: Atheneum, 1963.

Hoffer, Eric. *The True Believer: Thoughts on the Nature of Mass Movements.* New York: Harper and Row, 1951.

Hofstadter, Richard. *Anti-Intellectualism in American Life*. New York: Knopf, 1963.

Ignatieff, Michael. *Blood and Belonging: Journeys into the New Nationalism*. New York: Farrar, Straus, and Giroux, 1994.

Jacobson, Matthew Frye. *Roots Too: White Ethnic Revival in Post–Civil Rights America*. Cambridge, MA: Harvard University Press, 2006.

James, William. *The Will to Believe, and Other Essays in Popular Philosophy, and Human Immortality*. New York: Dover Publications, 1960.

Jefferson, Thomas, and Thomas Jefferson Randolph. *Memoir, Correspondence, and Miscellanies Volume I*. Charlottesville, VA: F. Carr, 1829.

Johnson, Barbara. *A World of Difference*. Baltimore: Johns Hopkins University Press, 1987.

Kallen, Horace Meyer, and Stephen J. Whitfield. *Culture and Democracy in the United States*. New Brunswick, NJ: Transaction, 1997.

Kars, Marjoleine. *Breaking Loose Together the Regulator Rebellion in Pre-Revolutionary North Carolina*. Chapel Hill: University of North Carolina Press, 2002.

Kasson, John F. *Rudeness and Civility: Manners in Nineteenth-Century Urban America*. New York: Hill and Wang, 1990.

Kesey, Ken. *Sometimes a Great Notion*. New York: Viking Press, 1964.

Kessner, Thomas. *The Flight of the Century: Charles Lindbergh and the Rise of American Aviation*. New York: Oxford University Press, 2010.

Klein, Alexander, ed. *Empire City: A Treasury of New York*. Manchester, NH: Ayers, 1955.

Klein, Herbert. *A Population History of the United States*. Cambridge: Cambridge University Press, 2004.

Larkin, Jack. *The Reshaping of Everyday Life, 1790–1840*. New York: Harper and Row, 1988.

Lasch, Christopher. *The Culture of Narcissism: American Life in an Age of Diminishing Expectations*. New York: Norton, 1978.

Lenihan, John. *Showdown: Confronting Modern America in the Western Film*. Urbana: University of Illinois Press, 1980.

Lewis, R. W. B. *The American Adam: Innocence, Tragedy, and Tradition in the Nineteenth Century*. Chicago: University of Chicago Press, 1955.

Leyburn, James. *The Scotch-Irish: A Social History*. Chapel Hill: University of North Carolina Press, 1962.

Lippmann, Walter. *Public Opinion*. New York: Harcourt, Brace, 1922.

Lippmann, Walter. *The Public Philosophy*. New York: New American Library, 1955.

Luedtke, Luther S. *Making America: The Society and Culture of the United States*. Chapel Hill: University of North Carolina Press, 1992.

Lukes, Steven. *Individualism*. Oxford: Blackwell, 1973.

Mannoni, Octave. *Prospero and Caliban: The Psychology of Colonization*. Ann Arbor: University of Michigan Press, 1990.

Marin, Peter. *Freedom and Its Discontents: Reflections on Four Decades of American Moral Experience*. South Royalton, VT: Steerforth Press, 1995.

Marin, Peter. "The New Narcissism." *Harper's Monthly*, October 1975.

Marx, Leo. *The Machine in the Garden: Technology and the Pastoral Ideal in America*. New York: Oxford University Press, 1964.

Mayes, Herbert R. *Alger: A Biography without a Hero*. Des Plaines, IL: G. K. Westgard II, 1978.

Mead, Margaret. *And Keep Your Powder Dry: An Anthropologist Looks at America*. New York: Berghahn Books, 2000.

Merton, Robert. "Insiders and Outsiders: A Chapter in the Sociology of Knowledge." *American Journal of Sociology* 79, no. 1 (July 1972): 9–47.

Mettler, Suzanne. *The Submerged State: How Invisible Government Policies Undermine American Democracy*. Chicago: University of Chicago Press, 2011.

Mitchell, Lee Clark. *Westerns: Making the Man in Fiction and Film*. Chicago: University of Chicago Press, 1996.

Morgan, Robert. *Boone: A Biography*. Chapel Hill, NC: Algonquin Books of Chapel Hill, 2007.

Mosser, Jason. *The Participatory Journalism of Michael Herr, Norman Mailer, Hunter S. Thompson, and Joan Didion: Creating New Reporting Styles*. Lewiston, NY: Edwin Mellen Press, 2012.

Murray, Charles A. *Coming Apart: The State of White America, 1960–2010*. New York: Crown Forum, 2012.

Ong, Walter. *Orality and Literacy: The Technologizing of the Word*. London: Routledge, 2002.

Painter, Nell Irvin. *The History of White People*. New York: Norton, 2010.

Peale, Norman Vincent. *The Power of Positive Thinking*. New York: Fawcett Crest, 1987.

Rand, Ayn. *Atlas Shrugged*. New York, NY: Signet, 2007.

Rand, Ayn. *The Fountainhead*. New York: Signet, 1993.

Rand, Ayn, and Nathaniel Branden. *The Virtue of Selfishness, a New Concept of Egoism*. New York: New American Library, 1964.

Rand, Ayn, David Harriman, and Leonard Peikoff, eds. *Journals of Ayn Rand*. New York: Dutton, 1999.

Ridner, Judith A. *A Town In-Between: Carlisle, Pennsylvania, and the Early Mid-Atlantic Interior*. Philadelphia: University of Pennsylvania Press, 2010.

Riesman, David. *The Lonely Crowd: A Study of the Changing American Character*. New Haven, CT: Yale University Press, 1950.

Rischin, Moses. *The American Gospel of Success: Individualism and Beyond.* Chicago: Quadrangle Books, 1965.

Rogin, Michael. *Fathers and Children: Andrew Jackson and the Subjugation of the American Indian.* New York: Knopf, 1975.

Rorty, Richard. *Contingency, Irony, and Solidarity.* Cambridge: Cambridge University Press, 1989.

Rorty, Richard. *Philosophy and Social Hope.* New York: Penguin Books, 1999.

Roth, Philip. *The Plot against America.* Boston: Houghton Mifflin, 2004.

Scharnhorst, Gary, and Jack Bales. *The Lost Life of Horatio Alger, Jr.* Bloomington: Indiana University Press, 1985.

Schulberg, Budd. *What Makes Sammy Run?* New York: Random House, 1952.

Server, Lee. *Robert Mitchum: "Baby, I Don't Care."* New York: St. Martin's Press, 2001.

Shain, Barry Alan. *The Myth of American Individualism: The Protestant Origins of American Political Thought.* Princeton, NJ: Princeton University Press, 1994.

Shapiro, Henry D. *Appalachia on Our Mind: The Southern Mountains and Mountaineers in the American Consciousness, 1870–1920.* Chapel Hill: University of North Carolina Press, 1978.

Slaughter, Thomas P. *The Whiskey Rebellion: Frontier Epilogue to the American Revolution.* New York: Oxford University Press, 1986.

Slotkin, Richard. *Gunfighter Nation: The Myth of the Frontier in Twentieth-Century America.* Norman: University of Oklahoma Press, 1992.

Smith, Henry Nash. *Virgin Land: The American West as Symbol and Myth.* Cambridge, MA: Harvard University Press, 1950.

Sonnie, Amy, and James Tracy. *Hillbilly Nationalists, Urban Race Rebels, and Black Power: Community Organizing in Radical Times.* Brooklyn, NY: Melville House, 2011.

Sowell, Thomas. *Race and Culture: A World View.* New York: Basic Books, 1994.

Stanfield, Peter. *Hollywood, Westerns and the 1930s: The Lost Trail.* Exeter: University of Exeter Press, 2001.

Tesler, Michael, and David Sears. "President Obama and Growing Polarization of Partisan Attachments by Racial Attitudes and Race." Paper presented at the annual meeting of the American Political Science Association, Washington, D.C., September 2010.

Thoreau, Henry David. *Walden, and Other Writings.* New York: Modern Library, 1950.

Tocqueville, Alexis de, Harvey Claflin Mansfield, and Delba Winthrop. *Democracy in America.* Chicago: University of Chicago Press, 2007.

Trollope, Frances Milton. *Domestic Manners of the Americans.* New York: Dodd, Mead, 1901

Turner, Frederick Jackson. *The Frontier in American History*. New York: Holt, Rinehart and Winston, 1962.

Walls, Stephanie M. *The Impact of Individualism on Political and Community Participation*. Dissertation, University of Cincinnati, 2008. http://www.ohiolink.edu/etd/view.cgi?acc_num=ucin1204053177.

Warshaw, Robert. *The Immediate Experience: Movies, Comics, Theatre and Other Aspects of Popular Culture*. Garden City, NY: Doubleday, 1962.

Webb, James H. *Born Fighting: How the Scots-Irish Shaped America*. New York: Broadway Books, 2004.

Weber, Max. *The Essential Weber: A Reader*. New York: Routledge, 2004.

Weber, Max, Peter Baehr, and Gordon C. Wells. *The Protestant Ethic and the "Spirit" of Capitalism and Other Writings*. New York: Penguin Books, 2002.

Weiss, Richard. *The American Myth of Success: From Horatio Alger to Norman Vincent Peale*. New York: Basic Books, 1969.

Whisnant, David E. *All That Is Native and Fine: The Politics of Culture in an American Region*. Chapel Hill: University of North Carolina Press, 1983.

Williamson, J. W. *Hillbillyland: What the Movies Did to the Mountains and What the Mountains Did to the Movies*. Chapel Hill: University of North Carolina Press, 1995.

Wilson, Edward O. *On Human Nature*. Cambridge, MA: Harvard University Press, 1978.

Woodard, Colin. *American Nations: A History of the Eleven Rival Regional Cultures of North America*. New York: Viking, 2011.

Woodmason, Charles, and Richard James Hooker. *The Carolina Backcountry on the Eve of the Revolution: The Journal and Other Writings of Charles Woodmason, Anglican Itinerant*. Chapel Hill: Published for the Institute of Early American History and Culture at Williamsburg, Virginia, by the University of North Carolina Press, 1953.

Index

About the Author

AARON BARLOW, associate professor of English at New York City College of Technology, is the author of five books relating to American culture, journalism, new media, and film, including *The Rise of the Blogosphere*, *Beyond the Blogosphere*, and *Blogging America*—all from Praeger.